T0285406

A Time for Wisdom
Advance Praise

"McLaughlin and McMinn provide a sound review of what wisdom is and the context in which wisdom is understood. We live in an age of data and information, but little is written on the value of wisdom. For decades I have heard supervisors say that you manage people with data. There is some truth to that, but you make decisions about people with wisdom. We need more wisdom in our culture today. If you work with people (manager, teacher, supervisor, coach, pastor, etc.), you could benefit from this book. It will help you understand the importance of wisdom, what it is, and how to apply it in various ways."

—**Clark D. Campbell**, PhD, senior associate provost and professor of psychology, Biola University

"When night falls, it is certain that I will be a day older. Does it follow that I will be one increment wiser? The likelihood of this desirable outcome increases when the virtue-enhancing strategies collected in *A Time for Wisdom* are absorbed and applied. There are pathways to train our inner selves—embodied souls—to embrace timeless principles of wisdom humbly. McLaughlin and McMinn supply an accessible primer on the psychological structures and processes to grow wiser no matter what the day brings. Why be satisfied with merely growing older? The time before us is to deepen our wisdom layers."

—**Rev. Stephen P. Greggo**, PsyD, author of *Assessment for Counseling in Christian Perspective* (IVP).

"Integrating modern research with insights from the world's religious and philosophical traditions, *A Time for Wisdom* shows us how to live ethically satisfying lives in a world that can at times cater to our worst instincts. The principles that McLaughlin and McMinn present are ageless and universal, making their book a resource you can turn to whenever you need a restorative perspective on the ups and downs of life."

—**Lisa Miller**, PhD, professor of psychology at Columbia University, director of the Spirituality & Mind Body Institute, and author of *The Awakened Brain*

"McLaughlin and McMinn weave together the best ideas from religion, psychology, and philosophy to engage the reader in wisdom. They do it with the lessons of wise mentors, sage spiritual leaders, gems of famous quotes, cutting-edge research, and current events that alone make the book worth reading. But then there are practical ideas for developing wisdom, broken down in simple ways for anyone to follow. From the scenarios the authors describe, I gained insights for applying concepts of wisdom to my life and relationships, and I learned how wisdom fits with other character traits like humility, joy, and peace. This book is not limited to the ivory tower; it is fully embodied in the real world. This is a wise book on wisdom."

—**Jennifer Ripley**, PhD, professor of psychology and Hughes Chair of Christian Integration, Regent University

"In *A Time for Wisdom*, McLaughlin and McMinn bring a sober, careful, and hospitable study of wisdom that gathers folk intuition, philosophical reflection, and spiritual tradition and holds them up to the findings of psychological science. The result is a field guide for readers who seek wisdom. There are no false promises, no stepwise programs, and no simplistic answers. Instead, the authors suggest a definition of wisdom that takes long-standing religious traditions seriously, offering evidence-based interventions for guiding true philosophers—lovers of wisdom—along their journey."

—**Evan Rosa**, assistant director for public engagement, Yale Center for Faith & Culture

"I applaud McLaughlin and McMinn for their outstanding and aptly titled book, *A Time for Wisdom*. They make a lively and compelling case for cultivating the virtue of wisdom during these highly anxious and polarizing times. Drawing on an amazing array of disciplines and literary voices—both ancient and contemporary—this highly textured book makes the development of wisdom an inspiring and practical goal. As a psychologist, I have read many books on this general topic, but *A Time for Wisdom* makes a wonderfully unique contribution that weaves together some of the best science, philosophy, and spirituality. The authors invite us to become grounded, quiet our egos, gain perspective and accurate understanding, and grow in compassion, humility, and other strengths of human wholeness. The insights and practices they offer will foster healthier individuals and communities."

—**Steven J. Sandage**, PhD, Albert and Jessie Danielsen Professor of Psychology of Religion and Theology, Boston University

"In a historical period of deep political and religious polarization, what is desperately needed is wisdom. That is exactly what McLaughlin and McMinn give us in their new book. They bring together the best of scientific research alongside ancient sources to both define wisdom and to model how to become wise. Their wisdom model (Knowledge, Detachment, Tranquility, and Transcendence) is neither simple nor easy, but it is immediately practical and implementable. This book is like a training manual on becoming wise, and it should be read in academic, religious, and political settings. Engaging with the model presented in *A Time for Wisdom* might make us not only a wiser culture, but a kinder, humbler, and more hospitable one as well."

—**Brad D. Strawn**, PhD, Evelyn and Frank Freed Chief of Spiritual Formation & Integration, Fuller Theological Seminary

"In our time of divisiveness and polarization, this book is a clarion call for wisdom. Wisdom is perspective—the ability to identify what matters most—and I believe this volume provides a way for its readers to do just that. It encourages an attitude of tranquil listening, even to those voices that make us feel uncomfortable. As the authors point out, 'Wisdom sees common ground for a common good,' and I believe this book can help readers identify what matters most in their lives and in the lives of others. In 'such a time as this,' we ought to listen to the lessons *A Time for Wisdom* offers us with a quiet and receptive heart."

—**Philip Watkins**, PhD, professor of psychology, Eastern Washington University

"A Time for Wisdom, by Paul McLaughlin and Mark McMinn is simply a great book. Excellent treatment of research. Practical suggestions. New insights. Fresh metaphors. Fantastic writing. Buy and read this book. It is a wise choice."

—**Everett L. Worthington, Jr.**, PhD, Commonwealth Professor Emeritus, Virginia Commonwealth University

A TIME FOR WISDOM

A
TIME
FOR
WISDOM

KNOWLEDGE, DETACHMENT,
TRANQUILITY, TRANSCENDENCE

PAUL T. McLAUGHLIN, PsyD
MARK R. McMINN, PhD

TEMPLETON PRESS

TEMPLETON PRESS
300 Conshohocken State Road, Suite 500
West Conshohocken, PA 19428
www.templetonpress.org

Set in Adobe Caslon and Proxima Nova by Westchester Publishing Services

This paper meets the requirements of ANSI/NISO Z39.48-1992 (Permanence of Paper).

ISBN: 978-1-59947-587-5 (cloth)
ISBN: 978-1-59947-588-2 (ebook)

Library of Congress Control Number: 2021945401

A catalogue record for this book is available from the Library of Congress.

Printed in the United States of America.

22 23 24 25 26   10 9 8 7 6 5 4 3 2 1

To my parents,
*for your steadfast and
unconditional love*

—Paul

To Bruce and Di,
*who guided me in paths of wisdom
at a time when I had so little*

—Mark

Contents

TRANSCENDENCE

A TIME FOR WISDOM

INTRODUCTION

Whoever came up with the term "ideological bubble" was an optimist. Bubbles are soft, pliable, transparent things, but in today's world it seems more fitting to say we segregate into our ideological fortresses, or bunkers, or armories, or silos. Inside, it seems safe and comfortable as we interact with like-minded souls who share our basic worldviews, assumptions, and beliefs. These souls become our Facebook friends, confidants, and exemplars. We join them for dinner and drinks while enjoying stimulating conversations, we worship beside them, and we offer help when their plumbing clogs. These neighbors and friends provide us with all the affirmation we need to know that we are good people with solid values, even as others outside are poorly informed and less virtuous.

These days fortress interiors even come with tailored advertisements, newsfeeds, and Google searches so that we can easily see how correct we are about matters of ultimate importance. We can rally together and celebrate that we are not much like those who live in the fortress across the way, or maybe we forget the other exists at all—a peaceful *Truman Show* life. Sheltered, confident, and strident in our convictions, we find safety in knowing our ideological communities are strong and amply supplied. If we pop our head outside at all, it is for the purpose of lobbing a grenade. But then again, why risk that when we can launch those grenades from inside the safety of our own fortress, in 280 characters or less?

Social psychologist Jonathan Haidt warns that, "team membership blinds people to the motives and morals of their opponents—and to the wisdom that is to be found scattered among diverse political ideologies" (2013, p. 318). Yet it seems that today we are increasingly pressured to be part of a team and to trumpet the virtues of our team's ideologies without considering that other perspectives might also have merit.

In earlier days, a free press could stand outside the fray, glance inside the transparent enclaves, and report something that seemed like transcendent truth-telling. This was the backbone of a healthy democracy, being able to challenge and scrutinize ideas freely without fear of control by the government or other powerful organizations. Similarly, universities were places of relatively free exploration and inquiry, housing researchers and professors who enjoyed enough academic freedom to make their students ponder new and exciting frontiers. Many faith communities were also able to function above the bubbles as people met in synagogues and temples and churches throughout the world to explore and celebrate the possibility of a Truth that transcends human squabbles and differences.

In today's era of ideological fortresses, media outlets are increasingly recruited to set up shop inside whatever sanctuary will increase their ratings and pay their bills. And today's university is under siege, facing intense scrutiny to raise the banner of safety above critical analysis and free thinking. Faith communities also feel the pressure to align with particular political ideologies. Transcendent Truth is increasingly seen through the lens of polarized human experience.

Where are the truth-tellers now? Who will dare to move outside of their fortresses to have genuine curiosity and conversations with other daring souls? How many are willing to choose wisdom over safety so that we can learn to truly listen to one another, to consider multiple perspectives, to endure messy places, to hold ideas with humility and openness, and ultimately to offer the world a better way to live?

This is a dangerous book. Put it down now and send it back to Amazon, or take it back to your local bookstore if you are not willing to step outside the door of your fortress. Wisdom calls us out—out of our comfort zones, out of preconceptions, out of the constant flow of media enabling us to believe we are always reasonable and others always crazy, out of our self-complacency, out of our natural circles of conversation. And then wisdom calls us in—into a long tradition of those who have walked in humility and grace in complicated times, into a fellowship of diversity and disagreement and growth, into a place of tranquility and peace with ourselves and others that transcends our differences, into a place of curiosity and awe and wonder at how complex and beautiful and amazing this life can be.

Few concepts allure and baffle the mind as much as wisdom does, yet few are as worthy of pursuit. Wisdom is the apex of intellectual and moral judgment, experienced in the orchestration of emotions, desires, and life-experience. It calls us to a higher self and a more noble way of existing in the world, and if there has ever been a time where we need higher selves, it is now.

We have good news for all who hope for wisdom. In spite of its complexity and elusiveness, wisdom has been studied by social scientists for quite some time, and there is now a substantial body of evidence uncovering the inherent qualities and function of wisdom. Today's research allows for a fresh approach to an ancient virtue by placing wisdom in a contemporary framework and familiar language.

We are big fans of wisdom science, but for us the most exciting thing about studying wisdom is the adventure of it. How can wisdom propel us forward into new frontiers and understanding and growth? How might wisdom expand our consciousness, bringing a deep and abiding curiosity that ultimately leads to new discoveries and insights with potential to heal fractures in the self, interpersonal relationships, and society?

If you are feeling suspicious about science and wisdom, that seems reasonable. We value the science of wisdom and hope you will, too, by the end of this book, but we will be the first to acknowledge that science does not automatically clear the path to a life full of wisdom. Still, scientific knowledge can clear the brush a bit, making paths of wisdom a little easier to traverse than they might otherwise be.

We conducted a scientific study a few years back to see if young adults in a faith community could become wiser through a mentoring program. They could, and they did, as we will explain later, but for now it is better to ponder the story of one of the mentors in that study. Marcile, in her late seventies at the time of the study, is the sort of woman who exudes grace and peace. Just being in her presence is healing. Her life has not been easy. She lost a husband in a tragic plane crash early in her life and dealt with a serious health crisis around the same time. Somehow, rather than becoming bitter, she learned to walk quietly and faithfully through life, holding tightly to friendships and faith communities where she served and allowed others to serve her. When she agreed to be a mentor in our scientific study on wisdom, she could not have known that just a few years later she would face Stage 4 melanoma, a crisis in her faith community, a pandemic, and wildfires unlike anything ever experienced in her home state of Oregon. Not surprisingly, she has faced all this with grace, tranquility, and hope. Did the young people she mentored become wiser because they were participating in a standardized wisdom curriculum based on the latest social science of wisdom, or maybe just because they were in Marcile's presence, in her home, sharing meals with her? Science cannot answer that particular question, but we suspect it was both. Wisdom is both a virtue out there to be explored and attained, and an embodied presence that we experience through relationships with those who have found wisdom through their years of living and suffering and loving.

This example raises various questions. Does one need to be old to be wise? Not necessarily, as we explore in Chapter 8. Does wisdom require suffering? Probably. We explore this more in Chapters 5 and 6. Is wisdom a spiritual task? Perhaps. We explore this in Chapters 10, 11, and 12. Can we learn to be wiser with intentional effort? We think so. How does a person go about gaining wisdom? Well, that is the point of the whole book. It is a journey, and we have four steps to suggest and practical strategies to help you grow in wisdom.

WHO ARE WE?

Believing wisdom has a relational dimension, as does writing, it seems proper to tell you something about us and how this book came about.

One quality of wisdom is the ability to hold multiple perspectives as simultaneously true. The story of this book starts in a faculty office in the Pacific Northwest of the United States, and requires embracing two different perspectives. Consider this the first practice exercise of this book on wisdom—holding both Paul's and Mark's perspectives of how this came to be.

Paul's perspective. I approached my education with the hope of gaining more than mere information and knowledge, and while I am not sure I gained wisdom to anywhere near the degree I gained student loan debt, I remain stubbornly persistent that seeking wisdom is not a bad way to spend one's time. At the beginning of my doctoral work in clinical psychology, I was asked to consider topics to study for my dissertation by my mentor and advisor, Mark. After a rather brief reflection, I knew I wanted to pursue wisdom. Up to that point in my life I had been a student of religion, philosophy, and theology, so the chance to investigate wisdom— an idea more commonly at home in the humanities than in the social sciences—through a scientific lens was exhilarating.

Mark's perspective. Yes, I always have my doctoral students ponder topics for their dissertations early in their training. I especially encourage topics connected to my interests in positive psychology and the integration of psychology and faith. After considering this for a short while, Paul came to my office announcing that he wanted to study wisdom. My response was quite dismissive: "Paul, that sounds like a great topic, but psychologists do not really study wisdom." So, he went to the library and proved me wrong. It turns out many psychologists have been studying wisdom for quite a long time.

Paul's perspective. Once I got the green light from Mark on wisdom, I began pondering such questions as, *What are the psychological components of wisdom? Can wisdom be taught? What are the attributes of wise people and how might they think and feel differently from the rest of us? How does the science of wisdom relate to philosophical and religious views of it?* In addition to finding answers to these questions, I was motivated by another factor. As someone interested in the relationship between religion, spirituality, and psychology, could the science of wisdom further explicate the view that faith and reason are complementary? I believed so.

In my own religious tradition, theological truths based on faith and divine revelation provide knowledge beyond, but not opposed to, reason, and this knowledge can be used to explicate and enhance our understanding of the natural world. With this background, I approached wisdom from a multidisciplinary perspective and undertook a dissertation that integrated the current psychology of wisdom within a Christian context. As I dug into the literature on wisdom, I found a rather shocking absence of religion and spirituality in psychological studies of wisdom. This may appear obvious to some, considering these were scientific journals, yet it appeared that in their attempt to create a secular field of wisdom they stripped wisdom from its natural environment and overlooked the importance of the transcendent. My dissertation involved putting the pieces back together again.

Mark and I worked with religious leaders from a local church to write a faith-informed curriculum for promoting wisdom. The curriculum included religious and spiritual practices, community mentorship, and psychological exercises intended to increase cognitive flexibility, detached objectivity, and problem solving—precursors to the four steps toward wisdom we describe in this book. We took academic theories of wisdom and brought them into the actual lives of people. Once the curriculum was developed, my research was not conducted in a laboratory or any university ivory towers, but right in the community. In relation to a comparison group, the young adults who participated in our wisdom-mentoring program showed increases in practical wisdom, daily spiritual experiences, life satisfaction, and the ability to see complexity beyond abstract concepts.

The project was a success, and I graduated with a deep sense of gratitude and satisfaction with it.

After finishing my doctorate I began working as a psychologist and continued pondering the research on wisdom, following up on academic literature, news articles, and books. But studying wisdom and practicing it are sometimes different. A series of career decisions—some of them beyond my control and some not—brought me to a job I loathed. My education felt useless, and I felt trapped, isolated, and doubtful of myself. I struggled to see beyond my tainted vision of despair and helplessness. All that I had learned about wisdom in over a decade of studying theology, philosophy, and psychology helped alert me to just how far adrift I seemed to be. Wisdom does not prevent difficulties, but it does help provide an internal alarm system for times such as these. I needed to turn the head knowledge I had accumulated toward my heart and my own life. How is wisdom accessible to the real-world struggles people face? How might the science of wisdom come off the shelves and work to improve the everyday lives of people?

After making some necessary changes in my career trajectory, I landed happily in a psychology practice where I regularly have opportunity to walk alongside people as they navigate the challenges of life. One of those people I will call Jason. My work with Jason helped cure me of the disillusionment I had felt. It reinstalled the belief that this work of psychotherapy can work, that insight can light the flame of change.

Jason was a highly intelligent young man I treated for depression and anxiety. His life was plagued with past traumas. An only child, he grew up with very strict and aloof caregivers. Over the years he internalized a deep sense of resentment, became obsessively paranoid at times, and often battled addiction issues. The world appeared an unpredictable and cold place. He struggled to manage a sense of safety and healthy dependency. Our work included building basic trust as relationships of any sort had often been a cause of much pain and disappointment. Early sessions included extensive time in silence. Jason would likely be considered to have what is known as a schizoid personality style, which is characteristically found among people with a low tolerance for intimacy and closeness, and who often seek solace in a solitary life and fantasy. Slowly we were able to make contact, and he allowed me to see to a certain extent some of his deep sadness, yet he remained sullen and disconnected.

Jason often talked about one area of enjoyment in his life, that of taking long walks through a local graveyard. He found solace being in the cemetery both day and night. With time, Jason came to realize that knowledge of his own story and life was deeply connected with his graveyard musings, that thinking about his past represented confronting an unknown realm where the grief for what could have been resided. The work staggered along. Then one day he told me that he came to see something during one of his most recent cemetery strolls that had surprised him. He went on to describe a sense of awe and amazement at the simple presence of the life of trees that had apparently evaded his awareness. Something changed for Jason, treatment flowed much easier, and Jason seemed to have expanded emotionally; his own presence felt lighter and at ease.

William James, the father of American psychology, in writing about religious conversion stated:

> To be converted, to be regenerated, to receive grace, to experience religion, to gain an assurance, are so many phrases which denote the process, gradual or sudden, by which a self hitherto divided, and consciously wrong inferior and unhappy, becomes unified and consciously right superior and happy, in consequence of its firmer hold upon religious realities. (1902, p. 186)

I doubt Jason would say he had a religious conversion, but this description by James is not far off from the changes that seemed to follow. The relationship between psychology, wisdom, and spirituality continued to intrigue and haunt me, ultimately compelling me to develop the four-level model presented in this book. But before getting to the four steps toward wisdom, let's muddle through the challenging task of defining what we mean by wisdom.

WHAT IS WISDOM?

We are about to offer a definition for something that cannot be defined. Wisdom is beyond definition in at least two ways. First, scholars cannot agree what it is. This is not for a lack of effort, but still, after decades of science and over two millennia of philosophy we still do not have precise words to capture the essence of wisdom. An international group of researchers who recently met described wisdom as "morally grounded excellence in social-cognitive processing" (Grossmann et al., 2020, p. 103). In response, one of the world's leading scientific experts on wisdom, Judith Glück, wrote:

> Having studied wisdom for over twenty years now, I think I have learned quite a bit from my own research. If someone describes a difficult life problem to me, I can produce a response that would probably be scored as wise. I consider myself as rather morally grounded, and I have become quite skilled at considering different perspectives, balancing interests, appreciating broader contexts, and knowing the limits of my knowledge. Yet there are moments in my life—family conflicts, endless and useless meetings, interactions with difficult students—where I yell, slam doors, and curse (or at least would like to do so) and where I am neither wise nor act wisely. How is that possible . . . ? (Glück, 2020, p. 144)

Glück's point is that social-cognitive processing is not enough; emotional regulation needs to be considered also. Perhaps the larger point is that any definition slips through our fingers because wisdom is elusive, multifaceted, and too big to capture with words.

Glück's words also hint at the second way wisdom is beyond definition: it is even harder to live wisdom than to describe it. Her humble admission resonates with how real life feels. Reason and analytical thinking do not ensure or fully capture the lived, embodied, relational reality of wisdom.

Here is a checklist to underscore Glück's point. In the last month, how often have you . . .

- Slipped into a frantic or anxious place rather than maintaining peace of mind?
- Acted in a way contrary to your values?
- Failed to listen well to another person's perspective?
- Run away from conflict, or raged through it, rather than looking for creative solutions?
- Lost track of your values?
- Chosen not to ask for help when you really needed it?
- Taken yourself too seriously?
- Given poor advice to another?
- Filled your life so full that you lacked time for deep reflection?
- Spoken words too quickly, without considering the impact they might have?

Each of these are inverted self-report items that show up on scientific tests of wisdom (Webster, 2019, pp. 302–304), but who among us could possibly answer never to all of these? These are common human struggles that undermine wisdom for most of us, at least from time to time. You will notice the subtitle to this book is not, "Four Easy Steps to Wisdom." That is because wisdom is not easy. Still, we believe it is a virtuous and important journey, especially in today's cultural moment where it seems so difficult to listen well to one another, hold complexity, and work toward Shalom in our divided and contentious societies.

Wisdom is beyond definition for both of the reasons we have just described, but we are about to offer a definition anyway. Why? Because it can still be helpful to wrap words around such a vital virtue. We offer this definition with empathy, knowing life is messy and living in wisdom is more difficult than any of us might have imagined earlier in life. And we offer it with humility, knowing it is only an approximation because any words we offer fall short of the fullness of wisdom.

Wisdom is an (1) embodied (2) disposition or act involving (3) critical contemplation, (4) purgation and purification of knowledge with practical implications, (5) leading to self-transcendence, tranquility, and elevated insight.[1]

Embodied

Wisdom is more than an academic topic for textbooks. It shows up in our bodies, pulsing from our brains toward our fingers and thumbs as we toss our tweets out into the world, type Facebook and Instagram posts, and leave comments in response to others. It resides in our hearts, as surely as in our brains, as we communicate with our partners and friends, seek mutual understanding in difficult times, delight in blessings of life, and strive to press forward toward maturity and virtue.

The embodied nature of wisdom is true from the earliest moments of life. Jerome is a 6-year-old who likes to bake with his father. When the bread comes out of the oven on a particular Saturday morning, his father warns him not to touch the bread pan because it is very hot and could hurt him. But remember, Jerome is 6, and being 6 entails a deep curiosity about the world and some persistent questions about how authority structures work. Not surprisingly, Jerome waits until his father is turned away, washing up some dishes in the sink, and then sneaks a quick touch of the bread pan. Drama ensues. So does wisdom.

We learn wisdom through engaging our whole selves, all of our senses, in the world around us. Sometimes this leads to wonder and delight, and sometimes it leads to struggle and pain. When Jerome touches that bread pan as a 6-year-old, he grows in wisdom even as he shrieks in agony.

Fortunately, we do not have to learn everything through trial and error, because wisdom also shows up in others we watch, observe, and admire.

---

[1] See Appendix for how this relates to other prominent definitions of wisdom.

Whom do you know, or have you known, who is extraordinarily wise? Take a moment and allow that person's face into your visual mind. Set the book down a moment and quietly ponder the face of wisdom. How would you describe this person to others? What relational and emotional qualities do you notice in this wise person? What is it like to be in this person's presence? What other virtues (e.g., humility, kindness, grit, hope, gratitude, forgiveness) describe this person? What emotions well up in you as you consider all this?

Without exemplars of wisdom, we would know very little about how to confront the complex world around us. Teenagers do not learn as much about driving by reading the driver's manual as they do by watching others drive. By the time they get their learner's permit, they know what happens when a brake pedal is pressed, which way the car turns when the steering wheel is turned clockwise, and what a signal light means. These skills are learned through relationship and observation, and not so much through semantics and written descriptions. Of course, teenagers also need to practice, make mistakes, enjoy successes, and try driving on their own before we consider them good drivers. So also with wisdom, we learn by knowing people who are wise, observing them, practicing what we learn, experiencing successes and failures, and trying out what we know in new situations.

But if we learn wisdom by observing others, we still need to consider *which* others we observe. Our natural tendency is to observe and learn from those who are like us, hold our same values, see the world as we see it. It is likely that when you pictured an exemplar of wisdom a few moments ago you chose someone quite similar to yourself. It may have been a family member, a teacher at a school you attended, a close friend, someone with the same skin color as yours, or a person in similar socioeconomic conditions. There is nothing wrong with learning wisdom from exemplars who share our life experiences, but if we only learn from like-minded souls what wisdom might we be missing as a result?

Disposition or Act

Is the capacity for wisdom some enduring quality we are born with (a trait), or something that shows up in particular times because of lessons we have learned in life (a state)? Those arguing for a trait perspective, also called an *essentialist* view of wisdom, argue that it exists more in some individuals than in others. Just as some people are more intelligent than others, so also some people are naturally wiser than others. Scholars offer interesting evidence for this perspective, including the finding that wisdom correlates with other well-established personality traits such as openness, conscientiousness, and agreeableness (Ardelt et al., 2019). Some have started studying the neurobiology of wisdom, which argues strongly for a trait perspective (Jeste & Lee, 2019). For example, the prefrontal cortex and the limbic system, both of which have implications for wisdom, have been "implicated in the neurobiology of character, and . . . linked with temperament studies in personality" (Jeste & Lee, 2019, p. 131).

Others prefer a state perspective, sometimes called a *constructivist* view, which suggests people can learn acts of wisdom with training and practice. In this view, wisdom is not so much a quality we are born with as a set of state-specific patterns that are developed over time and applied in particular situations and specific sociocultural contexts (Grossmann et al., 2019). This is supported by a number of studies showing people who exhibit wisdom in one situation are not necessarily inclined to show wisdom in unrelated situations.

We argue that wisdom exists as both a trait and a state (Grossmann et al., 2019). As a disposition, some people naturally have more wisdom than others. But whether or not we are generally wise, our actions vary widely from one situation to another. Sometimes wise people do foolish things, and foolish people do wise things. The good news about wisdom involving a trait or disposition is that we can hold up exemplars, as we did earlier in this chapter, and learn from those who are naturally wise.

And the good news about it being a state or set of actions is that we can grow in wisdom with thoughtful, repeated practice.

Wisdom can be learned. This is the premise of the model we present in this book, that people can become wiser with time and practice.

Critical Contemplation

In Paul's dissertation we found that young adults can grow in wisdom, and in a reasonably short period of time (McLaughlin et al., 2018). One might assume that a religiously based program to promote wisdom would try to instill answers to life's quagmires, but that is not what we did. We were more interested in promoting thoughtful contemplation than in providing a set of answers.

Imagine being a young adult coming to the first small-group meeting and being confronted with this situation:

> Your friend has been diagnosed with a serious form of cancer that will require difficult treatment with an unknown outcome. You want to remain hopeful and encouraging to your friend, but inwardly you are worried and sad. Your friend mentions that the cancer has been difficult for her faith. She wonders how a loving and powerful God could allow such a thing. You have been pondering this, too, and are not sure how to respond to your friend's questions about faith.

Can you notice inner tension in response to this scenario? Wouldn't it be nice to wrap up wisdom in a tidy package of words or advice? It might be helpful to pray or read books about why God allows bad things to happen, and while there is nothing wrong with these responses, they do not reach down into the depth of uncertainty and despair evident in this situation. It is important to let wisdom be bigger than words, and bigger than any answer that might be offered.

We selected mentors who themselves were able to navigate complexity in life without resorting to simplistic solutions. In the leader's manual, right after we had them present this scenario to their small groups, we wrote: "Please do not try to resolve the tension participants are feeling or answer the difficult questions they are asking. Allow participants to feel the discomfort and uncertainty of this situation." Mentors then ushered participants into a place where they could hold hard questions, asking them to notice their internal stirrings and desires to move toward quick answers. Leaders reminded the young adults that the shortest verse in the Bible, "Jesus wept," occurred because Jesus was so deeply stirred by emotion when his friend had died. They asked participants to sit in silence.

Rinse. Repeat. This happened for six sessions over two months. We wished it could have been more, but dissertations have timelines so the small group mentoring was a fairly brief intervention. Still, we found positive results and growth in wisdom for our participants in relation to a comparison group that did not participate in the wisdom mentoring. Why did this work?

One of the reasons we think it may have worked is because participants learned to engage in critical contemplation. At first glance, a phrase like "critical contemplation" may seem quite cerebral, but it is much more than that. Richard Rohr, founder of the Center for Action and Contemplation, puts it this way:

> Regardless how we practice . . . contemplation calls the ordinary thinking mind into question. We gradually come to recognize that this thing we call "thinking" does not enable us to love God and love others. We need a different operating system that begins with and leads to silence. (Rohr, 2020)

Similarly, our participants may have learned to think better about life's messiness, but even more, they learned how to sit quietly in the tension of complexity. Wisdom calls us to a full-bodied contemplation that involves a balance of thinking, feeling, quiet, and seeking the transcendent.

If our tendency is to retreat into ideological fortresses with likeminded people, contemplation pushes against this, compelling us to look both cognitively and empathically at multiple perspectives and varying opinions.

Critical contemplation requires balance and openness to differing perspectives, even in areas where we hold firm convictions.

The word "critical" may seem confusing at first. Shall we just post more vitriolic comments on YouTube and call it critical contemplation? Please, no. We are not advocating criticism of others. Instead, this is about carefully considering and weighing an idea or belief in relation to alternative views. In a sense, we are learning to be peacefully critical of our own thoughts and open to the possibility that they could change over time and in different contexts.

Sometimes the outcome of long contemplation is advocating for change. Jesus—normally peaceful and loving—once walked into the temple where money-changers were making an outrageous profit from weary travelers who had no other options and expressed his displeasure by flipping over the merchants' tables and driving them out with a whip. But notice this is not being critical out of personal inconvenience or offense, but a response to abusive power, corruption, and distortions of truth that work against wisdom.

Critical contemplation engages our emotions and bodies, and not just our brains. Rosa Parks sat at the back of the bus for years, and all that time she must have been pondering and imagining another world—one where Black people have the same rights and privileges as White people. Out of that long contemplation, on December 1, 1955, she let wisdom move her body to the front of the bus. On the one hand, it did not work out too well for her as she was arrested and prosecuted. On the other hand, it precipitated the Montgomery Bus Boycott, which brought attention to overt racism and systemic injustice. The struggle against oppression continues, but people like Rosa Parks have made society wiser as a whole.

In Rosa Parks's case, her critical contemplation moved her to believe and do something different from what she had done before. That is often the case with wisdom, but not always. Sometimes we continue to hold our same perspectives, but with greater awareness and compassion for the other. In her renowned *OnBeing* podcast (2013), Krista Tippett once interviewed Frances Kissling and David Gushee about their Pro-Choice and Pro-Life perspectives as part of the Civil Conversations Project. To hear Kissling and Gushee talk and truly listen to the other is a moving experience. When Tippett asks each of her guests to describe something they find important in the other's perspective, Gushee acknowledges:

> One of the things I'm attracted to and have really learned a lot from in dialogue with Frances and others in the pro-choice community is the sustained knowledgeable commitment to the well-being of women. And this issue, no progress can be made on it without that commitment.

With a similar humility, Kissling notes:

> I'm generally troubled by the one-value approach to the question. . . . What I get back from my movement is if the woman wants an abortion, there is no other factor or value that should be considered. . . . And I don't think you can make the fetus invisible in the abortion decision. I think abortion decision is a conflict value decision.

Neither changed their minds or their positions as a result of the conversation, but both demonstrated a beautiful capacity to consider the other's view. Listening to Tippett's podcast may not change your mind either, but it might change your heart, and it provides a great example of critical contemplation and civil engagement.

Consider the embodied face of wisdom we invited you to picture earlier in this chapter, or perhaps your own face as you journey toward wisdom. Is this a face that contorts in anger at the first sign of disagreement? Does this person rush to judgment without considering alternative views? Is this a tweet-first-think-later sort of person? Or is this the face of prudence, capable of anger and firm conviction but always considering other viewpoints and perspectives? James, the brother of Jesus, admonished his readers in the Christian New Testament to "be quick to listen, slow to speak, slow to anger" (New Revised Standard Version, James 1:19). Critical contemplation begins with excellent listening—considering multiple perspectives and viewpoints while recognizing the possibility that I may be wrong about a thing or two in life. Just as good listening affects our emotions and connections with one another, so too does critical contemplation.

Two exercises might be helpful. First, take a moment to imagine one of the most cognitively or emotionally rigid people you have encountered. What do they do when confronted with an idea different from their own? How do they respond relationally to those in a different camp, whether it be political, ideological, or religious? How do they express emotions when disappointed or frustrated? And now ponder the differences between the face of wisdom you identified earlier in this chapter and the face of rigidity that you just imagined. In which face are you most likely to find critical contemplation?

Second, consider a somewhat-controversial value or belief that you hold strongly. Perhaps you believe a certain way about second amendment rights or religious liberties or the role of the federal government vis-à-vis state governments. When thinking about your beliefs, you probably find it quite natural to think about why your views are better reasoned than the views others hold. Take some time in silence and try something that Krista Tippett did on her podcast with Frances Kissling and David Gushee. Ask yourself to identify the weakest argument for the view you hold and the strongest argument for the view someone else might hold. The goal is not to change your mind, but simply to sit silently with whatever tension arises in this act of critical contemplation.

A Process of Purgation and Purification of Knowledge

Imagine a cup of coffee brewed in a standard coffee machine, but without the filter in place. Life without filters is filled with messy grittiness. The process of purgation and purification assumes a lifelong filtering process that moves us toward living into our best selves, more authentically and congruently with our values, more attuned to others and the needs of a complex world. Purgation involves emptying out toxic thoughts in order to make space for clarity and peace of mind. Purification is a cleansing of the knowledge that reflects wisdom.

In Buddhism, the first step of the Noble Path is called "Right View." Hanh (2015) describes this as deliberately fostering the wholesome seeds in our character so that they might outgrow the unwholesome ones. "If you act in a wholesome way, you will be happy. If you act in an unwholesome way, you water the seeds of craving, anger, and violence in yourself" (p. 52). Right View also involves holding our perceptions lightly because many of our perceptions are incorrect and lead to suffering. Ultimately all views are at least partly wrong and fall short of reality.

Jared came to psychotherapy for help with a stifling depression, and it turned out the key to unlocking his dysphoria was helping him to hold his rigid perceptions more lightly. As a pastor, he had spent years teaching parishioners that faith is sufficient for any problem life brings us, including so-called mental health problems, so our first task was to confront the shame he felt about his own depression and to loosen his grip on these inflexible views about spirituality and mental health. At the beginning of treatment, he thought doubts about his faith reflected spiritual weakness and a lack of faith, so we worked on helping him hold his doubts with more tenderness and care. Jared viewed his marriage as the greatest jewel in his pastoral crown, believing that any flaws in this relationship reflected poorly on his ministry and his leadership, so we needed to normalize how common it is for relationships to encounter seasons of stagnation and struggle. In all these ways, psychotherapy helped Jared grow in wisdom, and to see how life is more nuanced than what he had once imagined and how we all live as deeply complex souls. As he came to terms with his depression and rigid assumptions, he experienced greater compassion toward himself and others, and learned a new gentleness as a human being and a faith leader.

Wisdom requires knowledge, as we explore in Chapters 1–3, but it also involves purging ourselves of incorrect knowledge. Just as we inhale oxygen and exhale carbon dioxide, so wisdom calls for a rhythm of absorbing and releasing, holding conviction and relinquishing unmerited dogma. This is a purifying process, learning to be wise as we traverse life holding our ideas humbly and being open to refining experiences. Wisdom involves holding up our ideas, beliefs, and emotional responses and viewing them in a mirror. How do they look to us? How do they look to others in our current time? How might they have looked to those in earlier times and different cultural contexts? How can we learn from our mistakes and misjudgments?

This is not easy. We simply do not like looking at our mistakes and misjudgments. It is far more natural to hide them (from ourselves and others), to pass them off as someone else's error, to simply deny or ignore them. Wisdom is excruciatingly difficult at times because of the brutal honesty it requires when looking at ourselves.

Self-reflection is considered an essential part of wisdom (Weststrate, 2019). Glück and colleagues found people in the general public view self-reflection and self-criticism as essential for wisdom (Glück & Bluck, 2011). Similarly, those who study wisdom as scholars see self-reflection as central to the concept (Jeste et al., 2010). On a scale of 1 (definitely not important) to 9 (definitely important), wisdom experts rated "Recognizing limits of one's own knowledge" at 8.8 and "Self-reflection" at 8.6 when rating characteristics of wisdom. Both were among the highest rated items in the survey (p. 672).

At this point we must confront a difficult question. We have argued that wisdom involves holding our views lightly, with humility, filtering our understanding and perceptions along the way. But doesn't this imply that some perspectives are better and more virtuous than others? And is not this an offensive thing to suggest in a pluralistic, diverse society? Yes, and yes.

It is an offensive thing to suggest some values might be better than others, but this is the basis of civil society. Allowing all people to sit in the front seat of a bus is better than allowing only White people to sit there. Treating a neighbor with respect is better than killing a neighbor in a fit of anger. Respect is better than hostility. Compassion is better than selfishness. Knowledge is better than ignorance. Love is better than hate. Exceptions could be argued, but generally these value assertions have been tested and refined throughout history in countless cultural contexts. We are not suggesting our beliefs (Paul's and Mark's) are perfectly correct and that everyone who reads this book should conform to them, but to fully embrace wisdom as a process of purgation and purification we need to hold the possibility that some perspectives truly are better than others.

Leading to Self-Transcendence, Tranquility, and Elevated Insight

Versions of the three-parachute story are posted all over the internet, so some variation of this will be familiar. Four people are on a descending, broken airplane with only three parachutes remaining. One person— usually a medical doctor or philanthropist—has a good rationale for being saved, so grabs a chute and bails. The second—typically a lawyer or a politician—proclaims himself to be the smartest person in the world and so grabs a parachute and jumps. That leaves just an old priest and a young child. The priest does the altruistic thing, offering the final chute to the child, at which point the child announces, "We can both have one because the smartest person in the world just took off with my backpack."

Humor emerges from familiar tensions—in this case, it is the tension of self-interest in relation to genuine care for others. Self-interest is complicated—and is not the point of this book—but we should note that it is hugely controversial among those who study this. Some degree of self-interest seems to be necessary for individual survival and for society to function, but when it goes too far it creates massive inequalities and injustices in a world with finite resources. This tension gets played out every day in various ways. Should I have my child vaccinated when I have serious qualms about doing so? If I ask for a larger pay raise, will this mean my co-workers may have less? When choosing what to eat, am I obligated to consider animal welfare or the effects on climate change? Should I apply for a federally subsidized program because I am eligible, even though I do not actually need the help? Is it best to look for every viable tax deduction? Wisdom allows us to raise these questions because nonwisdom (foolishness) marches forward without even considering an alternative to self-interest. This is what makes the joke work, because the incredibly smart man ends up being both morally and mortally foolish in his self-interest.

Self-transcendence is the ability to stand apart from vested self-interest, to see others, to recognize that something bigger than ourselves is at play in the universe. When you imagined a face of wisdom early in this chapter, was it a person capable of standing outside of herself or himself to see the needs of others, and the broader needs of a hurting world? It seems likely the wise person you imagined also had (or has) other virtuous qualities, such as kindness, generosity, humility, altruism, gratitude, love, and forgiveness. All these speak to an ability to transcend, to pursue something bigger and ultimately more noble than self-interest. We consider this more in Chapter 3 when we discuss the transcendentals (truth, beauty, goodness).

Maybe the more important point, instead of asking how much self-interest we need to survive, is whether self-interest drives us into small places of isolation and obsession or into rash and foolish decisions, such as grabbing the backpack, thinking it is a parachute. Wisdom calls us into large spaces where we can see and appreciate multiple perspectives and ultimately make informed decisions.

In our polarized political world, it is not difficult to imagine a political leader who pays attention to polls suggesting popularity while disregarding polls that seem more dire, perhaps even discounting them as "fake news." Inside this selective silo of desirable news, the leader can construct a narrative of unsurpassed excellence and approval, but it is not real and it will not lead to wise thinking and acting. Or let's say you get a performance evaluation at work every six months and you choose to only look at the positive comments while ignoring the growth edges your supervisor suggests. Over time, this will not go well. Those content with an isolated, egocentric vision lose touch with their truest and best selves.

I (Mark) recall a haunting memory from high school when our literature teacher assigned Edgar Allan Poe's "The Cask of Amontillado." Poe, always a bit of a gruesome story teller, spins a tale of a mason who gets revenge on a fellow nobleman by getting him drunk, chaining him to a wall, and then building a permanent brick encasement around him. As Montresor—the narrator and the murderer—walks away, he pro-

claims, "Rest in peace." As an overly empathic teenager, that story pen-
etrated my soul and has caused me many anxious reflections over the
years as to what it might be like to live out one's final hours in a brick
closet with no exit.

Being permanently trapped in a small space makes us claustropho-
bic, and rightly so because we intuitively know that we need space, relationships, perspective in order to function at our fullest. In isolating, we
lose touch with our truest and best selves. We say this compassionately,
knowing this isolation almost never comes from a desire to be self-focused
or alone, but typically emerges out of being hurt, from finding the world
unsafe and dangerous. We both see this as clinical psychologists where it
seems our work is often helping clients emerge from entombed places of
pain into the vast world of hope and possibility.

And so it is with wisdom—moving from small to large vision. This
can be true for both individuals and collectives. Just as individuals can be
foolishly self-focused, so too we can become entrapped in social collectives that are bound up in a small vision. When this happens, we often
polarize ourselves and segregate into our ideological fortresses. The world
closes in around us, and before we know it we are obsessing about a political leader or issue, a particular theological interpretation, a sports team,
or financial returns. Outside views are quickly dismissed as uninformed
or even stupid. Those inside the social collective feel wiser than others
because they know the truth, but it is a self-protective version of the truth
that deliberately shuts out those beyond the perimeter of the fortress.
Social psychologists call this groupthink, where agreement is required and
creativity is stifled. History is replete with examples of foolish decisions
made in these circumstances.

So how is it that we learn to self-transcend, to move beyond our own
self-interests, and what does this have to do with wisdom? This is one of
the steps in the model we present, and will be the main focus of Chapters 10 to 12. And yes, it is hard to do.

But what about slamming doors and cursing? Glück's provocative
quotation that began this section gets our attention because it feels so

honest and familiar. Shouldn't wisdom actually change the way we live in the world so that we can have some emotional balance in perceiving ourselves, others, and the world around? This is where tranquility becomes so important.

As we grow in wisdom, we not only learn new things, but we also understand and manage our emotions better, and our relationships evolve and flourish. It is not that we become perfect, as Glück so adeptly points out, but we at least start to notice where we are being wise and where we are struggling. We begin to see how difficult wisdom can be in the nitty-gritty stuff of life, and we feel challenged to improve however we can. Tranquility is one of the four steps toward wisdom that we will introduce soon.

Elevated insight is tricky because at first glance it may sound like quite a narcissistic claim, that one person can learn to see the world better than another. But rather than viewing others as the comparison point, which seems sort of pointless and arrogant, we find it more useful for each of us to use our own personal histories as the comparison. So if I can see the world differently today from the way I did a year ago, or a decade ago, because of growth in knowledge, detachment, tranquility, and transcendence, then I am becoming wiser over time.

Imagine you are in a situation, such as the one I (Paul) found myself in, where you dread going to work each morning. You wake one particular Monday morning and entertain the thought of quitting. Maybe, you think, I will just call and tell my supervisor right now that I am done. Or maybe I will not even call and let the proverbial chips fall where they may. Then you remember the work ethic instilled in you as a child, so you begrudgingly shower, pull on your work clothes, and take on another day. And now the wisdom alarms are blaring. What should I do? How should I manage my dissatisfaction? Isn't there more to life than this?

Elevated insight—and the moral grounding it entails—involves seeing yourself embedded in shared humanity. The reason you get out of bed and manage to get to work on this particular Monday is because you recognize the humanity of your supervisor and of all the others who rely on you to show up each day. Following up our commitments is a wise choice in most circumstances, in part because it is prosocial, making the world a more reliable and honorable place for all of us.

But let's make this a little more complicated. Perhaps one reason you do not like your job very much is that you feel the company you work for does not always deal ethically or truthfully with the public. You wonder if making a living the way you do contributes to greater dishonesty in the world. This also will be a factor in making wise choices because pursuing truth is also part of elevated insight. Now we have a dilemma. On the one hand, the most empathic and prosocial thing is to follow up on your commitments, to be a reliable and consistent employee. On the other hand, the desire to pursue truth and live consistently is precisely what makes your work so uncomfortable for you. How will you choose? The point of this illustration is not really to tell you what to choose, but to show how wisdom requires a high degree of insight.

This definition of wisdom sets a high bar, calling us beyond mere cognition to full-bodied living, beyond self-interest to the betterment of shared humanity, beyond simple solutions to holding complexity and nuance. There is no easy formula for this sort of wisdom, but there is a path forward. Yes, it is a difficult path, but walking it calls forth the best of what we have to offer ourselves and one another.

A FOURFOLD PATH TO WISDOM

No definition fully captures wisdom, but one reason to try is that defining wisdom helps us break it down into component parts, and then it starts to seem attainable. Maybe wisdom is not just a result of living a long life. Perhaps it is a virtue that can be developed, just as one can learn to be more forgiving or grateful or resilient. We believe so, which is why we offer a specific model for growing in wisdom. The fourfold path to wisdom that we outline in this book contains four ascending levels, each with its own specific purpose. The *KDTT* model is knowledge, detachment, tranquility, and transcendence.

Receiving Knowledge

We believe that any school of wisdom requires knowledge. In order for growth to occur, the soil has to receive the seed and allow the root to hold. Maddie is wise beyond her years. Diagnosed with Crohn's Disease at age 13, she has lived half a decade with this debilitating disease, already enduring more invasive medical procedures than most of us have in a lifetime. For long periods of time, her disease required her to abstain from solid foods and instead use a nasogastric tube to pump nutritional formula into her body. This is a stark and tragic reality for a teenager whose friends gather at pizza parlors and ice cream shops. Suffering is always difficult, and Maddie could have easily sunk into despair and self-pity, but with the help of a loving family and effective medical providers she chose a wisdom path instead. She began cooking and baking, even though she could not eat anything she made, and she soon became an artisan who loved to give away her art. I (Mark) have benefitted from many loaves of Maddie's amazing bread since she and my wife (four decades her senior) became unlikely friends. Maddie writes, "Giving food to other people also gave me a chance to explain my illness and to form new relationships with people. In this way, creating food was emotionally sustaining for me" (Huwe, 2018). Now in college, where she is preparing to become a health care provider, Maddie is evidence that growing in wisdom does not require old age.

The first part of wisdom is knowledge—holding the end in mind. Maddie, at age 13, needed to learn about her disease before making any steps toward wisdom. Think of this as remembering the map and destination of what is most important in life. All paths to wisdom start from some basic fundamental premises, certain principles that need to be ingrained in order to judge and discern the inevitable dilemmas and conflict of human life. This first level serves as the foundation for the development of wisdom by acknowledging the reality of a fundamental human nature and emphasizing transcendent values such as truth, beauty, and goodness. Knowledge also helps us consider what it means to grow into

our fullness as humans and how this relates to the coordination and ordering of human values toward the common good. We consider this level of
wisdom in Chapters 1 to 3.

Practicing Detachment

Negative capability, a term first used by the English poet John Keats, is
the ability to hold contrary notions in mind without resorting to simplistic solutions. This requires a degree of detachment, being able to stand
back from immediate circumstances and emotions, to refuse to be swallowed up in emotion, and to discern a larger perspective. When Maddie
faced Crohn's Disease at age 13, her world was turned upside-down as
she confronted challenges unlike her peers—ones that will never fully
be resolved. It would have been easy to slump into helplessness. The path
of wisdom called her elsewhere.

Or consider the ideological fortresses we began this chapter with. We
may be tempted to doggedly defend our beliefs rather than acknowledge
the possible veracity of others. Detachment from our most familiar ways
of being and thinking requires us to consider the ironies and contemplate
the messy and complicated parts of how we live and what we decide. This
step protects against a rigid self-idolization and narcissism as we learn
to refrain from myths of certainty. We discuss detachment in Chapters 4
to 6.

Experiencing Tranquility

The purpose of this level is finding equanimity, learning to regulate emotions amidst life's vicissitudes. Let's be clear: life is upsetting at times.
When confronted with new ideas, conflicts in relationships, frightening
medical diagnoses, or other personal tragedies, we naturally enter into
places of worry, fear, depression, and alarm. Becoming wise does not
numb us to these feelings, but it helps us move through them into places
of peace. We still notice our unwanted feelings and intense desires, but
they do not have to run our lives. The image of the Buddha under the
Bodhi Tree at the moment he achieved enlightenment beautifully

expresses this idea. After successfully defeating the demon Mara, a symbolic representation of desires and passions, the Buddha attains enlightenment. The image of awakened serenity found on the face of the Buddha remains an icon of psychological and emotional tranquility. This example also exemplifies the intimate relationship between detachment and tranquility, and the development from level 2 to level 3. Tranquility is found in balance, calm, and radical acceptance of the present moment. It follows from possession of deep knowledge and nonattachment to the outcomes of our actions. On this level, thoughts and feelings can be cleansed and purified. Tranquility is the focus of Chapters 7 to 9.

Cultivating Transcendence

The aim of this final level is stepping outside ourselves into some higher or elevated insight. To obtain wisdom requires a breakthrough of human consciousness that highlights the transcendent nature of existence. This final level represents an encounter with an absolute (e.g., the Divine, Tao, Brahman), and the goal is gaining new perspective from this encounter. Here is a spoiler alert: this is where we feel something is missing from current scientific definitions of wisdom. We spend the final portion of this book considering wisdom and transcendence.

THE HOPE OF WISDOM

We live in a time in which esoteric ideas historically reserved for a small number of elites are now being explored and facilitated by people of all walks of life. Consider the current surge of books, talks, and seminars involving the notion of mysticism—a term traditionally denoting years of religious devotion and ascetic practices often involving a mysterious transfer of knowledge not meant for mass consumption. Methods of mystical practice and development are now as readily available as cookbooks. It is easy to miss how strange this would appear to our ancient ancestors. This egalitarian dissemination of knowledge owes much to the social and natural sciences in their ability to break down and translate ideas into language easier to comprehend. In the chapters to follow, we communicate the language of wisdom from a psychological, scientific, and spiritual perspective, demystifying it and facilitating an approach that is informative and helpful in everyday life.

These are challenging days of polarization and vitriol. How can we start mending the wounds of the earth and those who inhabit it? Will political muscle solve the problem? It seems unlikely and has been well-tried. Will exhortations to love one another bring about harmony and peace? Apparently not. Will religious proselytizing and spiritual transformation bring us all together with a common vision and heart for justice? It does not seem likely. There is no panacea to today's quandary, but the best strategy forward seems to be the pathway of wisdom. Along this path we learn about ourselves and the other, we detach ourselves from the passions that drive our irrational ways of being in the world, and eventually we experience a degree of calm amidst the storm. This is a path that calls us outside of our silos, outside of our preconceptions and little ways of searching for truth, and into a broader flow of lived humanity, and perhaps even beyond humanity to some awareness of transcendent Truth.

PART 1

KNOWLEDGE

CHAPTER 1

KNOWLEDGE
AND WISDOM

O urs is a time of political and ideological polarization that easily shuts off discovery and wisdom, mutes curiosity, stifles creativity, and inhibits the adventure of daily learning. Wisdom moves us in the other direction, calling us into the unknown, asking us to learn from those who are unfamiliar, bringing adventure to life, and allowing us to change and grow as individuals, communities, and societies. And it all begins with knowledge.

Here is a brief true-false quiz:

Question 1: Wisdom is the same as knowledge.
Question 2: Knowledge requires wisdom.
Question 3: Wisdom requires knowledge.

In response to question 1, we have all heard adages and proclamations that wisdom is not the same as knowledge. It is easy to find an abundance of clever metaphors, such as knowledge is akin to nailing boards together while wisdom is building a sturdy and beautiful house. Or maybe it is the uncle at the Thanksgiving table complaining about how smart his young boss thinks she is, yet she lacks wisdom for how to manage a department. The boss may be wiser than the disgruntled uncle thinks, but in general we agree that wisdom and knowledge are not identical. Question 1 is false.

Question 2 is also mostly false. Most of us can think of a person with encyclopedic knowledge who seems quite ill-equipped to manage the dimensions of wisdom described in the previous chapter.

Question 3 is the point of this chapter, and we answer true. Wisdom requires knowledge. However a person may define the two, it is difficult to deny the intimate relationship between them. Knowledge most clearly distinguishes wisdom from other related virtues, but not just any knowledge will do. Just as not all food is equally nutritious, neither is all knowledge. In this chapter we explore nutrient-rich knowledge, which is likely to help us develop wisdom. Just as good eating becomes a habit with time and practice, so also seeking wisdom can become a heart-healthy habit as we learn to pursue enriched forms of knowledge. In the next chapter we consider why enriched knowledge is so difficult to find in our data-driven age, and in Chapter 3 we offer two strategies for clinging to helpful knowledge amidst the difficulties.

FACTUAL KNOWLEDGE

Without knowing the basic facts of how things work, wisdom is not possible. In the introduction we mentioned Maddie, diagnosed with Crohn's Disease at age 13, and how her first step toward wisdom was learning about her disease and how her body responds to it. Without that, she would not have developed the sort of wisdom that characterizes her young life.

Wisdom-related knowledge begins with understanding factual information. Annelise came to psychotherapy in a panic, thinking she might be going crazy. Over the previous several months she had fleeting experiences where she felt disconnected from her own body, as if she were watching herself from outside, like viewing a movie starring Annelise. Sometimes she perceived her feet to be huge (they were not), or had the sense that life is not real, that she is not real. It is all make-believe. Each time she experienced these episodes, her concerns about going crazy deepened, even to the point of considering suicide. Psychologists call these symptoms of depersonalization/derealization disorder, and they occur frequently among people under age 40. In Annelise's situation, all she needed was some factual information.

"You mean I'm not going crazy?" she asked, with tears of relief and gratitude.

"No, that's very unlikely. The symptoms you describe show up often, especially in times of stress. Somewhere close to half of the adults in our country have experienced something like what you describe."

With this basic information, Annelise felt immediate calm, and her worries about psychosis went away. We scheduled a follow-up appointment or two, and soon her depersonalization symptoms subsided and life got back to normal. All she needed was factual knowledge and a compassionate listener to help calm the anxiety symptoms. Most often psychotherapy doesn't work so quickly or easily, but every now and then some factual knowledge clears the way forward.

To be wise, we need to know some fundamental facts. If you're going to make a living as an attorney, you better learn the law. If you want to know about Dostoevsky, start reading. If you think you might have cancer, it's a good idea to see a doctor and have some testing done. If you're going to be a good spouse or partner, get to know the person you're with.

Factual knowledge is a good start, but we need other sorts of knowledge also. Once we have some factual knowledge, we need to know what to do with it.

PROCEDURAL KNOWLEDGE

One of the most prominent researchers of wisdom, Paul Baltes, suggested two key types of knowledge show up with wisdom: factual and procedural (Baltes & Staudinger, 2000). Procedural knowledge requires awareness of what to do, when to do it, and how to do it.

Assume your child is being bullied at school. What steps should you, as a wise parent, take? Factual knowledge means that you know the bullying is occurring and you know, at your core, that this is not okay because your child is a person of dignity and worth, and that you are obligated to make things better. You gather basic information: When is this happening? How often? Is there just one perpetrator? Who is doing the bullying? Procedural knowledge is required to make it stop. How is your child responding? Who is the best person to contact at the school? How will you help your child cope with the emotional trauma of this experience?

Factual and procedural knowledge go hand in hand with wisdom. Factual knowledge comes first, but it is often not enough on its own to facilitate wisdom. For that, we need to know what steps to take to manage the pragmatic demands life brings. It wasn't enough for Maddie to learn about Crohn's Disease at age 13, though that was an important first step. She also needed to go through a long, painful process of learning how to manage it, including how to feed herself with a nasogastric tube, how to refrain from eating solid food, no matter how delicious it may look, how to manage the complexities of being a teenager with a serious illness, how to reduce risks of contracting COVID-19 because of her risk, and how to deal with the grief and loss of such a dire diagnosis early in life (Huwe, 2018, 2019). Factual knowledge came first for Maddie, as it typically does, but wisdom also required her to gain procedural knowledge.

Imagine for a moment that you have a lucrative job that pays many thousands of dollars every month. Certainly your job requires factual knowledge—perhaps how to write lines of code that a smart phone can understand, diagnose and treat diseases, or exchange foreign currencies. Your job also requires some procedural knowledge, such as determining which cloud is best for storing your code, or when to recommend treatment A over treatment B, or how to anticipate valuation of different currencies based on current political situations. But now let's back up for a moment and consider the cascading levels of procedural knowledge connected with your job. What sort of time and energy do you allot to your job, and how does that impact relationships with friends and family? How much of your personal worth and identity do you associate with your job? What is it you do with the large amount of money you earn each month? Do you invest some of it in a 401(k) for retirement? Do you honestly report it when it comes time to pay taxes each year? Do you contribute some of it for the sake of those who earn less than you, to help make the world a better place? These decisions also require enriched procedural knowledge, requiring interpretative acumen that one might call wisdom, calling you to situate yourself outside of the work itself and the paycheck it provides to consider your values in relation to the direction life is taking you, the needs of others, and the world around. This bigger perspective-taking is an important part of wisdom. Indeed, some of the early scientific writers in positive psychology preferred the word "perspective" to the word "wisdom" (Peterson & Seligman, 2004). Perspective is a vital part of enriched knowledge.

ENRICHED KNOWLEDGE

So far, we have suggested that wisdom requires knowing things (factual knowledge), and knowing what to do with the circumstances life presents (procedural knowledge), but there is a key word used by Baltes and his colleagues that also must be considered. It is the word "rich." They wrote of *rich* factual knowledge and *rich* procedural knowledge. We can know what it means when the "check engine" light comes on in our car, and how to call the mechanic when it happens, but having a light show up on our dashboard isn't when we most yearn for wisdom. When a long-time partner leaves, when a child has a serious disease, when we suddenly lose a meaningful job, when an addicted friend reaches out for help, when faced with a terminal medical diagnosis, in these times we long for a deep sort of wisdom to guide us through the murkiest and most difficult seasons of life.

What makes knowledge enriched? There are many different views on this, but we turn to Grossmann's (2017) work on wise thinking and to others who have expanded on his ideas (Oakes et al., 2019) to describe four characteristics of enriched knowledge that lead to wise reasoning: seeking broader perspectives, integrating different perspectives, being humble, and recognizing uncertainty and change. Plus, we add a fifth

characteristic to the list—developing self-knowledge. As clinical psychologists, we see the importance of self-knowledge on a daily basis.

Seeking Broader Perspectives

In today's world, knowledge is often dispensed in an effort to persuade,
which makes it quite natural to present a particular part of the story and
leave out other parts. Vote for this candidate, we are told, because the other
once supported this legislation. But we're not told why the other candidate might have chosen a particular position or what complexities were
at play at the time. One of the most important habits of wisdom is to
look for broader perspectives. These broader perspectives come from two
places: deeply held values and considering views that others might hold.

Deeply Held Values

Have you developed a sense of what matters most in life? Do certain core
principles guide you during challenging times? Without a general knowledge about life and what makes it worthwhile, we are unable to critically
and thoughtfully examine the culture and circumstances around us, making us susceptible to being dominated by the current moment, the loud-
est voices, or the shallow forms of knowledge surrounding us.

Michael came for help with depression that fell suddenly on him when
his wife of many years decided to leave the marriage. The depth of his
surprise and pain were palpable, visiting him in dreams and early morning awakening, robbing him of his appetite and joy. At times he questioned everything about a 15-year marriage that meant so very much to
him. But over the course of 20 psychotherapy sessions Michael was able
to move through profound grief, face into his anger and loss, find a renewed
sense of hope and purpose in life, and overcome his depression. What
allowed him to make these changes? Good psychotherapy, we hope, but
beyond that, it reflected the depth of perspective that he developed over
many years prior to his marriage crisis. Throughout his marriage, Michael
determined to love his partner, to see the best in her, to yearn for her well-
being. All these values were tested to the limit when she decided to leave

the marriage, but as he moved through his grief and anger, Michael was able to reclaim the best in himself and wish his former partner well. These were orienting values, allowing him not only to experience some greater peace with his divorce but also to reclaim his own identity in the aftermath of life's greatest loss. He was not a hater, but a lover. He chose to stand up to his anger, but without letting it consume him. These values were forged in his 15-year marriage and before, and they continued to bring hope and meaning to his life when his marriage ended.

Considering Views Others Hold

The success of Dear Abby and other advice columnists suggests that in the liminal moments of life we want to hear from others. What might they have to teach us about the situation we are facing? This is an important part of enriched thinking, the desire to imagine and pursue the knowledge others might bring.

Consider the "only an idiot" phenomenon. "I think Donald Trump was the worst president in American history, and *only an idiot* would think otherwise." Or maybe, "Getting a COVID vaccine is an assault to my freedom, and *only an idiot* would hold this sort of freedom lightly." Be honest. Most of us have at least a few opinions that we hold like this, but these typically do not promote wisdom. Enriched knowledge leading to wisdom points us in the other direction, toward curiosity and appreciation for others' views. For example, "I'm not a fan of Donald Trump's presidency, but some think it helped bring about some important changes in economic policy." Or, "I am not going to get a vaccine, but some people consider this a matter of civic responsibility more than individual freedom." Here is where we find an openness to learn other perspectives, leading to enriched forms of knowledge.

Integrating Different Perspectives

It's one thing to understand that others may hold different knowledge from what we ourselves hold, and still another to actively integrate others' perspectives into our own worldview and decision making. This sounds incredibly difficult because it is, but the wisest among us often do exactly this.

In her book, *Team of Rivals: The Political Genius of Abraham Lincoln*, Doris Kearns Goodwin (2005) describes President Lincoln's decision to staff his presidential cabinet with a group of politicians who disagreed with one another. Some of the men chosen by Lincoln had recently been defeated by him, some were from his own Republican party, while others were in fact Democrats. These rivals surrounded Lincoln during the tumultuous times of his presidency. This was a shocking move on his part. Wouldn't it have been much easier to bring in like-minded political partisans, a bunch of yes men that would rally around and indulge his every wish? Yet Goodwin explains, "Abraham Lincoln would emerge the undisputed captain of this most unusual cabinet, truly a team of rivals. The powerful competitors who had originally disdained Lincoln became colleagues who helped him steer the country through its darkest days" (p. xvi). While this highlights the brilliant political tact and character of Lincoln, as we zoom in it also allows us to see another important psychological component of enriched knowledge that reflects wisdom: the ability to integrate others' perspectives into our own. The more ways we can think about an issue, approach a problem, or enter into disputed narratives, the more we are able to gain insight from opposing views that challenge our own preconceived notions.

This flies in the face of conventional practice. Since the 1960s psychologists have spoken and written of *confirmation bias*, which means we are naturally drawn to perspectives that align with our own. We subscribe to tweets and add Facebook friends if they share our basic worldview. And we avoid others. We read the news pundits with whom we already agree. When walking into a bookstore, our tendency is to pick up a book that aligns with our preconceived views, glance at the back cover, and conclude, "This looks like a good book." Wisdom pushes against this, taking us out of the comfort the confirmation bias offers, asking us to consider other vantage points.

It's important to identify and live into our deeply held values, yet it's equally important to avoid overly rigid thinking that is of no help when instability and complexity arise. Remaining obsessively fixated in our own thinking patterns and myopic worldview can lead to mental polarizing and radicalizing. If our understanding of reality becomes synonymous with reality itself, then knowledge simply serves as confirmation bias, and truth becomes merely a reflection of our assumptions. Without integrating other perspectives while exploring our own, it's inevitable that we will lose touch with nuance and balance in how we see the world. Psychoanalyst Thomas Ogden (2009) makes a helpful contrast between magical thinking and genuine thinking, the latter being "thinking that confronts reality in its fully, unforgiving alterity" (p. 169).

What about the idea of truth? We believe certain truths are innate and universal. But can we know these truths fully and without a healthy dose of skepticism? We suggest that we cannot. Because we are inherently limited by our own vantage point, we only see these truths partially and never in totality. We can acknowledge absolute truth while critically examining reality from various points of reference. Again, Ogden writes, "genuine thinking, though driven by the need to know what is true, is at the same time characterized by firm recognition that conclusions are always inconclusive, endings are always beginnings. . . ." (2009, p. 169).

Knowledge, when it is increased from multiple perspectives, not only expands one's frame of mind, it can also increase empathic understanding. This requires considering the experiences of others, empathizing with their emotions, and seeing how they are impacted by context and circumstances. There are lessons here for us in our current climate of toxic civic discourse. Are we listening to alternative viewpoints that may challenge our preconceived notions? If not, just how might we benefit from finding our own "team of rivals"? Maybe we should stop avoiding people who take different stances from what we do, instead intentionally seeking out those from different cultures, religious groups, and political parties. Maybe we should follow Lincoln's lead and invite our opponents into our house.

Being Humble

As we've already hinted, enriched thinking requires us to become aware of the limits to our knowledge and understanding and to humbly submit to what we cannot know. With wisdom, it's as important to acknowledge what we do *not* know as what we *do* know. The context of our own history, culture, and life experience colors the lens through which we see and interpret the world. We are all confined in ways by the contextual makings of our own lives, because we do not obtain knowledge in a pure unfiltered form. Just as language allows us to learn and communicate, while also falling short of conveying our thoughts and feelings, so it is with wisdom-related knowledge. Nonetheless, wisdom often is found in between the known and the unknown. *Wisdom lives in the liminal spaces.* If we can rest in the tension and not pull toward certainty too rashly, we might find something profound and new.

This conclusion about humility resonates with both new scholarship and old. In recent times, Dilip Jeste and his colleagues surveyed 57 international experts on wisdom (Jeste et al., 2010), and the highest-rated item on their survey turned out to be "recognizing limits of one's own knowledge." In days gone by, the ancient Greek philosopher Socrates, considered to be one of the wisest figures in western civilization, acknowledged his own lack of knowledge and his tireless search for someone wiser than himself. He approached wisdom from the standpoint of ignorance as intellectual humility. While the ancient Oracle of Delphi speaking on behalf of the god Apollo said that no one was wiser than Socrates, he himself struggled to accept this prophetic utterance.

Seeing this in light of modern psychology and certain cognitive aspects of wisdom, it seems reasonable to say that the more we know, the more aware we are of our ignorance. "Extension of knowledge provokes consciousness of one's ignorance" (Ruisel, 2005, p. 282). However, Socrates came to admit that perhaps he in fact was wise, since he was able to acknowledge his own ignorance where others would not. What we find in Socrates are not prescriptions about what is wise but a disproving of common notions of knowledge that fail to survive critical inspection.

Humility invites us to admit that our thinking isn't always correct, or at least that we can't be sure of how correct we are. Some of the most exciting social science research these days is on the topic of intellectual humility, which is all about our relationship to the knowledge we hold. For example, Pete and James both "know" that using cloth bags at the grocery store is preferable to using disposable plastic bags, but they have different relationships with that knowledge. Pete refuses to consider any arguments to the contrary while James is open to reading about the complexity of the issues involved, including the amount of natural resources and carbon emissions that go into producing cloth bags and how long they are typically used before being discarded.

People with intellectual humility are quicker than others to admit they're not sure about something, or that they may be wrong. They are also more curious, open-minded, and reflective in their thinking processes (Krumrei-Mancuso et al., 2020). In other words, intellectual humility promotes the sort of enriched knowledge associated with wisdom.

Though it may seem morbid to discuss, another sort of humility is recognizing that we all have a shelf-life. While this idea does not show up much in the psychology of wisdom, it is prominent in the religious and philosophical traditions of the world. One of us had a physician tell us that the United States is the only country in the world where we think death is optional. It also seems to be a place where we tolerate arrogant certainty, and even praise it. Wisdom pushes us the other way, toward the finitude of our days and knowledge. Only when we face our myths of immortality and omniscience are we able to embark on a quest for wisdom.

In the New Testament, the letter of James says "yet you do not even know what tomorrow will bring. What is your life? For you are a mist that appears for a little while and then vanishes" (New Revised Standard Version, James 4:14). The book of Ecclesiastes in the Hebrew Scriptures contains the word *hebel* 38 times—a word that connotes the fleeting, vaporous nature of life (Neff & McMinn, 2020). It's humbling and curious to realize how much attention we give to the tedious details of life, often causing us stress and zapping our vitality, when it is all a passing mist. We concur with the psalmist who writes, "so teach us to count our days that we may gain a wise heart" (New Revised Standard Version, Psalm 90:12).

In this same vein, the Latin term *memento mori* denotes a reminder of death. The tradition is found in many cultures, such as Roman Stoicism and medieval Christianity. A vast collection of European Renaissance oil paintings portray scholars and saints, such as St. Francis of Assisi holding a skull in reverential contemplation, appearing to signify the presence of death that always lingers close by. In Buddhism, one manifestation of *memento mori* is the *maranasati*, a meditation on death that comes traditionally from the Buddha himself. In the *maranasati*, "the Buddha says, 'Mindfulness of death developed and made much is very beneficial and ends in deathlessness. Bhikkhus [monks], do develop mindfulness of death'" (Moon, 2019, p. 2). This mindfulness practice is used to bring a conscious awareness of the reality of death, leading to an acceptance of mortality, improved vigor for living morally, and increased charity towards others (Moon, 2019). The idea of *memento mori* in both East and West is not to focus morbidly on death, but to gain a renewed sense of the fleeting and precious nature of life through self-examination and humble recognition of finitude.

Being humble involves recognizing that there are many things we do not know, that even the things we think we know may be less certain than we imagine, and that even our grip on life itself is impermanent. Perhaps this doesn't sound encouraging in a world that reveres power and control, but being aware of our limits is an essential part of the enriched knowledge that ultimately leads to detachment, tranquility, transcendence, and wisdom.

Recognizing Uncertainty and Change

Software developers writing in any computer language have something equivalent to an *if-then* statement. *If* this circumstance happens, *then* the phone or the computer should respond this way. This sounds fairly straightforward, but rarely is. An often-used variant of the *if-then* state-ment is the *if-then-else* statement, which can go on for dozens or hundreds of lines of code. *If* this happens, then do this, *else if* this happens, do this, *else if* this happens, and on and on and on. Enriched knowledge recognizes that simple if-then statements are rarely adequate in life. We need lots of *else* clauses because life circumstances are complicated, and change quickly.

Scientists who study wisdom might pose a question such as this: "A 14-year-old girl wants to leave her home for good. What would you advise?" An unwise response would be a simple reflexive statement, such as, "That's a terrible idea. If someone that young wants to leave home, the answer should always be no." Another unwise response would be the opposite reflex: "It should be her choice. If she wants to leave, then she should be allowed to do so." A wiser response would be to consider various possibilities and how each might be related to the situation in which this 14-year-old finds herself. Might there be something hap-pening at home that makes it important for her to leave? Does she have a safe place she is considering going? What sort of historical and cultural variables are at play?

Enriched knowledge calls for flexibility and nuance that is uniquely human. Though we began this section with a computer example, we're not really convinced software can capture this. Enriched knowledge does not reflect superhuman characteristics; quite the opposite, it highlights what's most deeply human in a simple, focused, and unclouded way. At their best, humans listen, struggle, feel deep empathy and compassion, consider nuance, change their minds, balance thoughts and feelings, and ultimately move forward with a degree of tentativeness and a deep desire to learn and adapt.

While enriched knowledge asks us to be flexible and adaptable, this does not mean that we simply adapt our views to whatever the current time and context expects of us. Consider again the person you imagined as the face of wisdom in the introduction. Does the person have all the latest gadgets and recognize quotes from all the best movies? Do they have lots of bumper stickers on their car? Do they spend hours reading or watching the news every day? Or is it possible that this person holds a certain ethereal or transcendent quality that seems outside their genera-tional and historical context? Is there a "just visiting" quality to them? Knowledge from a wisdom perspective involves pondering timeless truths and mysteries, drawing insights from both the beauty and limits of human nature. As such, wise thinkers may be mostly unimpressed with the latest advances and collective progress. It's as if they have freed themselves—at least somewhat—from the rigid confines of their his-torical and cultural age, and in so doing they discover individual and spiritual growth as well.

There is profound paradox here: wisdom calls us to adapt and be flex-ible, to be attuned to cultural and historical nuance, but it also calls us to stay steady and consider long, enduring truths. Developmental psycholo-gist Monika Ardelt (2000) describes this as the universal nature of wisdom-related knowledge, as opposed to merely intellectual knowledge. She writes that "wisdom-related knowledge is timeless and independent of scientific advancements or political and historical fluctuations because it provides universal answers to universal questions that concern the basic predicaments of the human condition" (p. 779).

Consider some of the timeless wisdom teachings in religious and spir-itual traditions. In the Hebrew Scriptures (Old Testament), King Solo-mon is approached by two women claiming a baby is theirs. He solves the problem by suggesting they cut the baby in half and give half to each woman. One woman agrees, the other objects and is even willing to give the child to the other. At that point Solomon recognizes who the true mother is and gives her the child (1 Kings 3: 16–28). Later in the Bible, in the New Testament, Jesus is confronted by an angry group of men who bring a woman caught in adultery. According to the religious law, the men believe they should stone the woman to death. Jesus quietly kneels in the sand and scribbles something before pronouncing, "let anyone among you who is without sin be the first to throw a stone at her" (New Revised Stan-dard Version, John 8:7). Both of these examples from the Bible have stood the test of time. They are "as powerful today as they were in a dis-tant past because they address universal issues of human emotions and behavior, such as the tendency to find fault in others but to be blind to one's own imperfections, feelings of envy and greed, and the protective instincts of a mother" (Ardelt, 2000, p. 779).

Knowledge about human worth and dignity resides at the core of what it means to be fully human, even as the applications of these principles vary from one culture to another. The United Nations Declaration of Human Rights, which has been translated into over 500 languages, is a historically significant example of an institution establishing core values and precepts that transcend individual nation-states and diverse cultures. "All human beings are born free and equal in dignity and rights. They are endowed with reason and conscience and should act towards one another in a spirit of brotherhood" (United Nations, art. 1, 1948). This maxim provides a wise core that guides how we understand and treat one another.

There is a straight line that runs through every human soul, a consistent essence in every person that we see from the earliest days of awareness until the final breath of life. We might call it personality or disposition or character, but whatever we call this straight line, it shows up on the school playground and in the vicissitudes of teenage years, as we establish career and relational patterns, and as we age and reflect and offer our expertise to future generations. As psychologists, we often find ourselves in the role of helping people remember who they are. The person sitting in the office is not just someone whose marriage recently failed, or who lost a job, or who has learned to numb pain with an addiction. No, this is a person with a particular story, a person of dignity and value—confused, perhaps, as we all are at times—but of deep importance and worth. There is something universal and ubiquitous here, and it reaches much deeper than the troubles that visit us and the false attachments we form in various seasons of life.

Yes, wisdom requires flexibility, critical judgment, and awareness of the relative nature of life. It calls us to embrace uncertainty and change, but it does so in a way that accentuates what it means to be fully human and to search for enduring underlying principles, even when forgotten truths may clash with the status quo. We explore this further in Chapter 3.

Developing Self-Knowledge

We have stayed relatively close to the wise thinking literature (Grossman, 2017; Oakes et al., 2019) on the first four strategies for enriched knowledge, but it's also important to consider what Staudinger (2019) calls *personal wisdom*. General wisdom involves applying general concepts of wisdom to changing situations in life and knowing how to navigate complexity. Personal wisdom, in contrast, involves knowing ourselves, our own history, the challenges unique to each of us as individuals, and developing sound judgment in decision making that will affect our life trajectories.

Seeking enriched knowledge outside ourselves by talking with other people, reading books, or sitting under the tutelage of those who are wise is a good start, but eventually we need to invite that knowledge into ourselves, personalize it, and bring it to bear in our own lives. This type of self-knowledge requires more than education or hanging out with wise mentors. It requires a willingness to explore and become intimate with the dark corners of our minds that are much easier to hide than to bring into the light. As clinical psychologists, we are painfully aware of this. Sitting across from patients in the consulting room, we are able to witness another's emotional conflict from just enough distance to be able to see what they cannot, to recognize the reality that, because of their absorption in it, they are missing.

For example, take Brandon, a bright young man who fails to understand just how much he does for other people and can't accept his own goodness and positive attributes because of anxious fear of disapproval and rejection. Or consider Kim, a middle-aged woman so absorbed by shame related to sexual trauma that she lacks the capacity to take in the love given by her husband and has come to interpret kindness and empathy as seduction and danger. What is evident to the therapist is too close for them to see. The subjective world we live in is often a well-designed illusion trapping us in a familiar affliction. We likely didn't create the affliction, but we perpetuate it by the narratives we carry. An outsider can give voice to, and increase understanding of, another, yet that knowledge has to be possessed and developed on one's own. It has to become personalized to be actualized.

Wisdom research in the social sciences started by incorporating views of wisdom found outside of the academic community, such as those in ancient literature and religious traditions, and by asking groups of participants what they perceive wisdom to be. In an aptly titled chapter, "Wisdom of the Crowd," researchers Weststrate, Bluck, and Glück (2019) boiled down common notions of wisdom to three components: cognitive, affective, and reflective. This last one—the reflective component—includes "deep insight, critical self-reflection, and humility" (p. 103). These are crucial in cultivating self-knowledge and growing in personal wisdom. Insight, self-reflection, and humility allow us to anticipate patterns of self-deception and ignorance and come to see reality more clearly and less filtered through our inherent biases.

Let's make this practical. What are you like when a friend or partner disagrees with you? Do you get sullen and silent? Do you defend yourself and try to prove why you are right? Do you acquiesce and agree with the other just to keep peace? How each of us answers these questions has a bearing on the knowledge we need for wisdom. Those who withdraw in the face of disagreement, nursing their wounds, may be prone to miss important perspectives that others have to offer, or even to miss their own perspective, because they retreat in pain rather than thinking more deeply about what might be valuable in their own viewpoint. The one who resorts to outspoken defensiveness won't be able to consider multiple perspectives because of their own self-protective armor. It's like the old adage: "There are two sides to every issue: my side and the wrong side." Those who give in quickly to the other, just to keep from rocking the boat, might fail to see the merit in their own perspectives and opinions, seeking peace at the expense of robust knowledge. Self-knowledge means we know how we respond when others disagree with us, and we find ways to correct for the gaps our natural tendencies may cause us.

Self-knowledge is not the same as self-absorption. Some might even say these are opposite. The famous novelist and social critic Aldous Huxley (1945/2009) wrote about the importance of self-knowledge as a way to free us from the torment of selfishness and fear by allowing us to develop as spiritual beings growing in awareness of our true nature. Self-knowledge, far from being mere obsession with our own thoughts, feelings, and identity, can show our dependent relationship to a higher power, thereby loosening our narcissistic grip. Self-knowledge is not primarily about who I am, but about who I am in relation to others and to ultimate reality.

In this chapter we have suggested that factual and procedural knowledge are the beginning points of wisdom, and that the quality and substance of knowledge matters. Enriched knowledge involves:

1. Seeking broad perspectives, both by looking to our deeply held values and the views of others.
2. Integrating those other perspectives into our own knowledge.
3. Being humble, recognizing that our knowledge may be wrong and is almost certainly insufficient, and that we ourselves are impermanent beings.
4. Acknowledging the uncertainty of life and how quickly things change while still holding steady and developing a wise core that resists fluttering in the wind.
5. Learning to know ourselves well.

But remember, wisdom is hard. It's not easy to hold enriched knowledge in the midst of our information age. It would be convenient if we could substitute a massive volume of information for the deep perspective-taking of wisdom, but if the volume of information we consume brings wisdom, then in our current days we would be surrounded by incredibly wise people. Are we? As we explore in the next chapter, being surrounded by vast amounts of data and information doesn't automatically bring rich knowledge or wisdom.

CHAPTER 2

DATA DRIVEN

W hile hiking through the hills of Vermont—which is a lovely thing to do—one notices long stretches of plastic tubing connected to maples and then heading downhill to holding tanks. Each spring, when the temperatures are below freezing at night and above during the daytime, sap drips from each individual tree, trickling downward until one plastic tube intersects with another, and then another, flowing, ultimately, toward a sophisticated evaporation process where every 40 gallons of sap will ultimately become 1 gallon of maple syrup.

Wisdom requires information, as Vermont syrup requires sap, but it is important not to confuse the two. Pouring sap, which is 98% water, on Sunday morning pancakes would be a grave disappointment. Information masquerading as wisdom is equally distasteful. The British poet, T. S. Eliot, pondered, "Where is the wisdom we have lost in knowledge? Where is the knowledge we have lost in information?" (Eliot, 1934, p. 7).

Eliot's words form the basis of this chapter, and hint at the reason it is so difficult to gain the enriched knowledge required for wisdom. In our data-driven world, we easily become so engulfed with information and knowledge that we settle for these rather than patiently allowing knowledge to distill into wisdom.

FLIPPING THE PYRAMID

Gravity being what it is, our maple syrup metaphor flips upside-down a more common metaphor of unknown origin known as the DIKW pyramid. Wisdom (W) is at the top of this pyramid, with knowledge (K), information (I), and data (D) sequentially beneath.

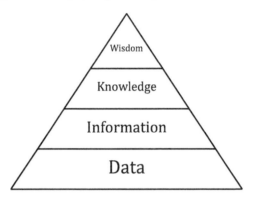

Our maple syrup example starts at the top of the hill, with sap from hundreds of trees (D) merging into tributaries of tubing (I), then held in storage tanks (K), and ultimately converted into wisdom. Whichever direction we take our metaphor—the uphill ancient Egyptian version or the downhill modern Vermont version—it is important to note that data is vastly more abundant than wisdom.

Data is the first and most basic level where something exists that can be perceived. For example, we might look out a window and see some trees, perhaps noticing that trees consist of trunks, branches, and leaves. These are basic observations that inform us of *what* things are or appear to be.

Information builds upon data and considers operations and functions. We learn that trees take in carbon dioxide and produce oxygen, which begins to inform us about *how* things work.

Knowledge goes further and shows connections and relationships between parts of information, and puts information in context. With knowledge we find increasing worth and meaning pertaining to what we are learning. For example, we see how trees relate to us as human beings and their association with the larger ecosystem.

Wisdom, the apex of our comprehension, requires meaningful reflection that points forward, toward solving problems and answering questions of *why*. Why is it important to protect our trees? What perspectives might we need to consider to hold the tension between the impact on valuable aspects of human life such as economic or labor concerns and aspects of flourishing unrelated to human life?

Perhaps an illustration not involving trees would also be helpful. Imagine being in a romantic relationship that seems to be getting more serious and heading toward commitment. Will you and your partner decide to get genetic testing and share your results with one another? The DNA *data* reside within you, in the saliva you could collect and submit for testing. The company that does the testing will provide you with *information* by way of an online report. You will obtain *knowledge* by reading your report and your partner's. *Wisdom* is harder and more complex. Should you do the testing in the first place? What will happen if you find discouraging news? What bearing will this have on your future plans together, including the possibility of having biological children?

Data, information, and knowledge are plentiful. This in itself is not bad—it may even be good—but it speaks to the importance of wisdom to help us manage the flurry of everything coming at us. Wise people take in data, gather information, develop enriched knowledge, and then think and act prudently in the situations and problems they encounter.

LIFE IN A DATA-DRIVEN WORLD

Because our world is saturated with data and information, we face unique challenges and opportunities. I (Mark) sometimes illustrate this to my students by having them take a brief quiz on the famous physiologist, Ivan Pavlov. Here is the quiz:

1. In what year was Pavlov born?
   a. 1756
   b. 1849

    c. 1889

    d. 1903

2. In what discipline was Pavlov's Nobel Prize?

    a. Psychology

    b. Physics

    c. Physiology or Medicine

    d. None of these because Pavlov did not win a Nobel Prize.

3. What nationality was Pavlov?

    a. American

    b. Austrian

    c. Swiss

    d. Russian

4. Which of the following is a picture of Pavlov's laboratory? (Here I include four pictures of old buildings, only one of which is a picture of Pavlov's actual lab in St. Petersburg.)

I encourage students to work in groups, use their smartphones, and be certain of each answer. And because students love a good competition, I always make it clear that each group is trying to answer the quiz as quickly and correctly as possible.

The point of this exercise is not really Ivan Pavlov, but how accessible information is in today's world. The quiz generally takes groups about 30 seconds to complete, and their answers are always correct. And then I guide them through an explanation of what would have been required to answer these same questions with certainty during my graduate school days in the early 1980s. I would have spent hours in the library to answer the first three questions, and the fourth question would have likely been unanswerable unless I flew to Russia. What students today can do with 30 seconds and an iPhone would have taken me at least a week and a thousand or more dollars to do in my graduate school days. Today we have more information in our handheld devices than we could have dreamed a few decades ago.

At this point my illustration also gets a little geeky, because I actually estimated how many volumes were housed in the Vanderbilt University library when I was a student and computed how many bytes of information that would have entailed. It was (and is) a massive research university library, which in 1980 contained about 1.7 terabytes of information. I recently ordered a 2 terabyte flash drive that fits on my keychain. It cost $29. Today it would be theoretically possible to hold all the information available to me in an impressive research library in 1980 on a keychain in my front pocket.

At the time we are writing this book, the most recent estimate we could find is that approximately 2.5 quintillion bytes of data are created on the internet every day (Domo, n.d.).[1] This includes social media posts, video and audio files, podcasts, news reports, and so on. I tried to graph this in relation to the amount of information available in the entire Vanderbilt Research library in 1980, and the Vanderbilt Library did not even show up on the graph! So then I multiplied the size of the library by 100,000 and it finally showed up on the bar graph.

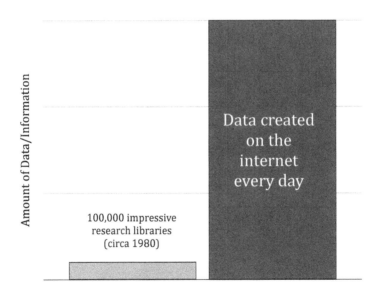

[1] This is likely an underestimate. Domo releases a fascinating infographic each year called "Data Never Sleeps." Version 5.0, released in 2017, was the last time they reported how many bytes of data are produced each day. It is undoubtedly higher now, as indicated by the growing number of worldwide users and increased use of social media revealed in subsequent versions of their annual infographic.

It would take 100,000 impressive research libraries in 1980 to even begin to compare with the amount of data generated on today's internet every single day.

Pause for a moment and consider the quality of data in this comparison. In an academic research library, almost every journal and book is peer-reviewed or otherwise vetted for veracity. When we multiply this by 100,000 to get the daily amount of data generated on the internet, a very small portion of this is of similar quality. Much of it is videos about cute dogs or how to cheat on a video game or change a car battery. This is not bad, per se, but clearly the ratio of internet data that points us toward meaning and wisdom is very low when compared to the sort of information available in libraries.

We will leave it up to you to decide if we are swimming or drowning in a sea of data, but we can agree that data and information engulf us. Life in this information age makes it difficult to gather the enriched knowledge necessary for cultivating wisdom. In the pages that follow, we suggest three reasons why living in our data-driven age makes wisdom so difficult to attain.

CHALLENGE #1: SETTLING FOR NONWISDOM

Richard Foster (1978) began his now-classic book on the spiritual disciplines by asserting, "Superficiality is the curse of our age" (p. 1). The same year, the Russian novelist Alexander Solzhenitsyn (1978) proclaimed in a Harvard University commencement address, "Hastiness and superficiality are the psychic diseases of the 20th Century." Four decades later, now armed with smartphones that put a world of information in our pockets, this continues to be an accurate diagnosis.

After a recent controversial presidential election—one where the incumbent had difficulty conceding his loss to his challenger amidst a flurry of claims about a fraudulent election—I (Mark) found myself reading news from multiple websites almost every evening. Sometimes I would spend hours doing this, looking at CNN, Fox News, ABC News,

NPR, BBC, CBS News, NBC News, *USA Today*. At some point I recognized how shallow my daily quest for information had become, as I read the same stories over and over, always hoping for new insight or awareness. In a turbulent political time, which coincided with the global coronavirus pandemic, I was hoping information and knowledge could somehow plug this gaping hole in my soul—a wound caused by division, fear, and uncertainty for the future more than a lack of information. I had known the Solzhenitsyn quote about superficiality for some time, but I went back and found it again and was stunned by the rest of what he proclaimed at Harvard. Here is the way Solzhenitsyn (1978) finished his thought:

> Hastiness and superficiality—these are the psychic diseases of the twentieth century and more than anywhere else this is manifested in the press. In-depth analysis of a problem is anathema to the press; it is contrary to its nature. The press merely picks out sensational formulas.

It occurred to me that my obsessive quest every evening was not helping me find wisdom. Drowning in information, I kept seeking more, like an addict looking for something to fix my discomfort. British mathematician and philosopher, Alfred North Whitehead, once wrote, "In a sense, knowledge shrinks as wisdom grows: for details are swallowed up in principles" (1929, p. 37). To seek wisdom in tumultuous days, we sometimes need to let the details shrink and reclaim the essence of what it means to be fully human in a complicated, conflicted world. We will write of this more in the next chapter as we consider how wisdom involves holding the end in mind and not getting overly absorbed in the minutiae.

Today there are many pressures moving us toward nonwisdom: distraction, apathy, boredom, and the overconsumption of information to name a few. John Francis Kavanaugh (2006) describes the modern predicament of our consumerist society and the depersonalizing nature of our commodified lives:

Marketing and consuming infiltrate every aspect of our lives and behavior. They filter all experience we have of ourselves. They become the standard of our final worth. Marketing and consuming ultimately reveal us to ourselves as things; and if we find ourselves revealed as things it will follow that our diverse capacities for knowing are reduced to the truncated conditions of thing-like or commodity knowledge. (p. 68)

Kavanaugh prophetically wrote this in 1981 before the rise of the internet and social media. How much more is that true today? The results of the commodification of knowledge, using marketplace strategies to manipulate human desires can lead to an erosion of wisdom's core. We become inundated with data and information that objectify us as consumers. It is not hard to see the emotional tax we are likely to pay here, anxiety and depression being common feelings when we fill ourselves with hollow content.

Robert Sternberg (2019), a renowned scholar who studies wisdom, wrote that nonwisdom shows up more than wisdom in today's world. One form of nonwisdom is quasi-wisdom, which is "incomplete reflection or insight" (p. 6). Someone might offer you words that seem wise on the surface, such as "go with your gut," and while this may work out well sometimes our guts are connected to our brains, and sometimes our brains are terribly misinformed. Quasi-wisdom is a great risk in a world so immersed in data, information, and knowledge. Everywhere we turn we have more words coming at us, some of them true, some of them not, most of them incomplete. These words lure us in as we seek to understand and live well in a complex world, but in the end they leave us confused and lost in a sea of words. This is particularly pernicious when considering the confirmation bias described in Chapter 1. Because we tend to seek information that confirms what we already believe and to avoid other information, it is far easier to change what we choose to read or view than to change our minds. If some evidence contradicts what we already believe, then we can always find some other source of information and call the evidence we do not like "fake news." This inherently limits our exposure to multiple perspectives and leads to nonwisdom, which can even result in the opposite of wisdom—foolishness.

A veneer of wisdom is another form of nonwisdom identified by Sternberg. This is where something appears to be wise—because of the authority of the one providing the information—when actually it is not. We jokingly say, "I read it on the internet, so it must be true." Especially if the source is a familiar news outlet, we are inclined to receive it as true and right. Here we must heed Solzhenitsyn's warning that we may just be reading or hearing "sensational formulas."

At first glance, a veneer of wisdom may seem harmless enough. "People will think what they want to," we pronounce. But when that veneer is financed by deep pockets intent on selling us a particular point of view for profit, then we have a bigger problem.

CHALLENGE #2: EXTREME POLARIZATION

The most troubling form of nonwisdom is what Sternberg calls pseudo-wisdom. This is when people try to appear wise, but do so out of self-interest. Regardless of whether Solzhenitsyn was overly critical of the press in 1978, what has happened since is a great polarization of news-related information, motivated by selling advertisements. News outlets have identified markets, based on extensive data collection and analyses, and now craft their stories to fit the interests and whims of the market to whom they appeal. This is not a problem of the political right or left—it is both. So we have conservative and liberal media now, designer news to appeal to our particular preconceptions—confirmation bias on steroids. If one source gives stories that do not quite fit our hopes or expectations, we simply find another source that does. In our data-driven world, we even have media bias ratings, so that we can discern whether our preferred news sources lean left or right, and then select the perspectives we prefer (see AllSides, n. d.).

For the first few decades of broadcast television, back when Walter Cronkite, Dan Rather, and Connie Chung graced American living rooms with daily news reports, the Federal Communications Commission (FCC) had a standard known as the Fairness Doctrine, which required television networks to identify controversial issues of critical importance to the country and provide contrasting viewpoints about the issue (Ruane, 2011). Further, if a broadcast said something critical about a person, that person had to be allowed equal airtime (Stefon, 2018). Two things happened.

First, amid growing complaints among broadcasters about how onerous the Fairness Doctrine had become, the United States Congress pushed the other way and voted to solidify the FCC Fairness Doctrine by making it federal law in 1987. President Reagan vetoed that bill. Later in 1987 the FCC repealed the doctrine. Second, cable happened. Before cable, the Fairness Doctrine was justified by a scarcity argument (Ruane, 2011). That is, people only had access to a few channels, so whatever these broadcast channels provided needed to be fair and balanced. Once cable came on the scene, and then satellite, and now internet, the idea of news scarcity is laughable. We have news everywhere! Plus, the FCC has different standards in relation to cable from what it has with broadcasting over public airwaves.

Whether or not one looks wistfully back to days when balance was mandated, it is clear that many news organizations now make no pretense of balance or fairness. This is further complicated by the so-called filter bubble, which means our internet search results are influenced by algorithms based on previous searches, purchases, and clicks. If you and I search for "gun control" on Google, we are likely to get different results based on what the algorithms predict we want to read (DuckDuckGo, 2018). Why would Google want to do this? Because they are funded through advertising sales, and advertisers want us to end up on sites where we are most likely to click and buy things.

The data business is booming, because in our economic system we are, after all, first and foremost considered consumers. With this underlying implicit structure come various forms of information, misinformation, knowledge, and nonwisdom. If we are not intentional and careful, our data-driven era can heighten superficiality, cheapen our understanding of complexity, and drive us into the echo chambers of our ideological fortresses. Rather than seeking any sort of fairness, we happily settle for partial truths and polarization.

CHALLENGE #3: LOSING THE BIG VIEW

One of the most impressive things about data is its specificity. The day after shopping for something online, we find ourselves bombarded with advertisements for similar products on our web searches. Based on algorithms of language use and our personal text histories, our smart devices anticipate the next word we will text. The same devices correct bad spelling for us, knowingly compensating for where our thumbs have been clumsy. And it is not just technological devices using data that is highly specific. Every dimension of business, health care, education, and public life contains and is influenced by data.

This specificity of data has allowed us to become highly focused and effective in our intellectual pursuits and our systems of care, something that brings both strengths and challenges. The idea of a liberal arts education—intentionally broad and general in focus—has largely given way to specialized and professionalized education. Similarly, the days of general family physicians in a solo office providing for the needs of a community are largely over. Our health care systems are managed by experts in business while many services are provided by those who have specialties and subspecialties. In one regard, this is excellent. If you or I are in the market for someone who can operate a laser in exactly the right way to successfully restore an eye to proper function, we will likely look for someone who knows how to zoom in and do one highly technical procedure with great expertise. But there also is a price to be paid for hyperspecialization, which is the ability to back up and see a bigger picture. In our data-driven world, we are better at zooming in than at zooming out.

Zooming in does not always promote wisdom, and sometimes it may even detract from it. Most of us have had the experience of calling a

company only to be met by a seemingly endless logic branch of auto-
mated telephone menus, each of them narrowing the focus for why we
may be calling. Presumably, the reason for this is to get us to a computer or person specializing in the very issue we need help with, but
how often in this process do we find ourselves proclaiming, "I just want
to talk with a real person!" A real person, in-person, is another recent
lament for some. That cry of exasperation—declaring our desire for
someone to really listen, to zoom out instead of in so to see us as an
actual person, to understand our needs, and to offer us help in a human-
to-human encounter—is ultimately a yearning for wisdom.

Remember the relationship of knowledge and wisdom discussed in
Chapter 1. Enriched knowledge, by its very nature, requires one to stand
back in humility, get a large view, recognize limits, understand complexity, and hold multiple perspectives. Wisdom requires the ability to zoom
out.

The need for zooming out to a place of wisdom is experienced in hos-
pitals around the world, every day, as desperately ill patients approach
death. Medical providers have the data, information, and knowledge necessary to sustain many of these lives through respirators, intravenous
nutrition and fluids, and dialysis. As families gather to face tragedy and
make difficult decisions, they need some basic knowledge about life
expectancy, chances of recovery, the family member's wishes, and so on,
but mostly they meet together for collective wisdom. Wisdom requires
them to consider all the knowledge they have obtained, to ponder questions of ethics, values, and transcendence, and to make a moral decision
on behalf of someone they love who is unable to make it for themselves.

As data drives us to specificity, wisdom calls us to hold large perspectives. Sternberg and Glück (2019) relate wisdom to moral decision making, which seems fitting because wisdom often involves issues of morality
in a complex world. Early developmental psychologists tended to look at
moral development through a series of cognitive abilities attained as one
matures (e.g., Kohlberg, 1984; Gilligan, 1982). While these developmental models are still valuable to consider, Sternberg and Glück (2019)

draw on more recent work to show how wisdom relates to moral deci-sions. We are oversimplifying a bit, but here is a three-step outline of how wise people might face a moral decision, such as what to do when a loved one is being maintained by life support.

Step 1 is to consider the moral intuitions that are built into human character. These are not so much cognitive as they are default values built into our nature, mediated by the cultures we inhabit. Haidt (2013) identifies values such as care (vs. harm), fairness (vs. cheating), loyalty (vs. betrayal), authority (vs. subversion), sanctity (vs. degradation), and lib-erty (vs. oppression) as moral foundations for how we naturally desire to live in the world. These moral foundations will be swirling in the souls of family members as they gather in a hospital room to make a difficult decision, whether or not they pause to think or talk about these specific moral principles.

Step 2 involves a slower reflection on what naturally emerges from our intuition. It is not enough just to rely on intuition about loyalty, for example, when trying to decide about whether to remove life support from the family member in the hospital bed. We need to hold deep questions about what is most loyal, and how values of loyalty may conflict with values of care and liberty. Greene (2013) suggests that our immediate moral intuitions are worth considering, but they should not be the final arbiter of the best decision.

Step 3 is to reflect even more, including a "self-distanced perspective on complex problems" (Sternberg & Glück, 2019, p. 561). We need to zoom out far enough to see things through another's perspective, think-ing in the third person. With the hospital decision, if the ill family mem-ber were able to express an opinion in light of the current diagnosis and prognosis, what would they have to say in this moment? How might others in the room understand morality in this context? In what ways could we grow in wisdom by considering the views of others in the room or around the world?

Data, information, and knowledge are good and necessary but not fully sufficient for living wisely. If we zoom in too far, we end up with a myopic, fractured, and fragmented approach to life that severs knowledge from social, cultural, and relational contexts, leads to isolated learning, and precludes the openness needed to see from multiple perspectives. But if we can learn to hold the big view wisdom requires, knowledge becomes our friend and ally.

WHY THIS CHAPTER IS (PARTLY) WRONG

We have used a couple of metaphors throughout this chapter—one about sap flowing downhill and one about a pyramid—to illustrate how much more data we have in the world than wisdom. And while this is true enough, all metaphors have limits, including the two we have used. With both metaphors it seems that data automatically and passively funnels into information, knowledge, and wisdom just as naturally as gravity causes sap to flow downhill or just as reliably as chiseled stones are placed on a large foundation. This oversimplifies the process of wisdom quite a lot because we have not yet explored the active process of hermeneutics.

Hermeneutics is the act, or perhaps art, of interpretation. Data does not automatically become information, nor information knowledge, because these transitions require an interpreter to craft a narrative and make sense of what is known. Some narratives truly are better than others, which means wisdom is not only the end state—the top of the pyramid or the gallon of maple syrup—but is actually part of the entire process.

Wise people engage in a hermeneutic of suspicion, which means they are open to the possibility of being wrong. Perhaps they are misinterpreting the data, not seeing important information, imagining the wrong story, coming to faulty conclusions. The hermeneutic of suspicion requires people to consider multiple perspectives rather than latching on to a single narrative and assuming it to be unquestionably true.

The flow from data to information, to knowledge, to wisdom is only as effective as the hermeneutics we employ along the way. A classic example of this is seen in the 1954 Seattle windshield pitting epidemic (Weeks, 2015). Some drivers in Bellingham, Washington, noticed some small pits on their windshields, about 1/16th of an inch deep. Some press reports picked this up, and soon other car owners in the Seattle area started noticing pits in their windshields also. Numerous police reports were filed. The data (windshield pits) had become information. But why was this happening? Some suggested vandalism. Others thought it might be related to nuclear testing (this was just 9 years after the bombing of Hiroshima and Nagasaki). More stories were released in the press and information started becoming "knowledge" about major problems in the world. Eventually the pitting epidemic escaped Seattle and started showing up in other U.S. cities as well. Theories started developing about small objects falling from the sky and damaging car windows, because house windows were not being harmed. And then as suddenly as the reports of pitted windshields started, they stopped.

The Seattle windshield pitting epidemic still shows up in psychology and sociology textbooks decades later because it is a classic example of mass delusion. Of course, some windshields were pitted, and that would still be the case if we all scrutinized our windshields carefully, especially if we drive on gravel roads as many did in 1954. Once the stories started, people began looking more closely, allowing their imaginations to run wild, and some vandals no doubt contributed to the problem. Once the mass delusion calmed down, the stories stopped suddenly and people went back to their normal lives without the neck strain of looking for falling objects from the sky.

We engage in an active interpretive process as data becomes information, knowledge, and wisdom. That interpretive process calls us to humility, self-restraint, intellectual discipline, and genuine curiosity. In other words, we need wisdom all along the way to become wise. If this sounds difficult, that is because it is. Yes, it can be distracting and overwhelming to live in our data-driven days, but these days also promote amazing possibilities if we can learn how to distill data, information, and knowledge into the sort of wisdom that brings out the best in us and others. This distilling process, though challenging, is still possible. We unpack this idea further in Chapter 3 as we explore holding the end in mind.

HOLDING THE
END IN MIND

C learly, we have a problem. To be wise we need knowledge, and not just any knowledge will do. It needs to be deeply enriched knowledge, broad in perspective, held by those who are steady while able to cope with change and brimming with humility and self-awareness. But this sort of knowledge is hard to come by in an age when we are engulfed with information, much of it shallow and often peddled to make a profit. What are we to do in the face of this sort of problem?

Sometimes the compulsive data-drivenness and hasty superficiality that Solzhenitsyn described keep us too busy and preoccupied to dive in and explore the deepest contours of our problem. The core of the problem is not a lack of information or willpower, but rather our difficulty teasing apart deeply meaningful, life-giving knowledge from the fatuous, frantic information that bombards us every day. As Henri Nouwen succinctly put it, "the great paradox of our time is that many of us are busy and bored at the same time" (Nouwen, 1981, pp. 23–24). Boredom is not so much a lack of things to do as it is a wandering and searching for something that matters more than what fills most of our days. We might call this spiritual boredom in that our daily interests and desires sometimes hold little value when contrasted with a life of deep meaning and purpose (Snell, 2015, p. 69).

Level one (Receiving Knowledge) concludes with holding the end in mind, which requires a bit of explanation. Often when we think of the word "end," we might readily associate it with the terminus, the finality of a thing. So a quick read of "holding the end in mind" might imply that we are talking about approaching death. What will matter when we are 85, sitting in a rocking chair and reflecting on the years gone by? That is not a bad topic, but it is not what we mean by "holding the end in mind." Another way the word "end" is used is to think of the fullness of something, the outcome, the natural conclusion. We call the end of a college degree "commencement" because it reflects a natural movement forward as a long, arduous process has brought maturity and fullness of understanding. This latter use of "end" is what we are discussing in this chapter. Holding the end in mind involves human flourishing, considering what gives life direction and purpose, and allowing our thoughts, feelings, and relationships to be guided by these principles. Enriched knowledge is a vital part of this. Because not all forms of knowledge have the same level of value, knowledge needs to be ordered, with proper weight given to the knowledge of greatest importance.

Perhaps most of us have a crazy closet at home, or even an entire room, stuffed full of merchandise and memories from years gone by. The unused tennis racket sits atop the obsolete desk chair, which also holds the compact disks we will likely never play again, unless we happen to pull out the CD player that is in the upper back corner, just beneath the Halloween decorations. The closet is so out of control that it is now managed by random stuffing—our optimistic effort of loading one more thing onto an overcrowded shelf or stacking something new on the floor with the hope that we can still close the door. This closet needs magic, which only happens on an otherwise quiet day when you have time and energy to pull everything out of the crazy closet, label the shelves, organize the things you will keep, create one pile for Good Will or the Salvation Army and fill the recycle bin and trash can with other piles. By the end of the day the magic is accomplished, and you experience the joy of order for however long the closet keeps from getting crazy again.

Similarly, knowledge leading to wisdom requires more than the stuffing of information into our brains. It calls for the discovery of an inherent structure and ordering of life around essential principles that serve as normative standards to guide and inform future choice and action. These principles become the foundation for a wise knowledge base, a framework to house wisdom.

Karl Jaspers, in his seminal book *Way to Wisdom*, writes, "if our lives are not to be diffuse and meaningless, they must find their place in an order" (1951/2003, p. 120). To break out of our banal situation, "we must find meaning in an edifice of work, fulfillment, and sublime moments, and by repetition we must gain in depth." (Jaspers, 1951/2003, p. 120). This way to wisdom sheds light on inherent principles that sustain the common good.

Holding the end in mind is not easy. A few years back I (Paul) sent my mother a message that no mom wants to see from her son: "Well, Mom, it's official, I'm going to prison." This was my cheeky way of conveying that I landed a job working as a psychologist at a nearby prison. She was less than thrilled. As for me, I was naively optimistic, curious, and slightly anxious about what I would face. As I passed through the mechanical gates and guard towers on my first day, I quickly started to notice that any idealistic sensibilities I had were immediately being drained from me. I had a cold and sober premonition: *This is a maximum security prison, and it is going to leave an impact on you far greater than you will leave on it.* The system is grueling, staff and guards face intense pressure, and for many of the inmates it is the end of the line. They have little to lose.

My time in the prison system taught me much about holding the end in mind. At its most basic level, this involves mental and emotional awareness of that which sustains us, especially when being confronted by difficulties that challenge our preconceived expectations. Maybe it is just plowing through a difficult shift at work, trying to keep in mind the image of your child's smiling face when you pick them up from school, or a hug from your significant other as you walk through the door. As you hold that image, it can help you keep perspective amidst all the daily tasks. For those on the front lines and for first responders, the end may be just getting home safe; certainly, for the custody officers I worked with, protecting themselves and their co-workers was a real concern, especially in a place where deadly violence is common. The prospect of making it to retirement, or for some of the inmates the hope of an early release, can make harsh conditions a little more bearable. Keeping the end in mind for many of the inmates with little or no prospect of going home is, however, a bit trickier. It is not surprising that for many inmates deemed LWOPs (life without parole) it was just staying alive, finding the will to go on living, most likely for a loved one on the outside, that became the only remaining self-preserving end.

For most people, the unique challenges of prison life will never be a reality. However, maintaining a healthy sense of purpose and meaning amidst the vicissitudes of life is a universal problem. How do we manage this dilemma of busyness and boredom? Some rare souls have responded by fleeing society and finding solace outside the norm, taking off to the Alaskan wild like Christopher McCandless or seeking retreat in monastic religious life like Thomas Merton. However alluring these austere fantasies of simplification may be, they are radical choices not likely suited for the majority of us. Another option is to remain planted where we are and put to use the privileges we have been given. People in the first world are challenged to make the most of their individual freedom and leverage their time and leisure to cultivate spiritual growth. In our data-driven world, advertisers constantly provoke and hijack our senses; as a result, our spiritual lives are dulled and deformed. This makes it much harder to identify our own self-worth and to allow ourselves to be guided by an end that is specific to our nature as human beings.

Our ancestors had something very powerful that we do not. They had *telos*, a Greek word that signifies purpose, end, and ultimate objective.

TELEOLOGY

Teleology is the idea that things in the universe, including human beings, have a clear function and goal for which they were created. Consider the rose in all its roseness, and the shark being a shark. *Telos* is the essence of things being what they intrinsically are. For humans, *telos* is seen in our internal force and natural pull toward a sort of happiness the Greeks called *eudaemonia*, a happiness only possible when someone knows, realizes, and embodies the fullness of their existence. When used at the service of wisdom *telos* guides actions towards the good. It motivates decisions to reflect truth.

Telos gradually slipped away with the Enlightenment of the 17th and 18th centuries. Though sometimes called The Age of Reason, Enlightenment reasoning ultimately moved philosophers and scientists toward rationality in the form of scientific materialism. "Reason," in the traditional sense, is a broad term that implies that cosmic order exists and that we can learn about it. If we pay attention and notice how things are ordered in the universe, reason frees us to explore cause-and-effect relationships, to search for answers as to why something exists. In contrast, scientific materialism assumes that physical realities are the only thing worth considering, and that they are best explored through systematic observation. In scientific materialism, there is no point in offering a metaphor about God or anything else about the divine, because the numinous cannot be known and observed through empirical methods.

One can be rational and yet detached from reason, sometimes with dire consequences. Consider, for example, the archetypal figure of the mad scientist, given literary life by Mary Shelley in her classic novel *Frankenstein*. Dr. Frankenstein, in his attempt to conquer death, creates an ill-fated monster, which comes to symbolize a myopic scientism driven to madness in its unwillingness to accept the natural order of things. This experiment, intended to be based on scientific principles, however ingenious, did not accord with reason, which includes other broader aspects of human nature, such as morality and spiritual realities. The 20th century is littered with examples where twisted rationality divorced from reason produced subhuman results. As children of the Enlightenment, we have inherited a grave limitation in our capacity for wisdom. The reductive definitions of what it means to be human, based almost purely on biology and psychology, keep discovery of a higher human purpose on the margins.

What if someone asks, "Tell me about your heart"? One could reply by checking a mobile app and reporting resting heart rate, heart rate variability, and cardio fitness, but such an answer reduces a complex question down to physical attributes. This would be an extreme example of scientific materialism. An answer involving reason would be integrative, seeing the self—and thus the heart—in relation to past knowledge, current experiences, and a sense of place in the big cosmic order of things. Perhaps you would answer, "My heart—like all human hearts—is sometimes confused, but is at its best when it is deeply connected to others and with a sense of purpose in living."

The plot has thickened in the 21st century as the rationality of the modern era is giving way to the age of individuality and emotion, which easily minimizes both reason and rationality. As a result, the purpose, aims, and ends we find are those we create in our own individual minds, and while self-definition is important, this can be a lonely liberation that does not answer the question of what it means to be human. Today we might answer the question about our heart based on immediate experience and emotion: "My heart is sad right now, and I'm not completely sure why."

In our postmodern day, we may learn what it means to be this or that human, but we easily miss the fullness of shared humanity. Charles Taylor (2007), widely considered the premier philosopher who discusses secularity, describes our situation as having a "buffered self," which is a boundary whereby we as individuals are cut off from the influence of external entities outside the mind, such as spirits, ancestors, magic spells, and other cosmic forces. This allows the possibility of, "disengaging from everything outside the mind" (p. 38). Taylor continues, "My ultimate purposes are those which arise within me, the crucial meaning of things are those defined in my response to them" (p. 38).

Returning to the idea of *telos*, when looking for meaning or purpose in life, today we tend to look inwardly. Whatever advantages the buffered self may bring, it makes it difficult to embrace the second step of Alcoholics Anonymous—which is also the first step of many systems of religion—to realize that a power greater than us exists, and that our very sanity depends on recognizing this. Rather than defining the fullness of being human by universal meaning that exists outside of ourselves, we have embraced a dangerous me-centric view.

Ask a child what they want to be when they grow up, and we are likely to hear about a career path—a physician or veterinarian for girls, and a police officer or firefighter for boys (Fatherly, 2017). Wouldn't it be surprising to ask an 8-year-old this question and hear, "When I grow up, I want to be kind, patient, loving, and courageous." Today we tend to think of how we define an individual self more than searching what it might mean to grow into the full commonality of our humanity. As a result, not only are wisdom and *telos* severed, but our understanding of morality now struggles to find solid ground. If we think about *telos* as being fully human, then this defines our common goal for living well and becomes the central premise of determining what is ethical and what is not. When we lost *telos*, our understanding of morality "withered as a vine with no root" (Cuddeback, 2013, p. 62).

Enriched knowledge asks us to consider big, existential questions with universal implications: Who am I? What am I living for? Is there meaning to life? Why is there something instead of nothing? Does God exist? These fundamental questions are bigger than what can be managed by the inward look of a buffered self or the reductionism of scientific materialism. Still, they are important to ponder as they surface over the course of our lives. As children, when our spirit to wonder is much more alive, we ask these big questions. Then, taken up with teenage angst, we may ask them again. Perhaps they swing back around to us in some required college philosophy course, as we quickly throw up our hands in agonizing frustration of the ambivalence and uncertainty. During our twilight years, as the end approaches, we find these questions again, seeking one final response.

One of the joys of working as psychologists is talking with people who are asking these big, difficult questions. It is not uncommon to sit with depressed clients who wonder aloud: "What is the point? Why am

I living? Why would it even matter if I stopped living?" Though we wish depression on no one—it is a dark tunnel of despair and pain—we recognize that in these liminal moments people often return to important teleological questions. The joy comes in helping people find their way through the tunnel, to see light and hope again, and ideally, to be changed for the better because they have been willing to ask these big, meaningful questions about what it means to be fully human. During our humdrum days we might easily live tone deaf to issues concerning *telos*, yet it is not uncommon to be immediately present to them during a particularly painful season when it is often the only thing we hear.

Even if we consciously reject addressing these big questions throughout much of our lives, we all offer implicit answers to them in the way we live. Consider the moment-by-moment actions of a day and how each reflects something about what we deem important and worthwhile for a life well-lived. You wake to the alarm clock and get out of bed, believing that something about the day ahead matters enough to get started. You care for yourself, whether by drinking a cup of coffee, eating breakfast, exercising, greeting a friend or partner, or all of the above, and in the process demonstrate that you care about your health and well-being. You head to work where your values are lived out each work day—earning enough to care for yourself and perhaps your family, being a responsible and helpful member of society, or being part of a team. During and after work you may eat meals or snacks that reflect commitments to health and longevity, or not, and to the place of pleasure and variety in daily living. You may spend time with friends, care for children, read books, watch television, or engage in spiritual practices, and each of these reflects something about how you understand a life well lived. The big questions about the important matters of life keep showing up in the little decisions and choices we make each day, whether or not we stop to pay attention to these questions.

Wise thinkers confront the questions. They neither settle for simplistic solutions nor ruminate neurotically about the questions, but they incorporate them into their critical contemplation and work creatively

with them. It is *telos* that provides an explanation, a reason for our existence. It is, to use a phrase from both ancient Christianity and Taoism,
the Way. Enriched knowledge should serve this *telos* and work within
it to clear the brush and light the path. Wisdom is a finger pointing us in
the right direction, a compass in the storm.

Memory serves a vital function in persevering with all that matters
most and protecting one from the tide of temporary trends and the tyranny of cultural sentiment. This is a vital aspect of various religious traditions. Liturgical ceremonies, mantras, litanies, and holy days all express
the importance of the ancestral collective, communal, and embodied experiences of divine wisdom. This is a tapping into timeless truths that many
modern spiritualities lack in their avoidance of religion. The importance
of remembering is significantly expressed in the Islamic tradition where
the Arabic word *dhikr*, which signifies "remembrance," and "mentioning,"
is vitally important to the spiritual beliefs and practices of the Sufis, the
mystical branch of Islam (Denny, 2006). The psychological and emotional
life become engulfed in the presence and rapture of the words understood
as coming directly from the mind of God, "that constant remembering
of God through recitation of the Qur'an, praise, and prayer came to con-
stitute a distinctive pattern of spiritual discipline known as *dhikr*" (Denny,
2006, p. 213). A similar case could be made for contemplatives in any
major world religion. As mystics attempt to hold wisdom as revealed by
God, they also touch the *telos* of human nature.

Not many of us are mystics, and many who read this book would not
consider themselves religious. Still, there are practices that can heighten
our awareness of teleology as we strive to establish a foundation of enriched
knowledge. Our ability to see *telos* is intimately related to our view of
human nature. Do we perceive an intelligible structure and order in life,
or is it simply blind forces in operation? We can avoid big, universal questions about human nature if we choose, likely because they raise fears of
inequality, imperfectability, determinism, or nihilism (Pinker, 2003), but
if we do, we may inadvertently limit what contributes to *eudaemonia*—a
good and happy life. We flounder in the abstraction of ourselves. "I

cannot merely make myself over in the image constructed by my intellect (particularly if that intellect is possessed by an ideology). I have a nature, and so do you, and so do we all" (Peterson, Doidge, & Van Sciver, 2018, p. 193).

Here are some questions we recommend for reclaiming some sense of teleology:

- *What is it that gives life meaning and purpose?*
- *What is the most important aspect of living well?*
- *What do you share in common with other people?*
- *Is there an ultimate aim or objective that you believe all people are destined for?*
- *How open are you to the possibility of transcendence?*

Wisdom brings us in contact with a core of human reason, an essential basis for building common ground and the common good. It reveals not just what is best for me but what is best for all.

COMMON GROUND AND COMMON GOOD

Cornel West and Robert P. George are two public intellectuals who, according to some current cultural trends, should have "canceled" each other years ago. West is a well-known philosopher, former Harvard professor, social critic and activist with an extensive career in fighting for liberal causes such as racial justice; George, a conservative legal scholar and Roman Catholic philosopher of natural law, heads the James Madison Program at Princeton University. Both men are bulwarks of their respective traditions. On the surface and based purely on identity politics, these men are supposed to be sworn enemies. Yet they have developed an inspiring friendship and become outspoken voices of intellectual freedom and public discourse. In a joint statement titled, "Truth Seeking, Democracy, and Freedom of Thought and Expression," they write:

The pursuit of knowledge and the maintenance of a free and democratic society require the cultivation and practice of the virtues of intellectual humility, openness of mind, and, above all, love of truth. These virtues will manifest themselves and be strengthened by one's willingness to listen attentively and respectfully to intelligent people who challenge one's beliefs and who represent causes one disagrees with and points of view one does not share. (George & West, 2017)

The virtues they describe establish common ground, based on respect, tolerance, and awareness of our shared humanity, which leads to a strengthening of the common good.

Similarly, Mahatma Gandhi and Abraham Lincoln may at first glance appear to be quite different types of men. Gandhi, a Hindu holy man dressed in a self-sewn robe preaching nonviolence, worked to free his country from the chains of colonialism. President Lincoln, a melancholic midwesterner, chose to preserve a powerful but young nation torn apart by civil strife. Regardless of their external and cultural differences, the lineage of these two men and their courage is one of the same pedigree. They seemed to grasp the essence of what mattered most. There is timelessness to their heroic lives, as both embody the causes to which they were martyrs. Both contributed to the common good.

Enriched knowledge, embedded in humility and self-awareness, calls us toward the common good as it turns decision making and judgments away from purely selfish motives and accentuates core ethical values that preserve and enhance the social fabric of society. Many social and civic freedoms that we have come to take for granted require and exist only within the common good (Schall, 2007). Voting is an example.

Marshall owns a home and lives in a community where schools are largely funded through a county property tax. Whenever a new bond measure is proposed to enhance school funding, Marshall has a choice to make: to vote for or against the tax. He has a simple algorithm for doing so. During the years when his own children attend the public schools, he votes in favor of the bonds, but when his children grow and no longer attend public schools, he votes against them. In other words, he votes based on his self-interest. This has become so common in American life and politics that it sometimes seems the only reasonable way to vote. It is not. Jeannette, who also owns a home in the same county, chooses instead to support the school bond measures regardless of the age of her own children. She believes education is profoundly important and wants to support it regardless of self-interest. Elena and Stewart feel differently and choose to vote against school bonds because they are concerned about fiscal management and the implications of rising property taxes for the disadvantaged in their community. They vote against the school bonds regardless of their children's ages. Though they disagree with Jeannette about how to vote, they agree that voting should be done for the common good rather than out of self-interest.

Shih-ying Yang (2013), a professor of psychology, sees wisdom as simultaneously building a good life for oneself and for others, and not just for the present moment but also for generations to come. This means wise people rock the boat sometimes, not for the sake of drawing attention to themselves or jumping onto a faddish bandwagon, but in order to respectfully question the status quo, knowing that some changes are necessary to consider for the good of all people, both now and in the future.

In today's combative political climate, it is easy to see conversations morph into arguments. This happens as both sides ping-pong perspectives back and forth that fail to draw attention to what lurks just beyond the passionate disagreements. One may appear to value social justice and the other personal freedom, but what is the higher end and purpose that both desire? Could it be that both sides want a just and fair society where individuals are free to live their lives? Explicating Aristotle's view of happiness in relation to human nature, Green (2012) writes: "because all humans share a common nature, we all have a common happiness we are called to, though individuals will necessarily vary in their specifics" (Green, 2012, p. 282). But it seems that now we are not so much conversing with fellow citizens with differing viewpoints about how to achieve the common good, we are othering opponents that need to be stopped and silenced. Rabbi, Lord Jonathan Sacks (2020) writes of this othering: "the sense that the other side is less than fully human, that its supporters are not part of the same moral community as us, that somehow their sensibilities are alien and threatening" (p. 216).

Much of the difficulty in finding constructive communication resides around the ideologies and identity politics that compromise free thinking. Political parties seek their own power and preservation. Simone Weil, the unorthodox and intriguing French philosopher and mystic, puts it this way: "once the growth of the party becomes a criterion of goodness, it follows inevitably that the party will exert a collective pressure upon people's minds. . . . It should horrify us, but we are already too much accustomed to it" (Weil & Leys, 1950/2013, p. 15–16). Weil is quite radical in her view, expressed in the title of her essay *On the Abolition of All Political Parties*. Still, her warnings seem prophetic and timely.

In the United States, we have experienced firsthand the negative effects of political divisiveness, culminating in early 2021 with the storming of the U.S. Capitol building by protestors, leaving five people dead. It is likely not a coincidence that this occurred during the days of COVID-19 where, unlike the initial response following 9/11, we did not come together as a nation, but instead our divisions widened and hardened. As we were driven inside, we became socially distant, isolated, and limited in our freedoms. As our communications became more and more electronic, anxiety crept in, and this only increased the pressure in our echo chambers. We sought solace in our own tribes, becoming even more entrenched and hardened against the other. This was a successful strategy of divide and conquer, by a virus that seemed to mysteriously exploit both our biological and psychological vulnerabilities. The more time we spent with our own fears—intensified by those thinking and feeling like us—the further away we moved from imagining a common good as we stopped listening to outsiders or considering other alternative perspectives.

U.S. 2020 gun sales surpassed that of any previous year on record, as we started hearing utterances about civil war. At the same time, diseases of despair, including drug and alcohol addiction and suicide, increased. While there were certainly other factors at play in the political and COVID–19 crisis of 2021, the lack of a common good degraded the social and moral soil in which mental health problems take root. Hopelessness and despair are influenced by what people see and imagine can be done to effectively improve their situation. Among those who feel unseen and unheard, illnesses are likely to worsen. Our anguished bodies and society are crying out for a common core, for a true collective unifying force. In the midst of this crisis, Pope Francis wrote in an encyclical letter, *Fratelli Tutti, On Fraternity and Social Friendship*:

> As silence and careful listening disappear, replaced by a frenzy of texting, this basic structure of sage human communication is at risk. A new lifestyle is emerging, where we create only what we want and exclude all that we cannot control or know instantly and superficially. This process, by its intrinsic logic, blocks the kind of serene reflection that could lead us to a shared wisdom. (Pope Francis, 2020, p. 43)

Wisdom sees common ground for a common good—and not just for a nation but for all people. Wisdom reveals transcendent knowledge that goes beyond space and time. More than just seeing, wisdom creates by a consistent thinking, feeling, and acting in accordance with higher principles.

But how do we do this? How do we rise out of the mire of social media bubbles and our ideological tunnels to find some of common humanity and hope? We lift our eyes up.

Embedded in the middle of the Hebrew Scriptures and Christian Bible are 15 psalms of ascent (Psalms 120–134). These are likely songs sung by the Hebrew people as they ascended the path toward Jerusalem to observe holy festivals each year. No doubt, they came from complicated lives in which they disagreed with neighbors and political regimes, where many lived in poverty, where injustice trampled the one and privileged the other, where they struggled with their own psychological and biological maladies. But each year—perhaps as many as three times each year—they emerged from their daily struggles, ascending to a place where they worshipped together in solidarity. They lifted up their eyes toward a common ground.

> I lift up my eyes to the hills—
> from where will my help come?
> My help comes from the Lord,
> who made heaven and earth.
> *(New Revised Standard Version, Psalm 121:1–2)*

We do not share a common faith these days, nor do we have many rituals that remind us of our shared common ground, but the wisest among us are still able to find ways to lift up their eyes.

THE TRANSCENDENTALS

Transcendence is a key part of wisdom, as will be explored further in the coming chapters. This is an elevation out of the mundane, a breaking through to higher ground, and it reflects spiritual realities that cannot be captured in scientific materialism (Ramos, 2012). As such, a full-blooded psychology of wisdom calls us to imagine the possibility that we are finite beings capable of connecting to the infinite.

During my time working at the prison, I often felt trapped, limited by the system, and dismayed by the callousness of the environment. Inside the prison lurked the reality of a closed system where concrete, gravel, and metal function as metaphors of institutional dominance over the natural rhythms of life and openness to transcendence. As time went by, I started recognizing similar patterns in life outside the prison. The German philosopher and psychiatrist Karl Jaspers diagnoses the existential dilemma of living within a closed system, as "a world which subsists only as an outward order, without symbolism and transcendence, which leaves the soul empty and is not adequate to man, which . . . thrusts him back upon his own resources, in lust and boredom, fear and indifference" (Jaspers, 1951/2003, p. 120).

Wisdom requires shifting perspective, lifting the eyes, tilting the head, to find the cracks where the light can penetrate. People with enriched knowledge, and the wisdom it brings, are able to find life-giving order in the cosmos—even in prison.

I remember a colleague who would stay into the evening, far past the end of his shift, printing mountains of handouts, editing paperwork, and doing all he could to ensure his patients were receiving the quality of care he felt they deserved. I also witnessed guards who would display patience and understanding that few mental health clinicians could rival, or moments I had with a supervisor who provided me with the space and support I needed to make it to the next day. These transcendent treasures of prison life remain mostly hidden and go largely unacknowledged. Still, they show the presence of something more in our world, even in the most unlikely of places.

Knowing and contemplating the transcendentals is crucial in developing enriched knowledge as a foundation for wisdom. G. K. Chesterton pondered, "Obviously, it ought to be the oldest things that are taught to the youngest people; the assured and experienced truths that are put first to the baby" (Chesterton, 1910/2007, p. 155). What might some of these old things and truths be? While he may not have been referring specifically to transcendental ideas, we doubt he would disagree about their significance.

What are the transcendentals? These are a priori truths or virtues that we intuitively know, probably because, as Chesterton implies, they are naturally passed on from one generation to the next, and perhaps even built into the primordial consciousness of being human. Classically, the three transcendentals are truth, beauty, and goodness, which are common strivings that unite all people. These inform our models and institutions of learning and higher education throughout the world. On a more personal level, we can think of these as general ways of assessing if particular thoughts, feelings, or actions align with wisdom.

If this seems a bit too abstract it is because it is. Still, these are essential abstractions that help us navigate when we are lost at sea.

Great minds of history, such as Plato, Kant, and Emerson gave voice to the importance of these transcendent notions. They had many names, yet refer to the same basic underlying features of human existence. William James described them in this way:

> Such ideas, and others equally abstract, form the background for all our facts, the fountain-head of all the possibilities we conceive of. They give its "nature," as we call it, to every special thing. Everything we know is "what" it is by sharing in the nature of one of these abstractions. We can never look directly at them, for they are bodiless and featureless and footless, but we grasp all other things by their means, and in handling the real world we should be stricken with helplessness in just so far forth as we might lose these mental objects, these adjectives and adverbs and predicates and head of classification and conception. (James, 1902, p. 56)

The transcendentals are both psychological capacities and spiritual strivings. Psychologically, they have a vital role in helping us discover what is most important, providing criteria for the common good, and guiding the ends of human action toward wisdom. They invisibly determine much of our lives whether we explicitly talk about them or not. We are likely to say we want to "be out in nature," "spend time with friends and family," or "learn something new" rather than "I want to feel the effects of beauty upon my soul as I gaze at a sunset"; or "I want to experience the sense of overall goodness around a campfire conversation"; or "I want to encounter truth as I listen to a moving and illuminating lecture or sermon." But whatever way we say it, we are trying to lift our eyes up to the places of transcendence.

Spiritually, it is not uncommon for people to speak about experiences where they felt at one with nature or connected to the goodness in the world. In other words, they have moved beyond the confines of their own individual existence to touch some larger presence or power in the cosmos. This applies to the religious and nonreligious alike. Ralph Waldo Emerson, the American intellectual giant who left orthodox Christianity and became a rogue scholar, poet, and social critic, writes from within the tradition that emphasizes transcendent spiritual principles: "the Transcendentalist adopts the whole connexion of spiritual doctrine. He believes in miracle, in the perpetual openness of the human mind to new influx of light and power; he believes in inspiration, and in ecstasy" (Emerson, 2006, p. 111). Furthermore, Emerson highlights the self-validating quality of the transcendentals. They do not depend on or need any external authority: "thus, the spiritual measure of inspiration is the depth of the thought, and never, *who* said it?" (Emerson, 2006, p. 111)

These are chords within the soul alerting us that we are in tune with our true selves. Wisdom prospers when we touch these innate transcendentals because they expand our horizon, allowing us to imagine some greater possibility than what we see around us in each emerging news cycle.

WISDOM, ENRICHED KNOWLEDGE, AND HOLDING THE END IN MIND

As we finish exploring the first step of the KDTT model, a brief summary seems fitting. We have argued that knowledge is necessary for wisdom, including basic factual knowledge and procedural knowledge, but not just any knowledge will do. We are suffocating in information, so much of it motivated by polarized or monetized self-interest, making it difficult to rise above, to lift our eyes toward enriched, life-giving knowledge.

Holding the end in mind calls us toward imposing some sort of ordering system for our knowing. Some things truly are more important to know than others. Part of this is reclaiming teleology, recognizing that humans are intrinsically made to flourish, to live individually and collectively in ways that bring *eudaemonia*. Some knowledge contributes to common ground and common good whereas other ways of "knowing" seem to perpetuate divisiveness and discontent. The transcendentals (truth, beauty, goodness) are a time-honored way of being in the world that brings together our existence with a deeper sense of purpose and direction, blending our psychological and spiritual selves as we dare to give voice to those big truths we intuitively know to be important.

A beautiful example of holding the end in mind showed up in the height of the 2020 coronavirus pandemic when Taylor Nichols, a Jewish emergency department physician, was called to treat a man begging not to die, whose skin happened to be covered with Nazi tattoos. Nichols, along with an African-American nurse and an Asian-American respiratory therapist quickly intubated the patient—even knowing that intubation can spray infectious droplets—and then continued to treat him. As Dr. Nichols spoke to CNN's John Berman, the essence of wisdom came shining through (Andrew, 2020). Though he felt a strong reaction to Nazi body art on the man in front of him, Dr. Nichols clearly and quickly lifted up his eyes to a higher plane, undoubtedly honed by his years of training and practice. He drew from what he described as a "well of compassion" instead of responding with disdain or vengeance toward his patient. He chose to be his best self rather than his vindictive self, recognizing what it means to be fully human. All of this was embedded in his profound awareness of common ground and common good. When Berman asked Dr. Nichols what might have happened if the roles were reversed (the doctor having Nazi tattoos and the patient being Jewish), there was a palpable pause for reflection, and then Dr. Nichols provided a winsome reply emphasizing how medical providers go into the job with a commitment to do their best for everyone—whoever walks through the door—and that he imagines the best care would have been provided if the roles had been reversed.

Enriched knowledge, and the wisdom it brings, shows up every day in surprising places: in emergency departments overwhelmed with COVID-19 patients, in prisons where hope seems so difficult to find, in neighborly conversations, in dinners around the kitchen table, in faith communities, in courtrooms, conference rooms, classrooms, and living rooms all over the world. This has the potential to heal our world, but the opposite is also true. Our capacity for wisdom can become a vortex that caves in on itself and devours that which it could have become. Knowledge itself is not enough. We also need the capacity to stand at the margins, observing ourselves and the world around with a degree of healthy, humble detachment.

PART 2

DETACHMENT

CHAPTER 4

DETACHMENT
AND WISDOM

B ecause this is a book about virtue, it seems important to mention
volunteer youth soccer coaching, which must be one of the great acts
of virtue in our day. Young children—a lot of them—show up with cleats,
a parent or two, exuberance, and more energy than can be described in
words. Somehow the volunteer coach manages all this energy while instill-
ing knowledge for the game, such as positions and strategy. Then the day
of the first game comes, emotions are heightened, and the presence of the
soccer ball is simply too compelling for the children to remember much
about positions and strategy. A two-team blob of 20 children (assuming
the two goalies stay put) follow the ball around the field wherever it may
go as coaches yell from both sidelines, "Play your positions!"

Knowledge is necessary to play soccer well, but so is disciplined distance that allows for perspective taking, planning, teamwork, and strategy. With wisdom, we call this detachment.

In the KDTT model, detachment sits between knowledge, its necessary precursor, and tranquility, its hoped for consequence. Detachment
is not an icy indifference or ignoring the serious matters of life. It is an
intentional practice and habit of distancing from thoughts and feelings
in order to bring peace, calm, and freedom from controlling desires and
passions. It is letting go and creating space for self-discovery beyond usual
patterns of behavior. Detachment has a long history in the religious and
philosophical traditions, both East and West.

If we moderns find detachment too forceful or harsh a concept, think about the degree to which most people are now intensely overattached and need a method of disentanglement capable of breaking unhealthy bonds to people, things, or ideas. The daily news cycle is the soccer ball, and the players on the field have red and blue jerseys, coming from their red and blue states. Doesn't it sometimes seem that we are all just clustered around the ball, kicking each other in the shins, without much discerning distance?

To lessen whatever misgivings you may have about detachment and to demystify the concept, here are four key ways that detachment contributes to wisdom.

1. Detachment *facilitates negative capability*, the suspension of judgment and the ability to remain in ambiguous spaces. This requires a separation from bias, assumption, and prejudice. Negative capability risks embracing the unknown in search for new levels of understanding.

2. Detachment brings *mental freedom* by peeling back the curtains on our lives. Without ample reflection, much of our lives can be lived in an illusory reality propelled by self-interest. We easily project our own struggles onto others, quickly divide the world into "us" and "them," and allow the approval of others to dictate who we become. With detachment, we learn to scrutinize, challenge, and purify our narratives, and in the process discover deeper truths about ourselves and the world around us.

3. Detachment *strengthens our capacity to grieve*. With the practice of detachment we can get the jump on the inevitability of change and anticipate the storms of life. This is perhaps the most familiar way in which detachment is traditionally understood.

4. Detachment allows us to *remain on the edges*. From just outside the mainstream we can see with an observing eye. Also, this frees us from being ruled by our passions and desires that might pressure us toward impulsive action. If we remain just outside

the pack, we can find our true likes and dislikes instead of those that are being pushed and sold to us. The view from the edges gives a greater awareness to perceive and unite with spiritual realities and experience transcendence.

NEGATIVE CAPABILITY

Any school of wisdom must include a curriculum confronting liminal space (the area of overlap between two different things) because befriending uncertainty leads to greater insight. If we can bear the discomfort of not knowing and of learning to loosen the grip on our desire for certainty, something new can happen. The ability to hold uncertainty and ambiguity with grace is called negative capability.

The Enneagram is an ancient archetypal framework (think personality test, but don't use that term around Enneagram fans) with a spiritual twist that is regaining popularity in some circles. Like olives, people tend to have strong feelings about the Enneagram one way or another. Websites, books, and apps are popping up everywhere and fans flock to these resources. Others are concerned by its lack of scientific evidence and cult-like popularity. It is fascinating to read comments on YouTube sites where the Enneagram is being discussed. Here are a few reactions to a YouTube conversation about the Enneagram and Christianity:

> "No offense, but this is garbage . . ."
> "The Enneagram does nothing for me . . . I think it's total nonsense."
> "He just compared Proverbs to the Enneagram? God's inerrant word compared to man's errant words? This guy is ridiculous and has dangerous thinking."

Neither of us are Enneagram experts or fans, but it strikes us as a poignant example of how people tend to polarize so quickly these days, and over so many different things. What might it be like to hold curiosity instead of judgment? I wonder why this tool has regained such popularity?

It is curious that there is not more science about the uses and misuses of the Enneagram—why might that be? How might considering Enneagram types help me understand myself or others better? How might it hinder my understanding of self or others to assign a particular type to someone as complex as a human being? These curious questions are only possible if we refuse to become an ardent advocate or opponent of the Enneagram and then take a position of negative capability.

The term "negative capability" is first associated with the poet, John Keats, who noted that some of the greatest writers and artists of all time are those who can hold tension, mystery, and paradox, without having to cinch down certainty. Keats lived a short life of 26 years at the tail end of what we now call the Age of Enlightenment. While intellectuals were scrambling for certainty and confidence in human reason, Keats noted in an 1817 letter to his brother that some of the greatest artists of all time demonstrated remarkable comfort with uncertainty.

> At once it struck me, what quality went to form a Man [*sic*] of Achievement especially in Literature & which Shakespeare possessed so enormously—I mean Negative Capability, that is when man is capable of being in uncertainties, Mysteries, doubts, without any irritable reaching after fact & reason. (Barnard, 2015, p. 79)

Sometimes we may naively associate wisdom with certainty, as if wise people hold the answers to fix the problems of those around them, and perhaps all the problems of the world. This might be possible if wisdom were fully defined by knowledge, but it is not.

In the West, we have lost a sense of mystery and often fail to see the physical world as having a hidden or sacramental meaning. We are radically materialistic in every meaning of the word. Ronald Rolheiser (2004) describes a "non-contemplative personality" that is suggestive of a common approach in our age, where "reality holds no dimensions of mystery beyond the empirical, which is the basis of all that is considered valid within human experience" (p. 52). This noncontemplative approach stands in contrast to detachment, which allows us to grasp more than just the utility of an object. Detachment takes the time and has the ability to allow things to reveal themselves, to slowly unfurl, to give an impression on the mind. Artists, poets, and musicians reflect a detachment from the merely pragmatic sense and see further into hidden aspects, whether in the form of words, musical sounds, or visual stimuli.

The point of the KDTT model is to see with a curious sense of wonderment, as a contemplative or an artist sees the world. A detached and nonintrusive approach gives depth, and a new level of knowledge emerges. When we look from our own preconceived notions and judgments, we see one thing, but if we are able to exercise negative capability, the world we encounter seems very different, and "there is a fundamental shift in our attitude. . . . From wondering how and wondering whether, we begin a wondering at" (Rolheiser, 2004, p. 63).

Negative capability is brought to light in the work of Wilfred Bion, the British psychoanalyst whose technique consisted of approaching sessions with a deliberate detachment from previous thoughts and feelings (Bion, 1977). Detachment on the part of the therapist facilitates greater room for listening and awareness of the patients' thoughts and feelings. For Bion, in each session the therapist should focus anew on the unknown aspects of the patient. This may appear odd. Doesn't therapy involve a clinician understanding more and more about the patient over time? Isn't remembering material from previous sessions extremely important in this regard? Well, yes, but Bion's idea also allows for open space, as much as is realistically possible, free of expectations and subjective bias. With this, it is possible that psychological and emotional growth can break through untainted by previous ideas.

Think of the implications of this for other relationships in life also. If we approach people attentively and without prejudice, we can see them in a new light, and new realities about them and ourselves can be revealed. Even people we have known well for a long time can start taking on new dimensions if we are able to detach from our previous assumptions and conceptions of who they are.

We may even be able to relate to ourselves differently if we learn to detach and hold negative capability. Pauline sought psychological help because of suffocating panic attacks, which she described as "like being in hell." In the midst of the attacks she had difficulty breathing, perspired heavily, and believed she might be dying. To make matters worse, her work involved many public meetings where she was charged with helping people in conflict find peaceable solutions. Heavy sweating, difficulty breathing, and thoughts of dying did not play well in the conference room where others counted on her to help them stay calm. As bad as the panic attacks were—and they were awful—the bigger issue in treatment was helping Pauline confront her fear about when and where she might have her next one. Fortunately, psychologists have good empirically supported treatments for panic attacks, so those eased up fairly quickly. Then the treatment shifted to Pauline's anxiety about anxiety. When might she have another attack? If it happens in the conference room, what will people think? How might this impact the people she is trying to help? How will this affect her consulting business? She wanted answers to these questions, which seems reasonable enough, but the treatment could only move forward when Pauline came to recognize that she could never answer any of these questions with certainty.

Stop and ponder this for a moment. None of us can know if we might have a panic attack in the next week. We cannot know for certain whether cancer cells are growing somewhere in our bodies. We do not know the future of the relationships that are most important to us. We want to know these things, and we do whatever we can to achieve some degree of confidence, but the truth is we do not, and cannot, know with certainty. And if we cannot even know our own lives with certainty, how much less can we know others with certainty?

MENTAL FREEDOM

The Matrix, a 1999 blockbuster movie, received enormous attention for its allegorical meaning in contemporary life. And while we will not repeat the plot or its alleged meaning here, it is worth recalling that the hero of the movie, Neo, has a choice of taking a blue pill, which will return him to his familiar illusion of life (living in the Matrix), or the dangerous red pill, which will allow him to step outside his illusion and see things as they truly are. It is not much of a spoiler alert to tell you that Neo chooses detachment, via the red pill. Otherwise it would be a short and boring movie.

One thing about living in a blue-pill world of illusion is that it does not feel at all like illusion when we are in the midst of it. Only as we are able to step back into the red-pill moments of detachment can we see the falseness of the illusion. Scientists studying wisdom emphasize the importance of self-reflection—what Westrate (2019) calls, "the mirror of wisdom." Self-reflection does not mean simply pausing to reflect on the self, which could be quite a narcissistic exercise: "How am I feeling right now?" "What am I thinking?" "What do I need to do to become happier or more fulfilled in life?" While these might be reasonable questions, the bigger point of self-reflection is to consider the self from a more detached perspective, as if we were stepping outside of our skin for a moment to observe what is going on.

We all struggle to see things as they truly are, and the less we self-reflect, the more we struggle. Our loss of objectivity leads to an inflated sense of subjective self-importance as our thoughts and feelings take center stage. Over time, our perceptions of reality are composed more and more of subjective projections, and the film we see is that of our fears rather than something we encounter in its own right. In *Thoughts in Solitude*, Thomas Merton wisely writes about the need for detachment from this illusory existence:

> The death by which we enter into life is not an escape from reality but a complete gift of ourselves which involves a total commitment to reality. It begins by renouncing the illusory reality which created things acquire when they are seen only in their relation to our own selfish interests. (1961, p. 17)

The commitment to reality Merton describes requires a detached, self-reflective perspective where we can see created things as innately valuable, even apart from our vested personal interests.

Merton refers to illusory realities and selfish interests. What might these be? For one thing, much of what we dislike in others reflects aspects of ourselves that cause us conflict. We humans are quick to project our own inner battles onto other people—who seem to be easier targets for our insights—rather than point them toward ourselves. This shadow side of our personality, as Carl Jung famously referred to it, keeps us from knowing our true selves.

Detachment unmasks our illusory selves and increases mental freedom by expanding the psychological qualities of metacognition and mentalization. "Metacognition" refers to an ability to think about thinking. We can imagine sitting above our mind looking down on our thoughts with a birds eye view, as we are above (meta) thinking (cognition). "Metacognitive monitoring involves a stance of active self-scrutiny that situates us at once inside and outside our experience" (Wallin, 2007, p. 41), and by way of "forming a representation of one's own mind; becoming aware of sensations, images, and beliefs about the self; and reflecting on the nature of emotion and perception" (Siegel, 2012, p. 294). Mentalization is similar and involves expanding our thoughts about our feelings in growing awareness of the context, or matrix, in which our minds exist; it is an increased knowledge about one's own emotional world. This concept, "denotes that the mind interprets reality and utilizes skills that produce self-understanding and understanding of others" (Jurist, 2018, p. 2). This is important in psychotherapy since many both desire and struggle to identify, modulate, and express their emotions (Jurist, 2018). In detachment, we pause our usual reactions; we stop, look, and listen; and we strengthen our metacognitive and mentalizing abilities, thus allowing ourselves to gain an increased willingness to delve deeper into reality.

Another illusory reality is found in our natural inclination to categorize things and put people in groups that makes it easier to handle life's ambiguities. It is tough to sit in anxiety and have our assumptions challenged. We are much more complicated and inconsistent in our own views than we may initially think. These opposing sides of ourselves are hard to admit. We do not like internal inconsistency, and we falsely pull toward one side or the other in an attempt to appear consistent.

Political parties, the media, and advertisers exploit this vulnerability. Threats, real or perceived, can easily push us toward survival mode, where instead of confronting our internal fears we externalize them onto a scapegoat. The results of a recent CBS News poll showed that Americans see other Americans as the biggest threat to themselves and their way of life (Salvanto et al., 2021). It was not climate change, COVID-19, or foreign threats. It was "them," those other Americans that are the real danger. This suspicious sentiment leads to a hardening of prejudice. We want our opponents to have an open mind so we can fill it with what we are certain is true.

A related illusory reality is the need to be right and constantly affirmed in our rightness, which makes us susceptible to lending others more power than we should. If they approve, then life is good. If they do not, then we have a big problem. Our happiness becomes dependent on others' views of us. In *The Imitation of Christ*, a classic of Christian spirituality, Thomas à Kempis writes:

> Our judgments frequently depend on our likes and dislikes and thus are far from true because we make them conform to our personal prejudices. If God were our one and only desire we would not be so easily upset when our opinions do not find outside acceptance. (Thomas à Kempis, 1998, p. 18)

The more importance we give to the opinion of others, the more easily this need can be manipulated and put to use by malicious forces. Thomas à Kempis offers an approach to wisdom that sees emotional attachment to the divine as a means to detachment in the here and now.

This blue-pill world of illusory reality all sounds quite depressing, but this is where the wisdom practice of detachment can give us hope and freedom. Yes, it involves risk of potentially having to consider ideas that actually change our minds. Wisdom does not simply avoid participation and choose not to take sides. But when it does, it keeps in mind the more important principles underneath the arguments.

Wise persons are able to temper, through detachment, the craving for omniscience. They recognize that being all knowing is not in the cards. Life happens in color and complexity, and we can only ever know a limited view of things. Consider for a moment how many of us would not fit into typical categories if our beliefs, voting records, relationships, and honest desires were placed under a microscope. The complexity of life does not allow for things to fit smoothly into the dichotomies of red vs. blue, black vs. white, privileged vs. oppressed that are so prevalent in our day. When forced between these binaries, we often begrudgingly and maybe rashly make a choice, swallow the bitter pill, and get shoved on one side or the other. Unfortunately, this collapses the more nuanced and creative contexts where wisdom lives. Detachment lights the way out of these constricting conditions that suffocate free thinking and honest emotional expression.

Those who are wisest are able to simultaneously experience and observe their feelings and thoughts. It is not that they do not have them, but rather that they learn to reflect on their thoughts and feelings so they can be considered in a larger context. Writing about the integration of the various behavioral elements of wisdom, Birren and Fisher (1990) observe: "the wise person is thought to show emotional mastery such that his or her decisions are not likely to be dominated by such passions as anger or fear" (p. 321). Both anger and fear are natural emotional responses to stressful or dangerous situations, yet the wise person is able to contain, regulate, and employ such feelings at a reflective distance. "However, the wise person is not entirely detached from the situation. This person will be able to maintain a reflective state of mind that generates alternative, if not novel, solutions to problems" (Birren & Fisher, 1990, p. 321).

This self-reflective and empathic form of detachment leads to mental freedom in two big ways. First, it frees the mind from overidentifying with our thoughts and feelings. This, in turn, widens our perspectives. New ideas arise in this context. Consider the Buddha and his discovery of the four noble truths, which both built upon and diverged from the ancient wisdom of India. Second, detachment facilitates equanimity, and this emotional balance allows for deeper comprehension, as a calm and clear pond reflects an image easier than disturbed waters.

GRIEVING LOSSES

Much of psychotherapy, like much of life, revolves around learning how to experience and accept loss. This is not limited to the loss of loved ones, but involves grieving over anything that was held close that has been taken. It is difficult to let go, like standing on a shore as a lover sets off across the ocean to an unknown future. When it is not a lover, we are saying good-bye to a parent, a child, a friend, to notions of how the world works, to a career, to hopes for reconciliation, to particular dreams for the future, to health, to simple solutions. Over and over, we say good-bye in life in the very moments when we wish we could latch on tighter and force a happily-ever-after ending. Over and over, we detach. Over and over, we face grief.

A woman I (Paul) will call Katherine, struggling from depression and anxiety, lived wrapped in sadness and regret. Past relational wounds and her grip on them prevented Katherine from being open to the present. During weekly psychotherapy sessions, we talked often about her resentment and bitterness for the way life had unfolded. Katherine and I had good rapport, but she often grew critical, saying that I could not understand the depth of her pain because I had not experienced that degree of loss yet; she being considerably older than I.

I liked Katherine. Her witty, dry sense of humor provided moments of reprieve, and she knew how to laugh at the tragic ironies of life. But as much as I enjoyed her humor, we came to see how it helped her keep other feelings suppressed. Beneath the humor lurked a deep pain over which she had not fully grieved. Quick to take on blame for a lost and dysfunctional love, it was only when she was able to admit and give voice to her long-held wish to reignite the relationship that she was able to let go of past injuries and feel free to move forward in her life. For years, she had lived as if she was still in relationship with a person who was long gone from her life, and in psychotherapy she came to see how memory makes a poor lover.

My role in this treatment was largely supportive, aligning with her need to grieve, and naming those hidden parts of her that yearned for another chance. I bore witness to her losses and invited her into a place of healthy detachment from the ghosts of her past. Over time, she allowed herself to hope and came to loosen an identity bounded by misplaced guilt and shame. Our dance of detachment, tears, and laughter included acknowledging the past, experiencing the loss, and learning to be open to life again.

Of the four steps in which wisdom develops in the KDTT model, detachment is likely to be the least enticing, especially when it calls us into places of deep grief. It is never easy letting go. Less is hardly as attractive as more in our time of excess, for "you can strip yourself, you can be stripped, but still you will reach out like an octopus to seek your own comfort, your untroubled time, your ease, your refreshment" (Day, 1963, p. 81). We do not like to separate from things and people, and we are wired to attach from the earliest moments in the womb.

Here we must face a choice: to grieve or to be blind to our need for grief. Change is happening all the time around us, and all change brings loss, even those changes that also carry excitement and joy. By cultivating a habit of detachment, we anticipate and familiarize ourselves with grief and the pain it brings. We are not unique in this. All people throughout time have lived with the cosmic, universal principle of entropy: the principle of disorder, randomness, and gradual decline to any system.

Yes, living in grief can be morbid and masochistic if we live in fear of what is to come, but a healthy detachment opens doors that knowledge alone cannot. Some light can only be found in the dark. In the end, the inescapable parting from what we hold dear happens whether we choose it or not, but intentional practice can make a difference as it tills the ground for tranquility and transcendence, as will be discussed in the coming chapters.

REMAINING ON THE EDGES

A deeply learned supervisor once explained to me (Paul) how in native tribes the shamans did not live directly among the people but remained just on the outside of the village. They would move in and out as needed, but they dwelt on the periphery.

Much can be seen on the edges, because sitting too close blurs the image. While it is more common these days to hear about healthy attachment styles and the importance of relational bonds, it is also true that a level of detachment is needed even with those with whom we are in close relationships. If we cannot see our loved ones with some reflective distance, then we cannot understand them as they are in themselves. They too become blurry. And we cannot see ourselves well either, because our self-understanding is always filtered through the responses and reactions of the other.

A perspective from the edge helps us come to wise judgments. When confronted with strong emotions, our natural tendency is to move right into the middle of the experience, flight or fright. We need to do something. Now. Remaining on the edge allows us to observe and consider from a more objective perspective.

Sometimes the experience of being on the edge is forced upon us, such as the surprising challenge of being distant from familiar routines during the COVID-19 pandemic. Not being able to travel, socialize, attend and participate in religious services was a loss experienced by large portions of the population around the world. But along with the barriers of isolation, this time of profound loss also opened unique opportunities to re-evaluate commitments and values. Maybe some meetings can occur virtually instead of making us travel for them. Some social gatherings are life-giving, and some are obligations that may be worth shedding. Some experiences were profoundly missed, and their importance became increasingly compelling as the pandemic raged on. For both of us, collective worship fell in this latter category, as we found ourselves longing for the familiarity of sacred spaces. We were forced to stand on the edge and observe something that had been part of each of our lives for many decades, and it made us appreciate it more. Absence can make the heart grow fonder. Standing on the edge allows us to see with new eyes. In this way, detachment expands knowledge.

A view from the edge highlights spiritual possibilities because detachment brings us outside of ourselves, our time, and allows us to see notions of human ambition and achievement in a new light. "The saint does not have to bring about great temporal achievements; he is one who succeeds in giving us at least a glimpse of eternity, despite the thick opacity of time" (Lubac, 1987, p. 81). How is this "glimpse of eternity" achieved?

Meister Eckhart, the great medieval German mystic, considered a saint by some and a heretic by others, goes so far as to place detachment above love as the pinnacle Christian virtue: "because the best thing about love is that it compels me to God, yet detachment compels God to love me" (Eckhart, 2005, p. 104). This provocative remark, which Eckhart is known for, shows that rather than attempting to climb to God through our own will power and virtues, detachment empties our desires in order for God to have the space to enter our lives right where we are. Detachment puts the impetus back on the absolute and divine power. According to Eckhart, it would appear that God is much better at finding and loving us than we are at finding God, and that happens through detachment.

If this sounds confusingly Zenlike, you are on the right track, and Eckhart is often considered a Christian mystic with Buddhist-like insights into the spiritual life. In both traditions, detachment, paradox, and irony are used as methods of perceiving the ineffable. Eckhart's perspective might not be for everyone, but he expands our capacity for love and detachment while showing the need to push towards the edge at times, to risk being disliked and unpopular, and the need to tilt our head sometimes to see upright.

Do you ever have the sense that almost everyone you encounter through the world of technology is trying to pull you in? Sometimes this is obvious, such as the advertisements that show up in Facebook, on television, or on your web browser. But other times it is more subtle, like the political pundit who wants you to see something through a particular lens, or the religious broadcaster who wants you to believe a particular view with absolute certainty, as if only a fool could possibly disagree. What might it be like to stand at the edge of all this, just paying attention and noticing how much people want us to adopt their particular view? And, yes, we can remain interested and curious, but we typically do not have to dive headlong into the latest meme or fad.

Another Christian mystic, Evelyn Underhill, describes detachment and its importance in the spiritual pursuit of transcendence: "all those who have felt themselves urged towards the attainment of this transcendental vision, have found that possessions interrupt the view; that claims, desires, attachments become centres of conflicting interest in the mind" (Underhill, 1990, p. 210). Living with palms open, refusing to cling to the faddish ideas and possessions constantly peddled around us, is essential in the pursuit of higher aims. A healthy separation, like the owl perched above, can bring a vantage point that allows for a broader view of the terrain.

It is not necessary to study mystics or travel to Tibetan monasteries to find detachment as essential in schemas of psychological healing and spiritual transformation. In words less traditionally religious, the Twelve Step recovery program highlights a certain common wisdom about the power of abandonment to the divine:

Yes, we of agnostic temperament have had these experiences. Let us make haste to reassure you. We found that as soon as we were able to lay aside prejudice and express even a willingness to believe in a Power greater than ourselves, we commenced to get results, even though it was impossible for any of us to fully define or comprehend that Power, which is God. (W. & Alcoholics Anonymous, 1976, p. 46)

Here we see an ability to observe from the edge, recognizing that something bigger than ourselves is happening in the cosmos, even if that something cannot be named or understood.

We have been emphasizing religious and spiritual perspectives here, but wisdom researchers who study self-transcendence—a concept similar to detachment—observe that some people are able to develop self-transcendence apart from a religious and spiritual context. This is accomplished through acts of generosity, practicing patience, developing self-regulation skills, meditation, determining to lessen self-focus, and working to confront negative personality qualities (Aldwin et al., 2019). In addition, the application of self-transcendence is vital in developing a common good and protection against exploitive economic forces and minimizing the cost on others, the environment, and threats to democracy. "Understanding one's own assumptions, blind spots, and often conflicting desires—in short, adult development and wisdom—is absolutely necessary to be able to perceive the common good, to weigh short- and long-term losses and gain, and the like" (Aldwin & Levenson, 2019, p. 299).

Religious or not, detachment is an important sequel to knowledge in stretching toward wisdom. At first glance detachment may appear as drifting away into the solitary abyss. This is not so in the KDTT model, as a detached approach is part of a larger wisdom schema, and wisdom itself is also at the service of something greater, namely, us. Keep in mind that each step of the KDTT model builds on the prior one, and that the process is incomplete without all four steps. The pursuit of knowledge without reflective distance and detachment leads to egotistical and narcissistic hubris. On the other hand, detachment without knowledge facilitates apathy and nihilism.

You are likely catching the rhythm of this book by now. In this chapter we have argued the importance of detachment in developing wisdom, but this is hard. In the next chapter we will explore why detachment is so difficult, especially in times of pain, and then in Chapter 6 we consider ways to work toward detachment despite the difficulties.

CHAPTER 5

PAIN, SUFFERING, AND DETACHMENT

When asked what he would do concerning his opponent's plan in an upcoming fight, Mike Tyson once stated, "everyone has a plan until they get punched in the mouth" (Berardino, 2012). Pain has a way of throwing us off our game. Wisdom is difficult because life surprises us with pain. Detachment is elusive because suffering is not.

The relationship among pain, suffering, and wisdom is complex. On the one hand, suffering serves as a catalyst to wisdom. Most would even say that suffering is a prerequisite to wisdom (Brady, 2019). In their MORE Life Experience Model of wisdom, Glück and Bluck (2013) explain how challenging life experiences set the context for learning wisdom. Without hardship, we have no opportunity to become wise. Those who become wise learn to hold their suffering gently in their hands, to observe and respect it, to grow in self-compassion and empathy toward others.

On the other hand, pain and suffering do not ensure wisdom. Even with ample hardship, most people fail to develop high levels of wisdom (Glück et al., 2019). Pain and suffering can detract from wisdom by making detachment difficult. When the rain comes, we often attempt to hold tight to things that have already gone. Detachment reminds us of loss. This is why the relationship is complex—the very thing that can promote wisdom can also make it difficult to find. In this chapter, we begin by briefly exploring domains of pain and suffering, including biological, psychological, social, and spiritual. Then we consider two reasons why pain and suffering can make detachment—and thus, wisdom—so difficult by impeding mental freedom. The first is that pain and suffering get right up into our face, like Mike Tyson's boxing glove. It makes it hard to see anything else. The second is our natural tendency to avoid anything that hurts, and despite whatever similarities may appear at first glance, avoidance is not the same as detachment. Not even close.

DOMAINS OF PAIN AND SUFFERING

Where does pain and suffering show up? Everywhere. Being punched in the mouth hurts in all sorts of ways. Well, yes, but let's try to be more specific. Consider four perspectives: biological, psychological, social, and spiritual (Engel, 1977; Sulmasy, 2002).

Put on a white coat for a moment and imagine yourself to be a physician in a primary care clinic. Your patient, whom we will call Felicia, presents with chronic neck pain and stiffness. At age 61, and especially given her work as a hair dresser, it seems likely that arthritis and overuse may be a factor. These are biological factors, but what about the psychological impact of recently losing a long marriage through divorce, including her ongoing sadness and anxiety for the future? Might the burdens of her soul also be felt in her neck? About 20% of adults in the United States struggle with some sort of psychological disorder in a given year (National Institute of Mental Health, n.d.), making psychological pain a major public health issue. Further, the loss of her marriage resulted in some serious financial challenges and relocating to a new home, far from her familiar neighborhood where she had known and been known. Humans live in collective groups, social units, and we find great comfort and meaning in this. From our earliest tribal histories we see the importance of belonging. How might Felicia's social challenges also show up in muscle tension around her spinal cord? In her anguish, Felicia is questioning and struggling with long-held beliefs regarding God's provision and benevolence. In this, she joins countless others throughout the ages who question why bad things happen to good people. If God is all-loving and all-powerful, then how can this be? Questions about spirituality bring people to painful pivot points in life where faith systems crumble and existential meaning is hard to find. Even those who remain in their religious or spiritual tradition encounter dissonance at times. When confronting the liminal moments of life, faith sometimes does not stand the test as well as people would like, and they end up with profound questions and disappointments. Consequently, they may become hardened and weaponize their faith traditions. Deep dissolution and pain often lurk beneath fanatical extremes, and tendencies toward addiction to certain components of religion can reveal an underlying "toxic faith" (Arterburn & Felton, 2001).

At first glance, this discussion of domains of pain may seem distal from where we started the book, considering how we live in a time of ideological fortresses where we band together with like-minded people and lob Twitter grenades at those who see things differently. We argue otherwise. Pain is central to this conversation, especially the social dimensions of pain. People have always been inclined to tribalism and group conflict, but what is relatively new is the information technology that surrounds us, allowing our squabbles and disagreements to be more public and socially painful than ever before. The pain of being scorned or unfriended on social media is both substantial and new in the course of human history.

But this moves beyond Facebook, and right into our living rooms. In the midst of today's virulent ideological conflicts, almost every extended family experiences painful division. Social groups also suffer, as well as neighborhoods and faith communities. So-and-so supports one political candidate and must not be trusted with conversation. One person is painted blue, and another red, and thus deemed to be untrustworthy. This sort of reflexive and dismissive rejection of the other is painful, especially to the outsider. But the insider is damaged, too, shutting out the other, labeling the outsider to be evil. In this, we do psychological damage to

ourselves and our like-minded peers by oversimplifying the complex problems of the world.

Does it ever seem that pain is the glue that holds our enclaves together?
One group coalesces around this issue or that, but soon the thing that
holds them tight is dislike—or even hatred—of the other group. Genuine, curious conversation with others seems to be waning as social media
attacks gain attention and popularity and we retreat into our silos of pain.

To find wisdom in pain, we turn to detachment, but this may be
exactly when detachment is most difficult because pain interferes with the
mental freedom that comes with healthy detachment.

PAIN AS A DEMANDING TYRANT

As explored in Chapter 4, detachment involves standing at the edge and
observing life even as we participate in it. It is almost like bilocation: we
live in the middle of our experience, but we simultaneously stand on the
margin, observing ourselves and the world around. But pain can be a
demanding tyrant, making it incredibly difficult to stand at any distance.
Before we know it, we are held captive by our pain, struggling to experience
mental freedom, finding it almost impossible to gain a broad perspective
on life.

Imagine sitting on an airplane next to a parent with a crying baby.
At first, you may be quite successful with detachment. You say to yourself, *Oh, that baby is unhappy. It may be difficult for anyone in this part of the
plane to rest or work for a while.* But over time, if the crying continues, it
draws you in so that not only the baby and the parent are experiencing
some undefined misery—you are, too. Once you have entered the misery
zone, the ability to detach and observe what is happening becomes almost
impossible.

Think of the many ways we shift into a misery zone—an intense
toothache, nerve pain shooting down our legs or across our arms with
stressed vertebrae, the sudden loss of a life-giving relationship, an unexpected job loss, learning of a nasty rumor that is tainting a hard-earned

reputation. Pain gets right up into our face, holding our gaze, demanding our full attention.

Have you had the experience of getting so engrossed in something—a conversation, book, television show, or table game—that you almost forget about your pain for a while? In these moments, distraction helps us slip outside of the misery zone. Detachment does the same thing, but with greater intention. With detachment, we learn to tenderly hold our pain, to observe it, even to learn from it. This detached perspective fosters wisdom, as explored in the next chapter.

When pain becomes suffering, because it is chronic and irresolvable, it requires people to adjust in one way or another. One person becomes dependent on opioids while another grows in wisdom. The key difference here is not just how we experience the pain itself, but how we experience our relationship to pain. If pain remains a demanding tyrant, always in the center of our focus, then we struggle to gain perspective and wisdom. But for those who are able to detach from their pain, observing and accepting it as an unwelcome stranger while continuing to live as fully as possible into their human values and commitments (recall the discussion of teleology in Chapter 3), they open the door to deep wisdom.

The idea of detaching ourselves from discomfort may sound impossible to those living in pain, as so many are, and we agree that it is exceedingly difficult. In the next chapter we will consider some practical ideas for how to tenderly hold pain while also gaining some distance from it. But first, we explore another way that pain can make it hard to find the detachment necessary for wisdom.

PAIN AS A PURSUING PREDATOR

Keith, a former student, was fishing in Alaska when a brown bear sniffed the salmon he had hanging from his fishing belt. Knowing something about these situations, Keith unhooked the fish from his belt, dropped it where the bear could reach it, and then backed up slowly. Thankfully, he did not run because bears can run as fast as racehorses, both uphill and down. It is good to figure this out in advance, before going to Alaska on a fishing trip, because the natural instinct is to turn and run when confronting obvious danger, and the outcome could have been dire.

When we run from pain, it often runs faster than we can. To be clear, there is good reason to avoid pain, if possible. If you can prevent a back spasm by not lifting the 120 pound rock, then by all means avoid it. But sometimes pain shows up anyway, despite our wisest efforts to keep it at bay, and then we have a choice to stop, back away gently, or to run in fear. When we run, we give into a fear-avoidance cycle.

The fear-avoidance model of pain explains how trying to flee pain actually makes the problem worse (Vlaeyen et al., 2016). In Chapter 4, we introduced Pauline, a once successful consultant who struggled with panic attacks. The attacks were so terrifying—and so disruptive to her work—that she spent her days in fear of having another. Her sympathetic nervous system was on constant guard, always in flight or fright mode, as she anticipated how bad it would be to experience another attack. She stopped scheduling so many consulting meetings, asking her colleagues to take them instead, but this did not end up helping. It only heightened her fear for those meetings that she still had to manage. She walked into those essential meetings with a sense of dread, making it hard to listen well to her clients or focus on the problems being discussed in the room. The more she missed conversation, the more she obsessed about the inner cues of what might be happening in her body, and this spiraled into more and more fear, less and less listening, and greater risk of panic. Her efforts to avoid panic were causing tension in her body, restriction in breathing, and cognitive narrowing. In essence, her fear of panic made it quite likely that she would, indeed, have an attack when she most dreaded it.

Recall that detachment involves a degree of mental freedom, but in Pauline's efforts to avoid her pain she moved toward mental captivity rather than freedom. If we think of pain as a pursuing predator, it makes detachment impossible. We have turned our back to what is happening in the present moment so that we can run away from pain, but we simply cannot outrun it. Trying to do so makes it worse. Detachment requires us to face our pain, to stand on the edge and curiously observe it even as we are experiencing it. We will explore 10 strategies for detaching from pain in the next chapter.

We have illustrated this with psychological pain, but the same patterns apply to other types of pain as well. Consider the biological pain that occurs with lower back injuries. Once an injury occurs and pain ensues, some people move into a state of low fear while others have high fear (Leeuw et al., 2006). Those with low fear typically recover over time, in conjunction with necessary treatments, but those in the high fear situation end up experiencing a heightened emotional state that leads them to avoidance responses. They cannot avoid the pain, but they can avoid situations they fear might exacerbate the pain. Scientists who study this report those experiencing high fear end up walking slower and engaging less vigorously in physical activities because they fear the consequences for their lower back. This, in turn, contributes to being sedentary and depressed, both of which add to the pain. The body and the mind conspire in some tragic fear cycle that adds to the pain and to the urgency to run from the pain (Leeuw et al., 2006).

One can make a similar case for social pain. When facing a social rift with someone, one option is to move forward toward genuine conversation. Detachment allows us to stand far enough away from the angst we feel to recognize that the other person may have something worth considering to say. Another option is to ostracize and alienate the other, nursing our narcissistic wound by trying to avoid the discomfort.

Or consider spiritual pain. When a faith system starts to crack around the edges, one choice is to delve in further, to speak with those who have faced similar challenges, to hold the mystery of the unknown with curiosity. This may well lead to changing beliefs, but from a place of genuine inquiry. Another choice is to abandon our quests and beliefs altogether, to scurry away in cynicism and frustration.

Then there is moral pain, which we take to be some combination of the psychological, social, and spiritual domains. With moral pain we encounter ethical challenges that bring us discomfort, or perhaps even despair. I (Mark) recall administering a standardized test to an 8-year-old, asking her what the right thing to do would be if she accidentally broke a prized toy that belonged to a friend. She quickly and unflinchingly replied, "Hide it!" It was not the answer I was hoping for in terms of moral development, but it was amusing enough that I had to suppress a chuckle. Her answer revealed our unpracticed, primal reflex when experiencing discomfort, which is to remove ourselves from it as far and as quickly as possible. But moral avoidance also has a way of catching up. How can we learn to stay present to the moral quandaries of our day, to hold the tensions they stir in us, and to do our best to find a compassionate, humane, and just way forward?

To the casual observer, it may appear that avoidance is similar to detachment, but in fact they are entirely different. Avoidance is counterfeit detachment: it is easier not to look at some things than to look because we do not like the discomfort it brings. In contrast, detachment requires us to look at both the harsh and beautiful things about ourselves, to stand back and honestly observe ourselves and the world around us. Avoidance tells us to hide or deny our mistakes. Detachment asks that we hold them compassionately and consider from an objective distance how to best move forward.

CHAPTER 6

Detachment
Strategies

In Chapter 5 we asked you to imagine putting on a white coat and becoming a medical provider for Felicia, a patient facing chronic pain. To begin this chapter, take off the white coat and put on a blazer if you must, though no jacket at all will be just fine. Imagine yourself a psychotherapist sitting with Jonathan, a patient struggling with chronic psychological discomfort, much of it stemming from chaotic early years involving trauma and abuse.

If you are picturing this well, you may already feel compassion and empathy for Jonathan—all the more so if you are actually in the room sitting with him. One of the main things psychotherapists offer is an empathic, compassionate presence in a world where people can feel isolated and alone in their suffering. It is not just that you know the skills to display empathy—you actually feel it as you sit with Jonathan, holding a deep, tender awareness of his losses and grief.

We have discussed how pain can inhibit detachment in at least two ways—if we allow it to get right up in our face, demanding our full attention, or if we try to outrun it, avoiding it at any cost. As a psychotherapist, you intuitively recognize this dilemma, and you do your best to prevent both errors. While in some sessions you may encourage Jonathan to recount some details of his early life trauma, you will not ask overly much for details, and you certainly will not spend every session on this. It would be too much to invite that pain into every moment of every therapy session. Therapy demands some distance from pain, even as you enter into it. Similarly, you will not try to outrun the pain with Jonathan. You both stay present to it, allowing the conversation to move in and out of old traumas as he chooses. That pain is right in the room with you, just as it is in Jonathan's life every day.

In your sessions with Jonathan, you glimpse how unjust the world can be, and how he stoops under the weight of sin perpetrated against him all those years ago. You are present, tenderly holding his pain. Over time, Jonathan learns to do this same thing with himself, as if he were his own therapist. He learns to hold his pain compassionately without its running or ruining his life. In other words, he learns how to hold a healthy detachment while still being fully alive to his past, present, and future.

An early and enigmatic set of scientific studies on wisdom coming out of the Max Planck Institute for Human Development and Education in Berlin, Germany, showed that clinical psychologists scored higher than other professionals on wisdom tests (Baltes et al., 1995; Smith et al., 1994). Explanations for this abound, but we wonder if one reason may be that clinical psychologists practice detachment every day, sitting in the midst of difficult situations without running from them or becoming consumed by them.

Now we will transfer this same skill set to other areas of discomfort or tension in life. As you are reading right now, what are the areas of concern you hold? Do you have financial worries? Are you in physical pain? Do political or ideological systems trouble you and cause you tension? Are you at odds with someone in a meaningful relationship? Is your workplace a problem right now? Here is the invitation of this chapter: can you take the same skills you imagined while sitting with Jonathan and apply them to your own life in the areas of discomfort you are feeling right now? Jonathan discloses how suffocating it feels to see his 6-year-old nephew, remembering the abuse he suffered around that age in life. You lean forward into his pain, giving him space to remember and to shed a few tears, and then as he is ready, you gently sit back in your chair and ask him more about his nephew. In this way, you remain present to his pain as he wants to speak of it, but you are also willing to move away from it as he needs. Now take this out of the therapy office and imagine that your mother-in-law is deeply troubled about a Supreme Court decision. Can you hold her discomfort compassionately and tenderly, listening to her perspectives, resisting the urge to dismiss them, yet without letting this taking over the entire conversation? This invitation to detachment is essential on the pathway to wisdom.

Because detachment is important in developing wisdom, here we offer 10 strategies for learning healthy detachment, even in the midst of life's difficulties. These strategies are distilled from scientific findings related to psychological flexibility (Hayes et al., 2012) and wisdom development (Aldwin et al., 2019; Glück & Bluck, 2013; Glück et al., 2019), with some insights from religious and spiritual leaders mixed in (Manney, 2011; Thurman, 1953).

STRATEGY #1: PICTURE YOURSELF AS A PLAYER-COACH

It would be impossible to capture in a paragraph all the impressive accomplishments of Bill Russell, a center with the Boston Celtics from 1956 to 1969. A 12-time All-Star, he was also named Most Valuable Player of the National Basketball Association (NBA) 5 times, and he won 11 NBA championships in his 13 years of playing. He once grabbed 51 rebounds in a single game. But one easily forgotten detail about Russell's illustrious career is that he served as a player-coach from 1966 to 1969, becoming the first Black coach in American professional sports and the first Black coach to win a championship.

Player-coaching almost never happens these days because professional sports teams have plenty of money to pay both players and coaches, but in Russell's day budgets were tighter, and every now and then a team would ask a player to coach. This serves as an ideal metaphor for maintaining a detached perspective on the pathway toward wisdom. We are simultaneously in the mix of our life, running up and down the court, and also standing on the sidelines, observing and noticing what is happening and considering strategies for how to make things more effective. The challenge is to be in both of these roles simultaneously—fully engaged in life, and still observing from a bit of a distance.

Emerging from the spirituality of the 16th-century saint Ignatius Loyola is a practice called Daily Examen. This end-of-the-day prayer ritual is now practiced by Christians of various denominations. It involves reviewing one's day by engaging in five steps (Manney, 2011). Notice how each of these puts the person praying in a detached position, both experiencing the day that has just passed and observing it.

1. Ask God for perspective, to illumine you, as you look at your day.
2. Give thanks. Remember today has been a gift. Settle into a place of gratitude for it.
3. Review the day. Consider what has happened, how you have experienced God's guidance.
4. Admit where you have fallen short.
5. Look ahead to tomorrow, and ask God for help.

Whether you use the Daily Examen or some nonreligious alternative, notice how a simple end-of-day ritual can place you in the role of player-coach. Each day you become a little better at seeing life from a detached perspective, reflecting on how your life is being lived even as you are living it.

Remember, too, that a good coach listens to other coaches and players. Wisdom often calls us to receive or even seek input from others so that we can learn to see ourselves more objectively. If a good friend tells me that I spoke abruptly to the server at the restaurant, I face a choice. I can dismiss my friend—perhaps even my friendship—as ridiculous, or I can receive the comment with curiosity and humility and allow it to help me learn a more detached, objective way of seeing myself and a more compassionate way of living in the world.

Most days bring various opportunities to observe ourselves from a detached perspective. As you are driving down the road, taking a break between work meetings to pour a cup of coffee or have a brief stroll, gardening, showering, working out, sitting in stillness after soothing a crying toddler to sleep, or waiting in line, ask yourself what you are feeling and thinking at this moment. What is weighing on your mind? What is bringing you joy and peace? Notice the sensations in your body. Observe yourself as if from the outside and pay attention to what you learn.

STRATEGY #2: NOTICE THAT YOU ARE NOT YOUR THOUGHTS AND FEELINGS

Acceptance and Commitment Therapy (ACT) is an approach to psychotherapy that bears similarity to this player-coach analogy (Hayes et al., 2012). The acceptance part of the approach is learning to be fully present to the realities of life, like being a player on the basketball court. The commitment part is more like being a coach. We get to manage our lives, even when we encounter unpleasant and unwanted circumstances. Are you feeling upset or anxious? Be fully aware and present to those feelings, but keep in mind that they do not get to dictate how you choose to live in this moment.

ACT uses a term called "cognitive fusion" to show we sometimes get too close to our thoughts. When this happens we lose a detached perspective in considering our lives. The person entering adulthood thinking, *I am a loser*, may find these words reverberating over and over for years into the future. If we get too close to this sort of belief, it starts to take over our identity, and soon we behave as if it were the only possible way to understand who we are in the world.

The essence of a human being can never be fully contained in a thought or feeling, even a devastating thought such as *I am a loser*. If we find ourselves having a troubling thought like that, one option is to turn ourselves over to it, allowing it to cut a swathe of damage on its way, but another option is to back up and simply observe what is happening. Instead of

I am a loser, one might think, *I'm saying that thing to myself again, that I'm a loser.* With this detached perspective, there is no need to prove if we are or are not a loser; it simply provides a larger view of ourselves and our experience. Notice the subtle but important differences in the following statements.

1a. I am depressed.
1b. I am a person experiencing depression.

2a. I am a failure.
2b. I failed at an important task, and now I am disappointed in myself.

3a. I always succeed.
3b. I tend to feel confident, and often it pays off for me.

4a. I am broke.
4b. Money is tight right now, and I'm feeling alarmed about it.

5a. My life is terrible.
5b. I've faced hard things in life, and sometimes I feel helpless.

In each of these cases, option b provides a perspective that is more detached than option a.

STRATEGY #3: EMBRACE PAIN AND SUFFERING WITH COMPASSION

The Vietnamese monk Thich Nhat Hanh has inspired awareness of Buddhist teachings throughout the world. In describing suffering as the first of Four Noble Truths, Hanh (2015) makes the compelling point that suffering is only holy if we embrace it and "look deeply into it" (p. 9). Otherwise suffering is the ocean in which we drown. This sort of response to suffering grows our ability to detach. If we can look deeply and kindly into our pain, this response suggests we are neither running from it nor allowing it to consume us.

Embracing suffering does not mean we love it, as if we were hugging a lover. Still, it does imply a tender holding, recognizing that suffering will come in life and that we will do better if we can make friends with it rather than if we try to fight it. Sure, if we can prevent or treat pain, then by all means we should do so, but some suffering can never be fixed with a pill, a surgery, a therapist, a self-help book, or anything else. Compassionately holding this sort of pain reduces its power over us. The idea of redemptive suffering in the Christian tradition—a theistic and communal view of participating in pain and suffering—expresses how "in my flesh I am completing what is lacking in Christ's afflictions for the sake of his body, that is, the church," as the apostle Paul writes in Colossians 1:24 (New Revised Standard Version). This verse highlights the opportunity and privilege for humans to connect their suffering to that of Jesus, and in a mysterious way, to understand their own pain and suffering as sacred and godly.

If we stop trying to scurry away from suffering, we have the opportunity to consider other values in how we live. Rather than having avoidance of pain as the main goal, we can choose other values to guide us forward in life. We do not mean to make this sound easy. It is not. Suffering is bitter. Still, a life lived in bitterness ferments into something worse than it would have otherwise been. Even in the face of bitter suffering, people can find guiding values by which they organize their lives. The more those values align with the transcendentals that we discussed earlier, the less likely they will be affected by the judgment of self and others.

In 2014 Thich That Hanh survived a major stroke, leaving him without speech and with some right-side paralysis. Still, those in his community describe his peaceful presence, his sharp mind, and his perceptive companionship (Hanh, 2020). A monk for 70 years, and an author and teacher for many of those years, Hanh prepared himself to live well in suffering.

For those seeking a values-based direction amidst life's challenges, a helpful online exercise is the values card sort. A number of values are listed, and you are asked to rank how important each is to you. Is curiosity an important value for you? Courage? Solitude? Spirituality? A number of websites are available for this, such as The Good Project (Good Project, n.d.). Consider taking some time to complete the values card sort exercise and then ponder your results. It might also be useful to share what you discover with a friend or family member. It will not solve any pain or suffering you are facing just now, but it might remind you of the guiding vision that motivates you through life's difficult times.

STRATEGY #4: HOLD THE CONTROL DIALECTIC

In Chapter 5 we mentioned the MORE Life Experience Model of wisdom developed by Judith Glück and her colleagues (Glück & Bluck, 2013; Glück et al., 2019). The model presumes that life brings challenges and that some people respond to difficulties by becoming wise, while most do not. What makes the path to wisdom possible in the face of suffering?

The M in the MORE model stands for *mastery*. Those who move toward wisdom are able to recognize they have some say in their lives, even when faced with suffering. They are active, willing agents who choose much about who they become, even as they recognize they cannot have full control over life circumstances. This is the dialectic: wise people take control over what they can control while recognizing that much of life is uncontrollable. This is reminiscent of the Serenity Prayer, adapted by Alcoholics Anonymous and attributed to Reinhold Niebuhr (Shapiro, 2014): "God, grant me the serenity to accept the things I cannot change, courage to change the things I can, and wisdom to know the difference."

One strategy for learning detachment is simply to say this prayer once or twice a day. Each time we repeat these words, we remind ourselves to seek mastery over areas of life we can influence and to release our grip on those things we cannot.

STRATEGY #5: CONSIDER MULTIPLE VIEWPOINTS

The O in MORE stands for *openness*. This is not to suggest a sloppy openness where anything goes and there is no room for values and expectations, but rather an awareness that every complex issue carries multiple perspectives.

In today's world, a compelling example comes in political perspectives. As we have discussed in previous chapters, we have become quite polarized in how we see the world. One person sees red, another blue. Those who fail at openness tend to compare the best logic of their own opinion with the worst logic of their opponent's. This makes it quite easy and natural to assume that "any reasonable person would agree with me." But this is not a fair or reasonable representation of the other side. Social media is overflowing with political posts and comments demonstrating this lopsided view of the other. To gain a detached perspective, one must consider the best arguments of the other side and the worst of one's own, as we discussed when considering critical contemplation in the introduction.

Most people simply cannot do this. A poster from the 1970s read, "There are two sides to every issue: my side and the wrong side." We chuckle, but if we are brutally honest, it is the way most of us approach life. This is one reason that Glück and Bluck (2013) conclude that "everyone has their share of challenges across life, however, most do not develop high levels of wisdom" (p. 79). It is not enough just to gather lots of life experiences, as one might collect coins or baseball cards. Wisdom requires us to grow and develop new insights, including the ability to see a thing from multiple angles.

Try having a conversation with an acquaintance about an issue you disagree on. This could be done on social media, but even better, try it in person, perhaps in a coffee shop where social norms will keep you from raising your voices. See if you can really listen, moving so deeply into the perspective of the other that it starts to make sense to you. This does not mean you must change your mind—you may or may not—but it is the perfect way to learn the skill of considering multiple perspectives.

STRATEGY #6: SEEK GENEROSITY TOWARD OTHERS AND QUIET THE EGO

Most of us have a proclivity to make simple, negative judgments about others and more generous judgments about ourselves. Social psychologists call this the *fundamental attribution error*. If something good happens to me, getting an A on an exam, for example, it is because I studied hard. Plus, I am really smart. But if you get an A, the professor must have given an easy test. Conversely, if something bad happens to me, such as getting a speeding ticket, it is because the police officer had a quota to fill and chose me as the mostly innocent target for a citation. If you get a speeding ticket, well, it is just good we have police officers around to hold irresponsible drivers like you accountable.

Detachment, and the wisdom it serves, requires us to lean the other way toward generous views of others and humble views of ourselves. The R in MORE stands for *reflectivity*, recognizing that the world is more complex than it seems at first glance. We may honk our horn and curse at the slow driver in front of us, assuming he is texting while driving, when in reality he is on his way home from a medical appointment where he just learned he has cancer. We cannot know this, of course, but if we hold open that possibility in a reflective posture toward the other, then we stand a bit detached from the anger that surges up in us when we miss the traffic light because the driver in front of us moved too slowly. Plus, it is just a more generous way to walk in the world, assuming that people are—as Brené Brown suggests—doing the best they can (Brown, 2015).

The E in MORE is a bit confusing because it stands for two things: *emotional regulation* and *empathy*. We will consider emotional regulation in the next chapters as we launch the idea of tranquility. Empathy requires us to view the other with generosity, to enter into their world with compassion and care, to listen well, to hold their pain, to be a true friend.

The other part of the fundamental attribution error is that we tend to ascribe internal attributes to our own good outcomes (we are smart, so we aced the test) and external attributes to bad outcomes (the police officer needed to fill a quota). Gaining awareness and detachment from this is no easy task, but it helps just knowing that this is our tendency. The next time you excuse yourself for some unfortunate outcome, or take credit for something good that happens, pause and entertain the possibility that you may be looking at yourself more generously than you would look at someone else experiencing the same circumstances. If you practice this skill of reflectivity enough, it eventually gives way to humility, and then to a healthy detachment from ego.

Speaking of ego, one of the most exciting developments in psychology in recent years is work on the *quiet ego* (Wayment & Bauer, 2008). In our untutored state, most of us have clamoring loud egos that fill our senses with personal demands and desires. But with practice we can learn to quiet our egos, to grow in humility and gratitude and generosity toward others. Wayment and Bauer (2008) discuss four qualities of a quiet ego, and the first is detached awareness, which is what we are discussing here. Detachment allows us to participate in the present moment without constantly questioning how this moment makes us feel about ourselves, and it allows us to be open to seeing and understanding the other. The other three qualities are interdependence, compassion, and growth—all topics we discuss in various places throughout this book. Not surprisingly, wisdom scholars also discuss quieting the ego as a way to get beyond the clamoring self and grow in wisdom (Aldwin et al., 2019). A quiet ego creates a beautiful space for wisdom to flourish.

STRATEGY #7: PRACTICE GENEROSITY

Another tool of self-transcendence—and thus detachment—described by Aldwin et al. (2019) is practicing generosity. Christian Smith and Hilary Davidson (2014), authors of *The Paradox of Generosity*, have a fantastic subtitle to their book: "Giving we receive, grasping we lose." They show compelling evidence that one path to human flourishing is by giving our-selves away to others. It may not make intuitive sense, but people who give financially and volunteer their time report feeling happier than others. Similarly, those who are attentive and responsive to others—relationally generous—experience similar happiness benefits. Generous people are more likely than others to be physically healthy and have a sense of their meaning and purpose in life (McMinn, 2017).

Why would this be? Giving away some of ourselves and our resources helps us stand outside of our immediate concerns and suffering, remind-ing us that others in the world are also hurting. When you write a check to a community service organization, you are remembering that people struggle with food security or with paying their rent and utility bills. It is not just that life is hard for each of us sometimes; it is hard for others, too. This detached perspective helps us grow in wisdom as we learn to be better citizens in a complicated and sometimes cruel world.

STRATEGY #8: MAKE FRIENDS WITH UNCERTAINTY

Recall the detachment quality of negative capability from Chapter 4, which is the capacity to stand in a place of uncertainty and ambiguity. It seems quite natural to grab on to an idea and clinch our fists around it in certainty. Cognitive psychologists—those who study how we think—point out that we are consistently more confident in the opinions we hold than we are correct. They call this the *overconfidence phenomenon*. Perhaps you have had a disagreement with a friend or partner about how some-thing happened in the past. You are both 100 percent sure you are right, but only one of you can be.

Try the discipline of saying, "I don't know" at least once a day. Omid Safi is a professor of Islamic studies at Duke University. In an OnBeing article he tells the story of a medieval saint that people sought out for wis-dom (Safi, 2017). One day someone asked the saint a question about the law, to which the saint answered, "I don't know." Someone else asked a philosophical question and received the same answer from the saint. Altogether, 30 people came to the saint that day, and only one received an answer. Safi observes, "One out of 30. The rest of the time, the saint realized that silence was an improvement over words." Safi's story is reminiscent of words attributed to Socrates: "The only true wisdom is in knowing you know nothing."

STRATEGY #9: REMEMBER PATIENCE IS A VIRTUE

Another tool of self-transcendence described by wisdom researchers is practicing patience (Aldwin et al., 2019). Patience requires a degree of detachment as we learn to step outside of the pressing demands of now and consider our situation from a fresh perspective.

Scattered across the internet is a story—apocryphal or true, who knows?—of a New York City cab driver who hurriedly stopped to pick up a fare, honked his horn at the door, and almost left before deciding to go knock and see if someone still wanted a ride. It was an old lady in her nineties, with a vinyl suitcase. He noticed through the open door that her house was buttoned up as if no one lived there, with covers on the furniture and no other decorations. She handed him an address, but then asked if he would drive a longer route through the city so she could take a look at the sights. As they talked, his passenger disclosed that this was her last journey, and that the address she handed him was for a hospice center. He turned off the meter, meandered through New York City with her, delivered her to a wheelchair waiting for her at the hospice center, hugged her good-bye, and did not charge a penny. As she parted, she said, "You gave an old woman a moment of joy." The cab driver did not pick up any more passengers that evening, drove around for a while, and pondered that this may have been the most important thing he had done in his life.

Amidst the pressure of making a living in one of the busiest cities in the world, this driver could have honked once then gone on to pick up another fare when his passenger failed to show. Instead, he practiced patience, went to the door, and touched a lonely woman's life with kindness. This is detachment at its best, turning off the meter and being present to the other when they need us to show up in the fullness of our humanity.

STRATEGY #10: LET PAIN HAVE A MINISTRY

If pain and suffering are great obstacles to detachment, and if—as we have argued in this chapter and earlier—cognitive flexibility is a great marker of wisdom, then this last strategy may simultaneously be both the most important and difficult one of all. Please hear us clearly that pain and suffering are not good things to be pursued, but they will find their way to us if we live long enough. And when they do visit us, whether for a short-term stay or for a long sojourn, they can minister to us. Yes, this is unusual language for what may seem an outrageous notion.

Howard Thurman was no stranger to pain and suffering. He watched a wife die of tuberculosis four years after they were married. His work as a Black theologian, and intellectual, and author writing during the 20th-century American civil rights movement must have been excruciatingly difficult at times. But Thurman was also a mystic, deeply committed to the practice of healthy detachment, and from this place of mystical detachment he offered profound words about the ministry of pain.

In *Meditations of the Heart*, Thurman (1953) wrote that all of life—including the pain we encounter—has the potential to form our souls more deeply. This soul-forming is what gives us depth and makes us most fully human. It makes us whole. Recall the notion of *telos*, described in Chapter 3, to understand what Thurman means by the wholeness of soul-forming. Of course, we look at our greatest joys and blessings when considering the formation of our souls, but what about pain and suffering? Even the events that lead to human misery, Thurman suggests, have a role in soul-making. He is quick to warn that this does not mean God sends us pain to form our souls, which leads to a sort of fatalism and destroys "basic faith in the goodness and wisdom of God" (p. 66). Rather, he argues that pain will find its way to us in life, and we have a choice to be bitter or to let it be our teacher.

Pain certainly found its way to one of Thurman's most outstanding students at Boston University: Martin Luther King, Jr. After Dr. King was stabbed in a hate crime at a 1958 book signing, Thurman came to visit him in the hospital where he encouraged King to "take the unexpected, if tragic, opportunity to meditate on his life and its purposes, and only then move forward" (Harvey, 2019). He encouraged King to take two extra weeks rather than rushing back into his public work (Harvey, 2019). King later referred to the meditative convalescence after his stabbing as important preparation for the work he was to do in confronting white supremacy. In his fascinating analysis of these events, American historian Paul Harvey (2019) concludes: "The relationship of Thurman's mysticism and King's activism provides a fascinating model for how spiritual and social transformation can work together in a person's life—and in society more generally."

Howard Thurman—a mystic familiar with healthy detachment—suggested that even pain can be our teacher. It is not the teacher we want, but sometimes it is the one we have. If we allow pain to be our minister, Thurman (1953) believed it will help us understand and love life. "To love life truly is to be whole in all one's parts; and to be whole in all one's parts is to be free and unafraid" (p. 66). This sounds a lot like tranquility.

PART 3

TRANQUILITY

CHAPTER 7

TRANQUILITY
AND WISDOM

S peaking as an Irish Catholic, though not always a very good one, I (Paul) can say that the Irish love a good fight, or even a bad one. The saying goes that an Irishman approached a brawl outside a bar and calmly asked, "Is this a private fight or can anyone join?" While we are arguing for wisdom as a peaceful and unifying means to overcome social ills and divisiveness, this strange story admits to the appeal of just jumping in and swinging away. This approach certainly has an allure. Fighting is not always bad, at least not if we consider the notion of fighting in a broad manner, referring to any kind of conflict or struggle. This combative spirit can be put to use in confronting challenges in the world around us and within ourselves, and persevering in the pursuit of wisdom. Learning to confront ourselves and others, to quarrel with control, while keeping the larger context in view protects against unbridled self-centeredness and being emotionally overtaken by the expectations of others.

This may seem a strange way to start a chapter on tranquility, but right from the beginning we want to be clear that tranquility is not passivity, apathy, or the absence of disagreement. A poet friend describes words as "slippery things," and indeed they are when it comes to a notion such as tranquility. One might think of tranquility as putting on noise-canceling headphones, latching the dead bolt, and settling into a hermit's existence where all the troubles of the world seem far away. This is not what we mean by tranquility. No, the notion of wisdom we present here is a full-bodied, fully engaged way of being in the world. It does not call us away from conflict or from the hustle and bustle of life, but rather it brings emotional regulation, even in the midst of the daily swirl, bringing a sense of calm to real life. The reason tranquility is so needed in our day is because we live in an age of emotion. The age of faith and the age of reason have passed. Today we find websites detailing the top 10 celebrity feuds of the year, watch reality television that stirs our anger and discontent, and subscribe to newsfeeds that do little more than attack opposing ideologies. Emotions are the major determining factors in our lives and pursuit of happiness, yet tranquility has never been so crucial and grossly lacking.

To give an example of what tranquility could look like, Emma has explained to Garrett, her 6-year-old son, that he is not to yell at his older sister, and that if he continues he will need to go to his bedroom until he calms down. He continues yelling, so Emma walks Garrett to his room and sits with him while he rages about how unfair it is and how the conflict is really all his sister's fault. Emma does not yell. She sits quietly and remains present to Garrett, but without reacting or yelling back. Emma has learned to be tranquil, to regulate her own emotions even when those around her do not, and her tranquility makes her an effective parent.

Like King Arthur's knights of the roundtable, tranquility that leads to wisdom is the Holy Grail, the emotional apotheosis, a peak state of peace, joy, and sublime serenity. This lost treasure of harmony between thoughts, feelings, and behaviors goes beyond the common notion of emotional intelligence (Goleman, 1995), even as we acknowledge that wise people have ample amounts of emotional intelligence. How can we move closer toward this lofty state of tranquility while pursuing wisdom? Can we find moments of tranquility in our daily lives?

PICTURING TRANQUILITY

As we return to the topic of tranquility, it might be helpful to move from a brawl outside a bar to a conversation with a friend over coffee. Let's say you and someone you like agree to meet to discuss a topic that you see differently. Perhaps it is related to gun control, or parenting strategies, or religion. It is a spirited conversation as both you and your friend have definite ideas, and you do not agree. At times people at nearby tables glance to make sure everything is okay because you are both clearly engaged—heart and mind—with the topic at hand. But the conversation is as civil as it is spirited. You both listen well, you are not gauging the success of the conversation on whether the other person comes to seeing things your way, and at times you both glimpse the wisdom of the other's perspective. You end the coffee conversation, still good friends, still disagreeing, and having enjoyed an invigorating dialog. As you leave, you offer a hug or a handshake to remind you both how much you care for one another. Neither of you have to win, and neither of you have to shrink into passivity or placating.

We offer this as a picture of tranquility, but with a disclaimer. Tranquility is not so much what is happening *between* you and your friend, which might be described as good conversation, mutual curiosity, kindness, or civil engagement. Tranquility is what is happening *within* you in the midst of the conversation, and *within* Emma as she sits with her 6-year-old son while he has his tantrum in his bedroom. Tranquility is being able to move into real-life places while finding a balanced equilibrium and not being overwhelmed by particular emotions. You likely feel frustrated at times with your friend's ideas in the coffee shop, but you also feel an abiding sense of shared humanity and love, which provides a tranquil center, an inner sanctum, as you engage in the regular routines of life.

Tranquility varies from person to person, even as it has general characteristics we might agree on, bringing a deep sense of calm to life in the midst of difficult times. The pictures we carry for tranquility—and the means to achieve it—are relative and highly personalized. Social scientists can learn to predict and anticipate behavior, cognition, and emotions, but much of the mystery of the psyche remains hidden. Each person has a unique relationship with their emotions, and the path to tranquility, like the art of psychotherapy, is never a one size fits all.

We brought you Emma's parenting and the coffee shop conversation with a friend because having specific examples of tranquility will be useful in working through this chapter, but if you have another picture of tranquility you prefer, please go there instead. Whenever we refer to the coffee shop, you can simply retreat to your picture instead, whether it be cutting vegetables, taking a well-earned Sunday afternoon nap, vacationing in the mountains, participating in corporate worship, connecting with a group of friends over deep conversation, or some other picture of blissful equanimity. An old classic psychotherapy technique is free association, to allow whatever comes to mind and to notice the related or associated thoughts and feelings. The intent is to gain insight into unconscious material. Try using this with the word "tranquility" and see what rises to the surface. What does it provoke? Whatever the web of images, words, and feelings may be says something about tranquility, but it also reveals specific things about each of us. This can be your picture to use throughout this chapter.

QUALITIES OF TRANQUILITY

Whatever picture we might prefer, let's try parsing our example of tranquility to look for some of its essential qualities.

Tranquility Is Not Apathy

One of the immediate things to notice about the coffee shop conversation is that you and your friend agree to meet to discuss your disagreements. Wouldn't it be easier just to avoid the dissonance and avoid your friend? Wisdom sometimes requires us to avoid chronic contentious conversations, but, generally speaking, tranquility is an active posture more than a passive one.

I recently heard a radio program describing a dispute involving law school students at a prominent university. The dispute centered around the students' feeling unfairly treated and emotionally activated because they were asked to argue from a perspective opposite of the one they personally held. We can imagine what these issues may have been: perhaps arguing for the death penalty while being personally opposed; having to defend lax immigration laws that open the borders when you think stricter laws are needed; or taking a different stance on abortion, military spending, or corporate taxes. This is a familiar pedagogical and ethical quandary for educators: should students be asked to consider—or even argue for—a perspective other than the one they already hold? There are reasonable perspectives on both sides of this issue, but consider what might be lost if students never had to take on a position other than the one they already hold. They will come to see conflict as private, personal, and pain-ful. They will miss the sheer enjoyment of civil disagreement, the thrill of debate, and constructive argumentation. Over time, they will lose respect for their ideological opponents and for the skill of dispassionate engagement. They will come to take disagreement personally, and taking things personally is a sign that the ego is working overtime and falsely protecting itself from taking in new information. In other words, they will miss out on learning.

Taking conflict too personally leads to spite and ill-will. Over time, this breeds resentment, hatred, and apathy. The apathetic sentiment so common in our day can appear like tranquility. It is not. If avoidance is false detachment, then apathy is twisted tranquility. Deep abiding peace and emotional calm that clear the path to wisdom are the goals. Still, tranquility requires the temerity of intentional engagement, even with ideas that are unsettling to us. If one wants to build a muscle it is neces-sary to put some pressure on it, to create tension so that growth can occur. While the path of least resistance is comforting, it circumvents the rock-ier path and misses out on the character building of those sages we admire and hope to emulate.

Tranquility Involves Shifting Our Inner Equilibrium

It is completely natural, and human, to believe we are right in our opin-ions and to imagine others who disagree to be primitive or uninformed. But what if we could challenge and shift this perspective toward calm equanimity even while having a spirited conversation in a coffee shop? Apart from the conversation, there are deep blessings to be observed and experienced—the company of a dear friend, the taste of freshly brewed coffee, the buzz of friendly conversation all about you. Rather than focusing on how uninformed and offensive your friend can be, you might choose to shift your inner equilibrium toward tranquility.

Tranquility takes us back again to the work of William James, who provides a rich and succinct definition:

> the transition from tenseness, self-responsibility, and worry, to equanimity, receptivity, and peace, is the most wonderful of all those shiftings of inner equilibrium, those changes of the personal centre of energy, which I have analyzed so often; and the chief wonder of it is that it so often comes about not by doing, but by simply relaxing and throwing the burden down. (James, 1902, p. 284)

Stopping our busy lives and releasing our burdens may sound attractive— but unrealistic—especially with problems that seem impossible to change, draining our emotional resources. It is hard to imagine this transition from anxiety and stress to relaxation when the household income continues to decline as day care costs go up, when a love relationship is slowly withering in spite of our many attempts to save it, while a loved one's Alzheimer's worsens, and when trying to get the kids to put the iPad down just long enough to have family dinner. Experiencing equilibrium may seem more of a platitude of the privileged than an ideal for people living amidst daily struggles. Still, we persist, tranquility is part and parcel of the pursuit of wisdom, and it can be achieved even amidst our frantic, hectic, and difficult lives.

If tranquility requires boldness, it also requires some intentionality to achieve this shifting of inner equilibrium—this moving a center of energy—that William James describes. It is not as simple as bingeing on Netflix and eating Oreos. So what is involved in this shift?

It begins with appreciating rest. Any biological entity requires rest. We need time to reset and rejuvenate. James speaks of relaxing, and yes, this sounds a lot like Netflix. But Howard Berenbaum and his colleagues recently found a negative relationship between what they dubbed entertainment activities and tranquility (Berenbaum et al., 2019). So when the *Nerd Bear* website offers someone $1000 to watch 24 James Bond films in 30 days, it is not likely to promote a lot of wisdom (Nerdbear, 2021). While we have ample freedom to pursue leisure in our day, we simultaneously have less space for tranquil rest. Leisure is often filled up with menial tasks or the pursuit of pleasure. For many, modern life has become a playground where desires are given free rein. These options are a wonderful smorgasbord for our inner hedonist, yet they often do not promote rest.

We might associate rest with sleep, and sleep is certainly part of health, wisdom, and tranquility, but there is another dimension to rest that involves what James calls, "throwing down a burden." Sometimes tranquility involves being actively countercultural, calling us to notice and release some of the driving energy that propels us forward. The same researchers who looked at entertainment activities and tranquility also found that tranquil people spend time nurturing others and taking care of basic needs, but are not particularly driven toward being the best at everything they take on. They can get Bs instead of As. They can be good-enough workers without getting Employee of the Year awards. They do not have to master the world. It is okay for them to be good enough at certain things.

We live in a world that celebrates drivenness and accomplishment. The word "driven" might even show up in a letter of recommendation. Walter Brueggemann, a Hebrew Scripture scholar, authored a provocative book titled, *Sabbath as Resistance: Saying No to the Culture of Now* where he compares the ancient culture of Egypt with our contemporary Western culture (Brueggemann, 2014). In both cases, the pressing message is *More! More! More!* Work harder, get more done, be more successful. The Ten Commandments in the book of Exodus provide an alternative to this driven way of being in the world. This alternative was essential for the Hebrew people as they escaped enslavement in ancient Egypt. Right in the middle of the commandments about the character of God (the first three commandments) and how to treat our neighbors (the final six commandments), we find this surprising mandate to rest. Honoring the Sabbath, Brueggemann argues, is one way to resist the culture of drivenness in which we live. Tranquility can be honed in Sabbath rest because it is a spiritual state of non-doing—an antidote to the dragon of narcissism that we explore in Chapter 8.

And as long as we are discussing religion, it is interesting that one of the strongest correlations Berenbaum and colleagues (2019) found in their study existed between tranquility and spiritual activities. Shifting our inner equilibrium toward tranquility calls us to something bigger than ourselves. But this is not a frantic effort to understand the divine or to accomplish all the requirements the divine might have for us. Rather, it is a space for spiritual awareness and contact with the transcendent, a sacred emptiness free of impulse and striving. This is a shift toward interior peace, the *shalom* of the Jewish tradition that expresses not just absence of conflict but deep and abiding wholeness and harmony. Ideally, tranquility brings a restoration of spirit and soulful energy. This interior peace is robust enough to stand tall as social and political trends gust, to enter into spirited conversation and disagreement without leading to disruption and inner turmoil.

Tranquility Ushers Us into the Unpredictable World of Emotions

As you consider the coffee shop conversation with your friend, do you feel a bit of anxiety rising within you? What might it be like if this spirited conversation devolves into an angry rant? Will you be able to control the strong emotions you hold about a topic you deem quite important?

Seeking tranquility requires us to venture into the world of our emotions, which is not always an easy trek. It would be nice if we could simply journey far enough to find calm equanimity, but that is not how emotions work. They come at us as a swirl, often in times of pain and uncertainty, and many times they are difficult to manage. They are not easily divided into positive and negative. For instance, even something as terrifying as skydiving or spinning upside down six times on a roller coaster or watching a tragically sad movie may bring people joy. Similarly, tranquility is not just quiet, serenity, or the absence of trouble. Tranquility would not be that useful if it did not show up in the midst of hard times.

Gina and Robert came for couples therapy in the aftermath of an affair. Both faced intense emotions. Gina felt deep anger, the sting of betrayal, and profound questions about the future of her relationship with Robert. For his part, Robert was overcome with shame and guilt, and fear that he might lose his long marriage to Gina. The work was difficult, mostly because the emotions were so persistent, sometimes showing up at unpredictable times and with frightening intensity. Their work was not to give up the emotions or set them aside, but to bring their feelings into the process of psychotherapy, to communicate honestly about them, and ultimately to seek a place of hard-earned peace, authenticity, and hope as they decided to move forward in their marriage.

Similarly, as you and your friend discuss your disagreements in the coffee shop, you will likely feel the stirring of intense feelings. There may be moments of exasperation, frustration, and anger. Acknowledging and accepting our own capacity for anger and impulsiveness is not easy. It is much easier to recognize these darker characteristics and behaviors in others than in ourselves, yet under the right—or wrong—circumstances, how might we actually act?

What if your coffee shop conversation ushers you into the world of political disagreement? The destabilization of the American political system and attacks on governmental institutions have been front and center as we write this book. The forces of radical change clash with reactionary movements as the ground seems to move beneath us. This instability stirs up a lot of mixed emotion. It can dislodge destructive forces in us all. Here again, it is easier to focus on how the other is being intense and unreasonable than to see these same characteristics in ourselves. It is very natural to see ourselves as mostly right, and those who disagree as mostly wrong, but this very natural tendency takes us to dangerous places.

In the next chapter, "Here Be Dragons," we explore the difficulty of finding tranquility in a narcissistic age. In order to open up and awaken to the calming waters of tranquility, it is necessary to come to terms with the fire present in each of us, to be mindful of the pervasive ego-inflating forces surrounding us. In concluding the previous chapter, Howard Thurman's words (1953) reminded us of the need "to be free, whole, and unafraid," though this requires a courageous confrontation with ourselves and—at times—the social fabric of our time. Tranquility may cause some inner and outer clashes with emotion in a society that promotes conformity to standards of status, wealth, and success—the breeding ground of narcissism.

Tranquility Requires Emotional Regulation

As strangers glance at you and your friend in the coffee shop, they are likely fretting that your disagreement could easily get out of control, leading to unbridled emotion and unpredictable words. They fret because this often happens when two people disagree on something, but that is not what is happening here. Tranquility involves regulating emotions without denying them or giving oneself over to them.

In the introduction we offered a compelling quote from one of the prominent wisdom researchers of our time. Judith Glück—the brilliant scholar who has the courage to admit she slams doors sometimes—argues that our current definitions of wisdom do not pay enough attention to emotional regulation (Glück, 2020). I may have immense knowledge and practice excellent detachment, but if I cannot manage my own emotions I still fall short of wisdom.

Just as a pressure regulator reduces a high-pressure source of water down to a manageable pressure that will not burst pipes, emotional regulation takes intense emotions and regulates them downward to make them manageable. A pressure regulator would not be useful if it shut off the water supply altogether, but that is what we sometimes do when implying that wisdom occurs in the absence of emotion. We need our emotions to be wise, but we need them to be regulated emotions. This is a paradox because intense emotions are often the thing deterring us from gaining clarity of thought and sound judgment, but the absence of emotion moves us away from real-life experiences where we most need wisdom. Kunzmann and Glück have noted that

> the small but growing number of studies on the relationship between wisdom and emotional competencies clearly confirms that wisdom, if conceptualized and assessed as knowledge and reasoning, is positively related to *emotional stability, certain positive emotions, emotion regulation*, and *a compassionate attitude toward other people* [emphasis added]. (Kunzmann & Glück, 2019, p. 593)

Positive, stable, well regulated emotions with compassion for others, these seem like words that could flash in neon above the office of any psychologist. These words stare narcissism in the face, suggesting a better way—a path that brings us closer to happiness with ourselves and others, allowing us to be the master of our emotional lives, not their minion.

While it seems a truism that facts exist regardless of feelings, at the same time feelings are facts in that they inform and influence real-life decisions. If you slowly start to feel negatively toward someone and choose to withdraw yourself from this person, then the facts of your relationship are in large part the result of your emotional sentiment about the other person. A heavy dose of old-fashioned impartiality, and less emoting in the marketplace of ideas, could serve as a corrective for many ills in our day, yet cold critical thinking and logic without the heat of emotions departs from the path to wisdom, which transcends mere rationality. Logical questions might bring satisfying logical answers, but full-bodied human questions require the embrace of head and heart.

Wisdom does not simply bracket emotions, but it does not get gobbled up by them either. Emotions serve a biological as well as a moral purpose. When you pass by someone on the street asking for a dollar, what emotions do you feel? Sad for the person's misfortunes? Compassion as you give over the dollar? Guilt for not giving it over? Indignation that the person is asking at all? Or perhaps you feel a combination of all these feelings—and more. Notice that wisdom is behavioral (whether you give the dollar or not), emotional (how you experience and understand this swirl of emotions), and moral (whether it is best to give the dollar or not, which is a difficult and debatable question).

It takes embodied awareness and regulation of our emotions to understand how they affect us and others, and sometimes we do not have much time to figure it out, such as with the person on the street asking for money. In his book, *Wisdom: From Philosophy to Neuroscience*, Stephen Hall (2010) observes: "emotional regulation may be the most powerful lens in human psychology; polished by time and curved by intimations of morality, it allows us to see what is really important in our lives" (p. 78). Value, meaning, love, and hate all stem from emotional input and resonance. Emotions inform us. They tell us what we are attracted to and repelled by. Thinkers following the line of Aristotle and Aquinas speak about the habit-forming nature of emotions and the resulting character they bring. "The grumpy individual becomes habitually alert to the opportunities for sarcastic remarks, and skilled in their delivery"; and in like manner, "the Boy Scout is quick to help an elderly woman cross the street, even after his daily good deed, and makes conversation with her easily" (Lombardo, 2011, p. 101).

Emotions play an essential role in the virtue of wisdom, yet unhealthy desires and attachments grow on the vine of emotion. For example, yearning for intimacy is a powerful and good human emotion—the beautiful glue that brings souls together—and yet when that yearning goes unregulated it can lead to all sorts of trouble, such as obsessions, relational intrusions, and poor boundaries. As such, emotions need to be considered, nurtured, pruned, and at times brought through the same purging fire—in much the same way that we gain knowledge. This sort of regulation is not accomplished through denial, ignorance, or suppression, but through a process of transformation and transcendence. Freud's image of regulation involved a watchman standing at the door between unconscious and conscious life (Kahn, 2002). Could this watchman help us learn wisdom? What might this look like, and how might it affect our own ego in an age of narcissism?

THE QUARTET: WHY TRANQUILITY MATTERS FOR WISDOM

Hopefully we have convinced you that tranquility is different from passivity, that it requires an inner shift of equilibrium, and that it involves plenty of emotions along with the need to regulate those emotions. But how does tranquility actually show up in the life of people who are becoming wise? We suggest four ways, using the image of a quartet because symphonic music may be one of the best images of tranquility—replete with dissonance, harmony, beauty, bliss, and peace.

Emotional Stability

Wisdom requires a frontal lobe—the part of the brain that promotes what is called "executive functioning." This is what allows us to consider our emotions without their taking over the whole show. Emotions can be strong-willed, and they do not naturally come in a stable form, but the frontal lobe helps moderate them and shape them into an acceptable form. When someone throws the television through a second-story window because his favorite team lost the Super Bowl, he is experiencing the same emotion as millions of people throughout the world, but failing to stabilize the emotion with adequate executive functioning. Looking through comments on blogs and social media sites, it seems increasingly common for emotions to burst through in ways that are not well stabilized. Where's a good frontal lobe when you need it?

In the last chapter we mentioned the idea of being a player-coach, which involves both living in an experience and standing outside it. Emotional stability involves a similar posture in which we fully experience emotion even as we can stand aside and consider other variables also.

Like executive functioning, wisdom involves emotion but is not ruled by emotion. This calls us toward a place of stability, which is what tranquility offers. The world may rage around us, but tranquility brings homeostasis where we are insulated from the pestering trouble of external and internal objects. People stare in the coffee shop because they are expecting your conversation to become tense and uncivil, but you and your friend have found something else is possible. You have found equanimity—that place where you are undisturbed and composed even as you experience your emotions fully.

Images of monks in meditative trance, yogis in perfect posture, or Dervishes gracefully in motion come to mind, and while most of us do not have years to devote to learning tranquility, we can learn from those who have mastered the art. One of the key lessons to learn is separating the link between our cravings and tranquility. We tend to overassociate pleasure and happiness with this or that thing, assuming we can be truly content and calm if some good event occurs. From a Buddhist perspective we see that "equanimity breaks the chain of suffering by separating the feeling tones of experience from the machinery of craving, neutralizing your reactions to those feeling tones" (Hanson & Mendius, 2009, p. 109). If we are less driven by our cravings, we learn to distinguish the way things are from our emotions toward them. A tranquil mind is honest and egalitarian in its appraisal of what truly satisfies our desires. The happiness dial might move up or down a bit with life circumstances, but tranquility rests in its own lack of need. We explore this further in Chapter 9.

Relatedly, the tranquil life of a monk reminds us of a simplicity that is not overwhelmed by indecision and a vast array of choices. Our minds constantly search for what can bring us pleasure and greater happiness. The problem of choice arises as we can envision different experiences, all of which we fantasize as being more enjoyable than they likely will be in the end. Should I marry this or that person, invest in stocks or bonds, should I take that job or this job? Is there a right or wrong choice here? Perhaps. Yet never before has simple choice been so torturous. This is due in large part to the simple range and freedom of choices we now have. Our world of dating apps provides a poignant example of this, where one can always imagine a more perfect match, making it difficult to make commitments without its feeling like settling on a less-than-optimal relationship.

Tranquility grows in simplicity. While psychotherapists are not typically called shrinks anymore, we have found that term quite well-suited for what happens in the consulting room: helping patients boil problems down and simplify issues in order gain a semblance of tranquility.

Holding the end in the mind has a role to play here, as discussed in Chapter 3. Rather than considering the "perfect partner" on a dating app to fit every possible category of one's wishes, perhaps it is better to first identify a short list of core, non-negotiable values. These core values help us to identify who we are, and who we are looking for, and they protect us from the onslaught of options. In a similar way, we can identify core, essential values that propel us forward as individuals in a complicated world, whether or not we are partnered or dating. These core values assist decision making as we root ourselves in transcendentals (truth, beauty, and goodness), which are not affected by external or environment changes. As we tap into these, we can find a stable presence outside of time, space, and the temporary conditions in which we find ourselves. This harnessing and consolidating of energy can lead to greater attention and presence. As the myriad of options in our day spark anxiety and fear of missing out, the problem becomes less about this or that choice when we allow knowledge of essentials to take root.

Also, the image of a monk in a meditative trance reminds us of peace. So does the coffee shop conversation where we love our friend despite the clear disagreements. These are difficult notions to accept in a time in which we tend to pit one group against another. In our particular cultural moment, there is great pressure to define ourselves in relation to a person or ideology. "I am this, and not that." "You are that, and not this." We are quick to perceive enemies these days, but when we do so, our enemy becomes our intimate partner, for by fixating on our conflict with them, we bring them closer to every waking moment. Tranquility creates a peaceful co-existing, and the distance it brings cools down the emotions of conflict that might otherwise occur.

Enjoyment of Being

Tranquility is an "enjoyment of joy itself" as a priest friend put it. Present to ourselves and separated from the urgent pressures demanding attention, we can find a mind at rest and enjoyment of itself. The more we crave and need to achieve a sense of peace through possessions or things outside of us, the more we are vulnerable to manipulation and seduction by others. Thankfully, joy is free.

As mentioned, tranquility is associated with simplicity and minimal need of external goods. To voluntarily choose to let go and to have less is challenging in any culture, yet ours is particularly hard on those who, either willingly or through no fault of their own, end up with lower means. Those who do not have as much as others easily feel shame in a society that claims everyone should go out and achieve the success promised to us (see de Botton, 2009). We have become accustomed to the idea that each individual is a mini corporate executive with their very own brand and marketing scheme. Becoming a person of influence is an imperative now. Yet if everyone was in fact a person of influence, there would be no such thing, which insures a sort of upward scramble, king-of-the-mountain sort of pressure for those who hope to achieve success.

More! More! More! is what we are taught in our high-pressure success culture (Brueggemann, 2014). And right here, in the midst of *More!*, we are offered the Sabbath of simplicity, of enjoying the moment, of good conversation with a friend in a coffee shop, of being satisfied without having a better job or the perfect partner. We equate *More!* with power and wealth, and have a wide array of defense mechanisms to help justify this. We stack up the most money and gain the highest level of status so that we can experience the greatest amount of pleasure. Aspects of this are even promoted in the wisdom literature found in the Bible, for if you live by these principles, then peace and prosperity will be yours. Who doesn't want these things for themselves and their family? The problem is that life does not play according to these rules.

For those who attempt to pursue other ways of living and being in the world, there are constant reminders of hypocrisy. Whether it is the environmentalist forced to use jet-fueled airplanes, the free-market capitalist endorsing the too big to fail campaign, or anyone willing to write a book on wisdom for that matter, everyone has their own cognitive dissonance to wrestle with. But in spite of our constant failure to be consistent and measure up to our own standards, the pursuit of wisdom, like the pursuit of happiness, creativity, or love is well worth the risk of appearing hypocritical. Tranquility helps bridge this divide by distinguishing needs from wants, desires, and strivings. It simplifies and focuses what is most important, and it gives us a simple enjoyment of being unaffected by conditions, or by the number of followers we have.

Mental Clarity

You have likely tried working in a coffee shop with the music blaring in the background. Sometimes this seems completely distracting, perhaps when the song playing was also played at your prom, or it is simply too loud or raucous to allow for concentration. At other times, though, you may be able to let the music settle into the background of consciousness and be able to focus quite well on the work at hand. Some people even prefer background noise as they work. This is the task of mental clarity—acknowledging the real and metaphoric noise around us and seeing the deeper work. Wise individuals approach problems with openness and dexterity that clear the brush on the path to mental clarity. In order to make decisions in a calm and clear-headed manner, they use tranquility and emotional balance to gaze deeper.

Clarity is clouded when emotions are in a state of upheaval, the way that it is harder to see down the road on a rainy day. Yes, there are examples where moments of acute distress are followed with bursts of insight, but most wisdom is stable and habitual. Flashy moments come and go, just as some talented athletes perform well under stress, but the skills and ability needed for a long journey toward wisdom are different.

Mental clarity allows for great openness, where we take in new information and learn. Perhaps arguing a novel perspective while in law school could actually promote awareness of a complex issue, but only for those who are able to set aside the emotional upheaval caused by being ask to do such a thing. Wisdom requires adaptation and assimilation as things develop and change.

Dare we say that mental clarity also calls us toward some semblance of objectivity? This is difficult to defend as postmodern research in many fields has shown us just how complicated and difficult true objectivity is. Still, it remains a worthy goal to bracket our biases in search of essentials. Do you ever find yourself longing for news that simply tells what happened that day, reporters reporting, rather than commenting? Although he went off air long ago, Walter Cronkite, once known as "the most trusted man in America," has remained an inspiration and model of honest candid journalism and news reporting. Watching old clips of him can seem strangely odd compared to our current never-ending onslaught of *breaking news* intended to get the viewers' attention and stoke the emotions. This entertainment version of reporting is quite different from Cronkite's famous sign off "and that's the way it is."

The virtue of objective openness brings a willingness to extend gratitude to the other side while not necessarily surrendering one's own view, the way you might do with a friend in a coffee shop. Tranquility regulates emotions in order to cool the jets and bring the mind into a relatively neutral space ready for exposure to new ideas.

Mental clarity also fosters subjective awareness and greater attention to particulars. Wisdom can zoom out, or zoom in, depending on what is needed at the time. It is easier to see truths that are minute or very specific when the clutter is removed. Again, looking through a Buddhist lens, wisdom "is experientially spacious, blissful, and clear, imbued with love; and inseparable from altruistic ethical conduct" (Goldfield, 2014, p. 111).

Wisdom defined thus brings a purification of knowledge and actions, which include emotions.

Receptivity to Transcendence

Tranquility is the bridge to transcendence. A tranquil mind creates an environment open to realities of a transcendent nature. Elevated insight is a manifestation of these realties when they are better understood. Although emotional stability, joy, and mental clarity are essential characteristics of tranquility, with transcendence we take flight and go beyond the level of human emotions and psychology. This illumination of the mind reflects the brightness that is already present, as a clear night reveals the brightness of stars all the more.

The experience of tranquility is akin to a "cleaning of the doors of perception," as William Blake so beautifully describes in his poem, *The Marriage of Heaven and Hell*: "If the doors of perception were cleansed every thing would appear to man as it is, Infinite. For man has closed himself up, till he sees all things thro' narrow chinks of his cavern" (1791/1977, p. 188). This phrase was made famous in our day by Aldous Huxley (1954/2009) who used it as the title of his classic book describing his experiences with mescaline. There are, of course, other paths to transcendence that do not involve psychedelics, which we will consider in later chapters.

Tranquility opens the doors. In its passive and balanced state, much can occur that otherwise would flee amidst the noise and distraction. Tranquility leads the way toward the important concept of *apatheia*, a Greek term meaning absence of pathology, suffering, emotional disturbance, and desire. We can see etymologically its relationship to the word apathy, but its meaning is quite different. Not intended to stop at a place of stoic dispassion, *apatheia* served the higher purpose of the passions. That is, *apatheia* was seen as leading to greater spiritual insight and unmediated knowledge. This knowledge, or heart knowledge, became the foundation for a union with the divine and even a deification (god-making) of the person. Writing about the teachings of the seventh-century theologian

Maximus the Confessor, Joseph Nguyen writes, "Maximus located the center of divine union in the heart where human desires originated . . . the passions were retained, transformed, and redirected to the love of God and others as created in God's image and likeness" (2018, p. 43). In this view, spiritual growth occurs with the inclusion of our natural human desires, drives, and embodied emotions, in whatever way they are given proper direction and guidance toward their teleological end. Wisdom is a human virtue capable of penetrating divine mysteries, and some would say it can reach heights of godlike proportions.

Calling on spiritual transcendence and god-likeness is a provocative end to a chapter on tranquility, but thankfully we will have the final portion of the book to explore and explain these concepts further. And we hope to leave ample room for debate and disagreement along the way.

CHAPTER 8

HERE BE DRAGONS

Maps of the medieval world would often show sea creatures and monsters with the Latin phrase *hic sunt dracones* (here be dragons) in unknown and far off territories. How many unknown dragons lurk within us and around us that stifle growth, wholeness, wisdom, and tranquility? In his book, *Facing the Dragon: Confronting Personal and Spiritual Grandiosity*, depth psychologists Robert Moore and Max Havlick (2003) write from a neo-Jungian perspective about the danger of ignoring our own capacity for evil, describing, "what we might call a 'Lucifer complex' that threatens to seduce and possess the human ego consciousness" (p. 9). How might we identify this toxicity in our day, and what does it mean to be seduced by something as nefarious as a "Lucifer complex"? The disturbing annoyance of the question may reveal part of the answer. The problem of our inflated ego and selfish desire to know and control has another name. It is called narcissism.

In our day we encounter the burden of ego inflation, sense of entitlement, power seeking, lack of empathy, and preoccupation with ideals of beauty and success—all of which are traits of narcissism. Admitting this, naming the dragon, is the first step toward tranquility.

If it feels as though we are critiquing you, our reader, may we try to clarify? This dragon has less to do with any of us as individuals and more to do with our highly evolved brains and cultural trends that impact, shape, and feed our greatest struggles. As psychologists, we hear enough about similar struggles and reoccurring issues that we begin seeing dragons

155

in society itself. We are told in preflight instructions to put our own mask on if the plane is going down before helping the person beside us, and doesn't this serve as a fitting metaphor for what we already believe and assume through most of our days. Personal happiness and self-actualization are high values in our time, especially in individualistic cultures, and these values come with various benefits and problems. Similarly, the famous Viennese psychoanalyst, Sigmund Freud, recognized in the minds of his patients certain unspoken and unexpressed desires that manifested neurotic pathology reflecting the general repressed nature and frigidity of his Victorian Austria. Sexual repression is less a problem these days, but still, our current societal pressures weigh heavily and compound existing issues, masking common psychological problems. Narcissism is not a disease that some have and others do not; it is a collection of characteristics and psychological tendencies present in all of us to a greater or lesser degree.

We may need some practice with this idea a bit before going further in this chapter. Narcissism is not just a label to slap on someone else, but rather is a part of the human condition. In our day we have become quite accustomed to using it as a label to identify the despised political candidate, to dismiss the demands of a controlling boss, to diminish the complexity of a former partner. It is true that some people have much more narcissism lurking in their souls than others, and it makes for difficult relationships. Still, at least for the sake of this chapter, try to avoid categorizing and dismissing others as narcissists. Narcissism is the water we swim in, it is all around us, and, yes, it is within each of us to some extent.

There are two halves to narcissism—one of them widely known, and one not—and thus two ways that narcissism impedes tranquility. The first half—the widely-known one—is self-interest. Narcissism means people think highly and often of themselves. We're so vain, as Carly Simon once reminded us. And, yes, we will reveal the second half of narcissism later in the chapter.

FACING THE INNER DRAGON

We sometimes think of the human brain like a computer, churning through bits and bytes of binary data to provide some consistent, objective output, but that is not what a brain does. Like all creatures, humans are built for survival, which means our brains are designed to be self-interested. And we do it very well. Consider a few examples.

Enhanced Self-Perception

These days it is an insult to be called average on anything, though it is statistically impossible for most people to be above average. Still, most of us in Western societies perceive ourselves to be above average on positive qualities. If we ask 100 people how good they are at driving, it would seem reasonable that 20 of those people would say they are in the top 20% in their driving ability, but in fact 46% of those sampled in the United States put themselves in the top echelon, and almost everyone (93%) believes they are above average in their driving ability (Svenson, 1981). Similar studies show that we believe ourselves to be better than average in all sorts of ways: more intelligent, better leaders, stronger social skills, more effective as parents and spouses, greater work ethic, a better friend, more skilled at managing money. The list goes on and on. More than 90% of college professors believe they are above average as teachers (Young, 2018). Likely even those who teach statistics fall prey to this statistical impossibility.

Holier than Thou

A series of studies coming out of Cornell University two decades ago show that we perceive ourselves as more generous, selfless, and kind than others (Epley & Dunning, 2000). This is not particularly surprising, given enhanced self-perception, but these researchers wanted to know if the holier-than-thou effect is because we perceive ourselves as better than we actually are, or maybe we are just quite cynical about the moral behavior of others. It turns out that our estimations of others tend to be fairly accurate. They are about as generous as we assume them to be, for example, but our estimations of our own morality far exceed reality.

Overconfidence Phenomenon

Imagine a series of multiple choice questions: How long is the Mississippi River? Who wrote *The Scarlet Letter?* How many pounds of beef are served at McDonald's restaurants every day? What is the most common language used on the internet? In each case you are asked to provide an answer and also estimate how confident you are that you chose the correct answer. When scientists do this study, they find a consistent result: people tend to be more confident than correct. Perhaps you have experienced this when recalling a distant memory with a friend or partner. One of you remembers it a certain way, and the other in a different way. You are both completely confident in your memory, but only one of you can be correct.

Future Focused

Our inner dragon keeps us obsessed with what lies ahead—gazing always towards the future where potential threats lurk. It seduces us into thinking we are at risk of some unknown calamity that we must slavishly work to prevent. The things we fear often do not manifest, not in the way we think they will, anyway, yet we continue to sacrifice our sense of tranquility to this modern idol. Thomas Merton gave witness to this in his book *The Way of Chuang Tzu* in which he interprets the teachings of the Taoist philosopher:

> The ambitious run day and night in the pursuit of honors, constantly in anguish about the success of their plans, dreading the miscalculation that may wreck everything. Thus they are alienated from themselves, exhausting their real life in service of the shadow created by their insatiable hope. (Merton, 1969, p. 100)

This is partially why psychotherapy can be so intimidating. It is hard to just sit and have one's own mind be the focus for an hour. It can appear like time focused too heavily on the present. When the process works well, it is not uncommon to experience a sense of active presence and stability in the therapeutic process. It becomes less of a grab and run in order to weaponize myself against looming threats and more of a time to face this inner dragon of the unknown.

Confirmation Bias

We have discussed this already, in Chapters 1 and 2, so we will not linger here other than to recall that we tend to seek out information that confirms what we already believe and avoid contradictory information. This leads us to believe that "everyone knows" we are right in the opinions we hold.

Fundamental Attribution Error

As discussed in Chapter 6, when something good happens to us, we tend to attribute it to internal causes. I get the job promotion because I am smart and hard working. But when something good happens for someone else, we tend to attribute it to external causes. My co-worker gets the promotion because she is lucky or just happens to be in the right place at the right time. When bad things happen, we tend to flip this attribution style upside down—external for self, and internal for the other. I get demoted because the boss just does not understand my value to the company. My co-worker gets demoted because he is a slacker.

We brushed up against Brené Brown's (2015) idea in Chapter 7, that people are basically doing the best they can. But when it comes right down to it, we tend to, generously, assume that we ourselves are doing the best we can while others mess up the world. This is the inner dragon of narcissism.

We could go on and on, but we won't. The human brain is designed for adaptation and survival. This makes us inclined toward self-interest. Lest we cast this as vile, keep in mind the evolutionary purpose for this. Those organisms who are able to put themselves first are most likely to survive in a fierce and competitive world. Our brains constantly scan the environment to determine threat and find ways to elevate ourselves above the dangers we perceive. You may have heard the old joke about two friends hiking in the woods and encountering an angry bear. One hiker bends over to tie his shoes and the other comments, "You can't outrun a bear, dude." The first hiker responds, "I don't have to outrun the bear. I just have to outrun you." After all, *survival of the fittest* is a euphemism for *destruction of everyone else.*

But this is not the whole story. Humans have also evolved to be social creatures, knowing that living in community is safer than isolated individualism. Relational neurobiology demonstrates how our brains are wired to connect and be in community with one another. And if we are to live in harmonious community, then we must learn to make determinations that are not purely self-interested. Paradoxically, it is in our best self-interest not to be fully self-interested. As such, we are able to be prosocial, to love, to be aware of, and concerned for, the other. Those who study the neurobiology of wisdom associate particular parts of the brain—specifically the medial prefrontal cortex, amygdala, nucleus accumbens, and ventral striatum—with the capacity to be prosocial in our attitudes and behaviors (Lee & Jeste, 2019).

At the risk of oversimplifying, consider two parts of the human brain in a tug of war. One is the individualist survival mode, elevating self above others, outrunning the friend rather than the bear. The other is the prosocial community mode, knowing that we function and survive best when we are in healthy relationships with others. We live in a state of tension between self-interest and self-transcendence. Human civilization is, and has always been, the story of working out this tension and learning how to live as well as possible in community with one another. When my friend gets cancer, I step forward in care and compassion, helping as I am able, even as I am silently relieved that it is not me with the cancer diagnosis.

The virtues—including the virtue of wisdom—help us transcend raw self-interest so that we can find a balanced way of caring for and about others. Wisdom calls us toward social perceptiveness, empathy, cooperation, healthy relationships, and strong communities, but its constant competitor is self-interested individualism fueled by the threat of destruction.

Let's picture the human brain tug of war during the coffee shop conversation in the previous chapter. Part of your brain is telling you how right you are and how wrong your friend is. You are completely confident in this, above average in your reasoning ability, thinking of all the people who would be happy to confirm your views. The inner narcissist is hard at work. Another part of your brain is calming you, experiencing peace in the presence of another, reminding you that your friend cares about you, that two minds truly are better than one, that you may have something to learn by considering another perspective. Self-interest and self-transcendence are competing in your brain, as they are in your heart.

Tranquility is difficult because part of our brain is like an angry, isolated dragon, happy to destroy everything and everyone in our path. At the same time, tranquility is possible because another part of our brain is like an elephant brain—living in herds, caring for one another, finding deep meaning in relationship. Thankfully, the massive cortical layer of the human brain allows us the ability to understand and shape our experiences so that we can exert some deliberate control over the sort of person we become. We can learn to shift our equilibrium from dragon to elephant. This is the capacity for virtue, for tranquility and wisdom. We explore this more in Chapter 9.

SURROUNDED BY DRAGON BREATH

It is not just that we face inner dragons, but we live in contexts where others are also facing theirs. These collectives are, in many ways, beautiful and life-giving. They help us build relationships, consider one another, transcend our self-interests, and grow in virtue. But our collectives are not perfect either, and so we are engulfed in systems that sometimes encourage our own narcissistic tendencies while also allowing the narcissism of others to spill over and make a mess.

Consider the contentious results of the 2020 presidential election in the United States. Believing that the incumbent, Donald Trump, was ousted from office because of an unfair election, people across the country perpetuated—along with Trump himself—what came to be known as "The Big Lie." Regardless of how you might feel about this occurrence from a political perspective, back up a step and notice what this communicates about our proneness to narcissism. The charisma of President Trump became the central focus, even outweighing the importance of democracy itself as insurrectionists on January 6, 2021, stormed the Capitol building with the hope of overturning the election results. A testimony to President Trump's magnetism was how he could make people believe that he was more credible, noble, and insightful than others, and the best president ever. He simply belonged at the top, and if voters thought otherwise, then someone must be committing election fraud. And it worked remarkably well. Despite being twice impeached and having the lowest average Gallup approval ratings since approval ratings started in the 1940s (Korte, 2021), less than a year after his term expired 36% of Republicans believed Donald Trump to be the best president in U.S. history, which far outshines any other president and is twice as many as those who nod to Ronald Reagan for that honor (Frankovic, 2021).

Our goal is not to take a precise political position here, and we would argue that Democrats are just as prone to narcissism as Republicans. You may be a big fan of the Trump administration and believe that he was unfairly ousted from office, but even if that is so, stop and notice how deeply engulfed we have all become in the narcissism of our particular enclaves.

It is hard to say whether ours is a more narcissistic time than previous times in history. Psychologists Jean Twenge and W. Keith Campbell thought so when they wrote *The Narcissism Epidemic* (2010). The authors demonstrate how scores on the Narcissistic Personality Inventory have increased sharply in recent decades while empathy and perspective-taking scores have decreased. At the same time, scores on self-esteem inventories have increased, almost to the point of making the scales meaningless because so many achieve the highest score possible. In his book, *The Road to Character*, and in a subsequent National Public Radio interview, David Brooks (2015) refers to Gallup poll data where 12% of high school seniors reported being a "very important person" in 1950 while 80% affirmed their importance in 2005.

Scholars vigorously debate whether it is truly an increase in narcissism or just the age-old cohort effect where older people always look at younger people as the most self-centered ever (Roberts et al., 2010). And, by the way, younger generations hate the label of narcissistic, even as they acknowledge it may be true (Grubbs et al., 2019). But whether our current levels of narcissism are worse than ever or just as bad as always, it still makes tranquility difficult. Consider a few of the social trends making it difficult to shift our equilibrium toward quiet, calm, centered places.

More! More! More!

Allow us to tie up two loose ends here. In the previous chapter we mentioned Walter Brueggemann, an Old Testament scholar who wrote about the radical countercultural nature of the Sabbath commandment. Brueggemann connects ancient Egyptian culture with contemporary culture in that both insist on growth and consumption and the urgency of now. In an online interview, Brueggemann puts it this way:

> We are caught up in a culture of restlessness, a market ideology in which the goal of life is to produce more and consume more. We consume more hours so we can produce more—and so we can be richer and more powerful and more effective and more well thought of. The market ideology is a rat-race that has infected us all. . . .
>
> The consumer culture defines everyone around us as a threat or competitor or as a rival for the same goods. Therefore, we don't think of other people as neighbors; we think of them as people who threaten our property, our way of life, our possessions, and our futures. In order to fend them off, we resort to many forms of violence. (Pattison, 2015)

We feel this, right? Upward mobility is the assumption. And if this means working early mornings and late nights, then so be it.

The second loose end comes from earlier in this chapter when we mentioned two parts to narcissism. The well-known part is that narcissism means heightened self-interest and excessively high valuations of ourselves. The lesser known part is that narcissism propels us forward in grandiosity. It is as if we are always building something spectacular— the brilliant career, the optimal marriage, the ideal family, the perfect body, the majestic estate, the carefree retirement. A good narcissism bumper sticker would be: "If you think I'm great now, just watch where I'm heading!"

Pull these two loose ends together and consider the narcissistic atmosphere of contemporary life. We peddle as fast as we can, but still expect ourselves to peddle faster. "You're great, but be greater," we are told.

Advertising

Advertising is not new. Archeological evidence suggests it has been around for centuries. What is relatively new is personalized advertising. If you do an internet search for a new gardening tool, advertisements for similar tools will pop up on Facebook and your internet browser for days to come, using a system called "personal data points."

We are not going to argue advertising is evil, but ponder for a moment the subtle psychological effect of being surrounded by continual marketing efforts. Here is the message: you may be reasonably happy now, or not, but if you buy this product it will make your life easier, happier, and better. No one explicitly says this in their marketing, but when we live and breathe in a world supersaturated with advertising, it is inevitable that it makes us discontented, yearning for the next purchase to help us achieve a state of wholeness.

The American Psychological Association commissioned a task force to consider the effects of the $12 billion spent annually in marketing aimed toward children (Wilcox et al., 2004). It turns out children and parents have more conflict because parents do not always purchase the advertised product and children eat less nutritional foods, and are more prone to obesity and other health problems, because many of the advertisements are for unhealthy foods. Further, youth smoking and drinking are promoted by advertisements allegedly targeted for adults but with images bound to appeal to children (think of the Budweiser frog, for example). Other advertisements almost certainly attract children to violent media and video games. The goal is to sell products, which is not evil, but the result shifts society toward self-absorption, violence, mindless consumption, and ill health.

The Individualism Shift

Sonja is a 15-year-old being raised in a suburb of Sacramento where she plays soccer and the saxophone and makes YouTube videos on how to write and illustrate graphic novels. She sees herself as bright, fun, and social, and so do her friends. She looks forward to gaining more freedom from her family as she grows older.

Ara is also 15, being raised in Seoul, where she spends many hours each day in school. She takes 30 minutes in the evening to chat with friends on the internet before the tutor comes to her home to help her with additional evening studies. She hopes to bring honor, and not shame, to her family as she grows older.

Sonja is being raised in an individualistic culture where independence and personal freedom are valued, while Ara's collectivistic culture values family ties, honor, and meeting expectations. Collectivistic cultures emphasize the welfare of the group over the individual, which makes the decisions of a 15-year-old less flexible than they are in an individualistic culture, where autonomy and personal freedom are highly valued.

At age 15, Sonja's life is bound to look better, but this might change if we fast-forward a few decades. In midlife and later, Ara will remain part of a collective that has always been central to her identity. Sonja will likely be connected to friends, but may have relocated and see family only rarely, perhaps to eat Thanksgiving dinner and have strained conversations. Ara may well live in a multigenerational home, she will be honored more and more as she ages, and there will be little chance of living and dying alone. In contrast, Sonja may struggle to feel connected as she ages, and with each passing year she may find her relevance and perceived value waning.

Individualism and collectivism are being studied and discussed extensively, both because these patterns vary from country to country, and even within countries, we see different cultural pockets. In the United States, for example, people of color are more likely to live in collectivist cultural pockets than European Americans, and, at least at one time, Protestants were perceived to be more individualistic than Catholics.

A recent study shows the world shifting more toward individualism, both in values and practices (Santos et al., 2017). This includes shifting focus toward friends over family, valuing independence of children over their obedience, and emphasizing the right of self-expression. From the years 1960 to 2010, the world has (overall) shifted from being slightly collectivistic to being slightly individualistic, though huge variations still exist from one country to another. These shifts appear to be related to socioeconomic development. As countries become more affluent, they also become more individualistic.

We write this book at what we hope is the back edge of the worst pandemic in a century, and from a country that is predominantly individualistic. Mask mandates and vaccines have been rolled out and remain controversial, yet it is striking how arguments on both sides are individualistic in nature. One person refuses to wear a mask because it impinges on individual freedom while another wears one to keep from getting sick. One person declines a vaccine because it might be personally dangerous while another gets the vaccine to prevent getting the illness. Rarely do we hear a collectivist argument, which might go like this: "I wear the mask and get the vaccine because I have been asked to do so, and because my community and my nation will be best served by us all complying with what has been asked of us." This is complicated by issues of trust, as some groups in a multicultural country have been asked to do things in the past that have not been in their best interests. At its best, collectivism rests on the assumption that those in authority are trustworthy.

There are various advantages to both individualism and collectivism, and our goal is not to advocate one system over the other, but for the sake of exploring how contemporary society unwittingly contributes to collective narcissism, it is worth considering how Sonja is likely to experience the next decade or two of her life. The good news is she will have ample amounts of freedom to go to the college of her choosing, or not, to marry the man or woman she wants to be with, or not, to have children, or not, and to name them whatever she chooses, to pursue a particular career path, to determine her social groups and identities, to maintain or jettison the religious values of her parents. But these freedoms will come at a cost, which is the bad news. She will be left to determine a set of values by which to live her life, and she may not always be prepared to do so. It will not be a path to follow for Sonja, but a trail to be blazed.

Individualism is increasing around the world, but at what cost? As we become more and more self-guiding, self-focused, self-directed, what might this mean for shifting our equilibrium toward tranquility, and for growing in wisdom? I (Mark) once led a workshop with Korean pastors who traveled to the United States to learn about pastoral counseling. The first evening of the workshop, as we sat around a table in a conference room, the leader of the Korean group asked me, "How old are you?" Having studied the culture a bit, and having spent some time in Korea the year before, I recognized the meaning of his question. He was really asking, "Why should we listen to you?" For the pastors in that room, wisdom is to be gleaned by looking to the older generations, finding sages who have walked this path before. In an individualistic culture, we are pretty much on our own to figure out wisdom as we go. This leads us to the fascinating and complex topic of aging, wisdom, and culture.

DO DRAGONS FLAME AND BURN?

So far we have considered how tranquility is a centered, balanced emotional state of equilibrium that does not require retreating from life, but actually shows up right in the middle of our busyness. But this is difficult because the dragon of narcissism lurks inside each of us, and most of us live in cultural contexts that feed the dragon. Wouldn't it be nice if this dragon of narcissism slowed down with age? Maybe that is why wisdom increases over the lifespan.

Or does it? The relationships between age, culture, narcissism, and wisdom are fascinating and complex. Two longitudinal studies have recently been published, which answer some questions people have been asking for a long time (Chopik & Grimm, 2019; Wetzel et al., 2020).

Two-and-a-half conclusions seem warranted. First, those who are most narcissistic early in life still seem to be more narcissistic than their peers later in life. At least to some extent, this seems to be a relatively stable personality trait. Second, people become less narcissistic as they age. If these conclusions seem inconsistent, consider 3 hypothetical people testing for narcissism on a 10-point scale:

	Age 20	Age 50
Monica	7	5
Nathaniel	8	6
June	4	3

At both age 20 and 50, Nathaniel scores the highest on the narcissism scale, which is the first conclusion, namely, that the trait is fairly stable over time. But notice also that all three people score lower at age 50 than at age 20, which is the second conclusion.

We still owe you half a conclusion. It is only worth half because it dovetails with the second conclusion, that narcissism decreases with age. It turns out that individual autonomy increases over the lifespan even as the more destructive forms of narcissism decrease. Destructive narcissism includes being highly defensive and grandiose. These decrease with time while independence and autonomy increase.

If narcissism decreases with age, then shouldn't wisdom increase? Folklore would certainly suggest so, but what does the science show? An early cross-sectional study in Germany shook things up when researchers found that wisdom grew dramatically during adolescence and young adulthood, but then remained quite stable over the remainder of life (Pasupathi et al., 2001). But we need to get away from straight lines in our minds. It is not just that wisdom is flat over adulthood, or that it goes up in a straight line, but rather it is what researchers call a curvilinear relationship. Wisdom tends to go up for a while, peaking sometime in the forties, and then turns downward again later in the lifespan (Ardelt et al., 2018).

We warned you this is complex. First, wisdom is not a single thing, but more a collection of different abilities. Some of those increase and decline differently over the lifespan. Abilities to be compassionate and reflective appear to increase after midlife whereas cognitive dimensions of wisdom show declines (Ardelt et al., 2018), and much remains unknown about how other dimensions of wisdom change over the lifespan (Lim & Yu, 2015). A second complexity is that all of the studies we have described consist of German participants. How might this look different in other cultures? Does culture even matter when considering wisdom and aging?

Well, yes, it does. Leading wisdom researcher, Igor Grossmann, and his colleagues (2012) conducted a cross-cultural study looking at wisdom in an American sample from the Midwestern United States and a Japanese sample from the Tokyo area. Participants in each country were given two wisdom tasks, one involving newspaper articles showing intergroup conflicts (e.g., ethnic tensions) and one involving interpersonal conflicts revealed in letters to an advice columnist. With both scenarios, participants were asked what might happen next and why they think it might unfold that way. All responses were transcribed, and expert coders rated the responses on six dimensions of wisdom. The researchers also went to great lengths to ensure cross-cultural consistency in how the two samples were evaluated. It turns out wisdom does increase with age in the United States, with a consistent upward trend from age 25 to 75. In Japan, however, wisdom looked the same across participants of various ages. The line is flat from ages 25 to 75. It is also interesting to note that the young adults in Japan are already as wise as a 50-something person in the United

States. Could it be that Japanese youth get wiser faster than youth in the United States?

There is still much we do not know about wisdom and aging, and you will likely notice that none of these studies are longitudinal. From what we do know, it is interesting to ponder how culture may play a role in wisdom development. Japan is historically a collectivist culture, though it has become more individualistic in recent decades than some other Asian countries. Still, when compared to the United States, Japan leans collectivist. It seems at least possible that wisdom happens faster in collectivist contexts because people look to their elders from early in life, learning and following their example.

Back to the question of whether dragons flame and burn? Maybe some, though there is much we do not know yet. It seems that narcissism decreases with age, which should help with tranquility, though the most narcissistic young people remain relatively high on the trait in relation to their midlife peers. Wisdom increases with time in some cultures, but not others, and it is a complex relationship where some dimensions of wisdom turn downward at midlife and others continue an upward path. It seems at least possible that collectivist cultures promote wisdom earlier in life than individualist cultures.

Like every step toward wisdom we discuss in this book, tranquility is difficult. This dragon lives right inside our minds, and in our neighborhoods, workplaces, states, and countries, insisting that we need to be special, to scramble and scratch and strive, to blaze a trail, to rise above the pack, to be upwardly mobile, to be above average in everything we do. Tranquility calls us in the other direction, toward rest and simplicity, and throwing off the burden of hustling to prove our worth. No wonder this is difficult.

We have some ideas for becoming tranquil, even though they are difficult.

CHAPTER 9

THREE TREASURES

The classic Taoist text, *Tao Te Ching*, dates back to the 6th century BCE. Credited to a sage named Laozi, the text marks the path to wisdom by following three treasures: gold, silver, and bronze. We are kidding about the treasures, but the rest is true. We might think of precious metals as treasures—things that bring honor and wealth and put us at the front of the line, but the three treasures in the *Tao Te Ching* point us in a different direction, toward *compassion, simplicity*, and *humility* and being content in the middle or at the end of the line (Oakes et al., 2019).

Remember Emma as she sat with Garrett as he had his tantrum in Chapter 7? Recall the coffee shop conversation with a dear friend who sees the world differently from you? These examples call us to shift our equilibrium toward a place of centered calm, peace, and repose, even as they exemplify the three treasures. Each of these treasures helps us face outward, whereas narcissism has an inward face. And, yes, there is a reason that tranquility follows detachment rather than the other way around. We need to loosen our emotional grip before we can shift toward equilibrium.

The convenient camera switch button on our tablets and mobile phones allows us to swap the inward-facing camera to the outward-facing one, and vice versa. The dragon of narcissism would have us spend all day in selfie mode, but that does not lend itself to tranquility—the emotional essence of wisdom. The tranquil life is one where our focus shifts readily from self to other, other to self, and in a way that ultimately becomes so natural that it hardly seems like any work at all.

The Taoist concept of Wu Wei (nonaction) brings an antidote to the inner dragons we saw in the last chapter. Nonaction is not doing nothing but a participation in the natural rhythms of nature and accepting the sweet with the sour portions of life. This is the concept behind the symbolism of yin and yang. It goes without saying that ours is a society of action and excessive doing. The more we do the more we are compelled to move by forces outside ourselves. "The non-action of the wise man is not inaction. It is not studied. It is not shaken by anything. The sage is quiet because he is not moved, Not because he wills to be quiet" (Merton, 1969, p. 80).

We are not Taoists or Chinese scholars, so we will not attempt to unpack the meaning of this ancient philosophy and religion. Still, we are drawn to these three treasures, so in this chapter we employ the same three concepts in presenting ideas about developing tranquility in a land of dragons.

COMPASSION

Those living in compassion begin by looking for spaces in life where calming, life-giving, broadening emotions naturally occur. They relish these spaces and seek out more of them, and they let them grow and build. Then they draw from this deep well of self-transcendent positivity to move outside of themselves, to notice both the beauty and the pain of the world around, and to be present to others. The more we experience emotions that take us outside of ourselves, the more we move toward deep tranquility and wisdom.

The Book of Joy showcases a fascinating conversation between the Dalai Lama XIV and Archbishop Desmond Tutu about human flourishing. As part of this conversation, the Dalai Lama observes:

> After meeting with so many people, thinkers, scientists, educators, health-care professionals, social workers and activists, it is clear that the only way

to truly change our world is through teaching compassion. Our society is lacking an adequate sense of compassion, sense of kindness, and genuine regard for others' well-being. So now many, many, people who seriously think about humanity all have the same view. We must promote basic human values, the inner values that lie at the heart of who we are as humans. (Tenzin Gyatso, Dalai Lama XIV, Tutu, & Abrams, 2016, pp. 273–274)

These words about society lacking compassion ring true. It seems more natural these days to be angry than to be compassionate, to focus on what goes wrong more than helping to make the world a better place. Amidst these days of cynicism and dispute, compassion truly is a treasure.

Compassion moves us outward, thinking beyond the selfie mode of our narcissistic urges. In contrast, anger and cynicism move us inward. Consider reading your favorite news site or paper and ponder which direction your heart moves. Most often the news is aggravating, pointing us inward to places of frustration and despair, and moving us away from tranquility. But what about those rare times when the news promotes compassion?

Geri Weis-Corbley worked for CNN when she mentioned to a colleague that someone should report good news. Her colleague replied matter-of-factly, "Good news doesn't sell." Years later, still inspired by this conversation, Weis-Corbley started the Good News Network (Good News Network, 2021), an online newspaper with inspiring stories from around the world: a woman starts a fund to help keep people from being evicted and ends up helping 3000 families, native tribes in Oklahoma open a COVID-19 vaccination clinic for all Oklahomans, a police officer buys food for a family in need, a major corporation launches a charity initiative to help get free prescriptions to Americans in need. On and on the stories go, demonstrating the best qualities of what it means to be human, showing the face of loving compassion. Contrast for a moment the inner experience of good news with the cynicism promoted by our normal news cycles. One leads outward, compassionately, toward a place of kindness and hope, and the other leads us inward where we easily stew on all that is wrong with the world. Which one best promotes a sense of tranquility? The answer seems clear.

The prophetic agrarian Wendell Berry (2002) once wrote, "I believe that the world was created and approved by love, that it subsists, coheres, and endures by love, and that, insofar as it is redeemable, it can be redeemed only by love" (p. 146). The Good News Network reminds us this is so.

Monika Ardelt (2019) is a leading researcher in the science of wisdom who also writes about compassion. Her Three-Dimensional Wisdom Model, as well as the scale she has developed to assess the three dimensions, has gained attention and respect in the field. Her first dimension of wisdom is *cognitive*, which bears similarity to the knowledge step discussed in Chapters 1–3 of this book. Second, she posits a *reflective* dimension, which allows people to take multiple perspectives, recognize complexity, and be self-aware while regulating their emotions. This leads, then, to the third dimension, *compassion*, which is where we move away from self-centeredness, to go out of our way to consider the needs of others and act accordingly. Notice how being wise starts to look like a verb more than a noun in this model—it is not so much something we possess or not, but it begins with appropriate knowledge then collects multiple perspectives while moving away from self-interest and eventually contributes to the well-being of others and the world around. The *telos* of wisdom is flipping the camera around, looking outward more than inward.

Let's say you are sitting quietly at home enjoying the latest Netflix sensation when your mother-in-law rings the doorbell. For the cognitive dimension of wisdom, you will need to know some things: she will likely want to visit, you prefer not to, and it is not entirely clear whether she can tell you are in the house or not. Then there is the reflective dimension, considering multiple viewpoints. On the one hand, this is your first day off in a long time, so it seems reasonable to maintain some privacy. On the other hand, this is your mother-in-law, and you want to maintain a good relationship with her. Perhaps she has something important to say— or perhaps not. Then there is compassion, which drives you out of your own inner world to consider the other—in this case, your mother-in-law. So in all likelihood, you put Netflix on pause, get up and answer the door, have a brief but warm conversation, then go back to your show with a bit of an inner warmth, knowing you did the right thing.

The cognitive dimension peaks around age 42, and then starts declining (Ardelt et al., 2018). If you are much older than 42, you probably can recall a time when your mental math skills were better than they are now, and perhaps your rote memory skills, too. Reflective wisdom tells a different story. It increases until about age 46, and then plateaus until age 71 when it starts increasing again. As we age, we seem to be increasingly capable of considering multiple perspectives, to be self-aware and insightful, and to regulate our emotions. Compassionate wisdom decreases slightly in early adulthood, reaching its lowest point in the mid-40s and then increases through the rest of life.[1] Perhaps as life simplifies, with careers established, relationships stabilized, children leaving home for some, we are able to be more mindful of others around us.

What might emerge in the world if more of us—like Laozi, The Dalai Lama, Geri Weis-Corbley, Wendell Berry, and Monika Ardent—became fascinated by love and compassion? How can we let these virtues take root and grow in our lives, making them lively and energizing forces in our day-to-day existence?

An ancient Eastern practice known as loving-kindness meditation may be helpful in this, and has been shown to increase compassion in those who practice it. Whereas all meditation involves tranquility—slowing our breathing, calming ourselves, finding calm and peace—loving-kindness meditation deliberately turns the focus from ourselves to

---

[1] This is more complex than we have suggested, because education also has a bearing on compassionate wisdom. What we have described reflects those with a high school or college education. In contrast, those with only elementary education show decreases in compassion over time. These findings are from a large sample of German adults, in which the percentage of people getting a high school degree is lower than it is in the United States.

others. First, sit comfortably, breathe deeply, and let your whole body relax. Once reaching a state of calm, imagine someone who loves you deeply standing in front of you, sending love and wishes for good to you. Soak in the feeling of being loved. Perhaps you imagine being surrounded by many people who love you, all of them sending love and positive wishes your way. Next, amidst this place of feeling loved, imagine sending love and kindness back to that person who loves you. Perhaps there are certain phrases you utter silently. The common ones are: "May you be happy," "may you be healthy," "may you be safe," "may you live with ease." As you become better at loving-kindness meditation, you then extend this love not only to people you already love, but to those with whom you have neutral relationships, perhaps a colleague or acquaintance or someone who helps you at the grocery store. Over time, and with ample practice, you then begin sending loving-kindness to all living beings, even to those you do not naturally experience with warmth and good will. This has similarities to meditative prayer in Western traditions, where the person praying holds people in mind and offers their well-being to God. Quakers have a term, "holding people in the Light," which is quite similar to both loving-kindness meditation and meditative prayer.

In a study with Stanford University students, even a brief 10-minute compassion exercise involving loving-kindness meditation increased personal well-being, a sense of connection with others, and decreased self-focus (Seppala et al., 2014). Other researchers found that a more extensive loving-kindness meditation practice in a corporate workplace led to positive emotions, greater social support, a deeper sense of purpose in life, and fewer symptoms of illness (Fredrickson et al., 2008).

Compassion is an example of what researchers call a self-transcendent positive emotion (STPE), a key part of Barbara Fredrickson's (2001) broaden-and-build model in positive psychology. Other STPEs include awe, joy, gratitude, and peacefulness. There are several ways STPEs help build health, tranquility, and wisdom by broadening our attention to the world around us, building resources and resilience, and moving us beyond self-interest.

STPEs Broaden Our Attention

STPEs broaden our focus so that we take in more of the world around us than we might otherwise notice. Imagine for a moment that the first thing you touch in the morning is your phone, where you encounter a painful and aggressive email from a former friend and news of another story of racial injustice. You sit and stare at both of these for a long time, feeling the stress surge through your body along with feelings of hopelessness and anger. You sit in this place a bit too long, making you late for an important meeting. You shower hastily, gobble a few bites of food, and head to your car before realizing you do not have your car keys. Suddenly you remember you left them outside on the back porch, so you race out the backdoor, grab your keys, rush to the car, and speed down the road to make your meeting. During this entire process your attention span is narrowed and focused. In your rush to find the keys, you do not even notice the dahlias that are blooming in the back yard, just next to the table where you placed your keys last night. The rising sun, blue sky, beautiful cloud formation, and birdsong fade into oblivion because your body is so focused on the painful news you just received. You rush past your partner without much of a greeting because, well, who has time for a greeting, plus you are in no mood for this. This narrowed focus is adaptive and helpful in times of stress as the cortisol flows through your body, but Fredrickson points us toward the converse of this.

What if you have nurtured a store of tranquility to help you greet a hard email and bad news in the morning? Perhaps you rise early in advance of the meeting, practice loving-kindness meditation, and enjoy a leisurely cup of coffee before checking your phone. Now your attention broadens rather than narrows. You revel in the beauty of the morning, the cheerful birds, the beautiful colors of the dahlias. Joy fills your soul as the vagus nerve sends calming signals from your brain to your heart. You still do not love the email and the news you read, but you are in a state of balance and preparedness for the hard things of the day. This example speaks to our need for spaciousness in a world filled with complexity.

Rick Rubin, the long-bearded, monumentally successful music producer, has worked with everyone from Run-DMC, the Beastie Boys, Adele, and the Red Hot Chili Peppers, to Johnny Cash, and that is the short list. In describing his creative process working with a wide variety of artists in different genres, he talks about spending time with them and getting to know them as people. When it comes time to record, he steps aside and does not interfere with every detail of the process. He listens. He creates space for the music to unfold, which in a way, already exists in the essence of the artist. Rubin's creative genius is a form of broadened attention, movement beyond ego, and a tapping into the potential of the present moment. This requires both tranquility and faith. Wisdom, like the making of good music, requires the right mixing and balancing of different parts. Its natural frequency evades us if we try too hard to force it.

STPEs Help Build Resources and Resilience

As you sip your cup of coffee in a state of broadened attention, you also build interpersonal relationships and become more attuned to the world around you. Instead of brushing past your partner, you smile, make eye contact, give a warm greeting. Enhanced connections with others then make us increasingly inclined to notice positive emotions and experiences.

Once we immerse ourselves in broadened attention and positive emotion, we start building other benefits as well. Those who fill their lives with STPEs are more optimistic, less depressed, more resilient, and, yes, more tranquil in the face of difficult times (Fredrickson et al., 2003). *On Being* host Krista Tippett (2017) notes that she has "yet to meet a wise person who does not know how to find some joy even in the midst of what is hard, and to smile and laugh easily, including at oneself" (p. 13).

All these benefits of STPEs are the *build* part of broaden-and-build, because broadened positive emotions build many individual and interpersonal benefits in a person's life, all of this working in a life-giving upward spiral.

STPEs Move Us Beyond Self-Interest

If we are not unhinged by the difficult emails and news of the day, we have more bandwidth to consider others around us, and if our relationships are enhanced because of the positive emotions we are encountering, then again, we are more inclined to think about others. As discussed in the introduction, self-transcendence is an important part of growing in wisdom.

Compassionately walking with others during life's difficulties helps foster wisdom. Judith Glück (2020) writes, "For many people, the most typical manifestation of wisdom is providing support, guidance, and (sometimes) advice to people facing difficult situations" (p. 144). Similarly, in her book, *Becoming Wise*, Krista Tippett (2017) writes, "Listening is about being present, not just about being quiet" (p. 5). Being truly present to another forces us out of our self-interested bubbles and into places of self-transcendence and greater wisdom.

There is a spiritual dimension here, too. Consider emotions such as awe, gratitude, love, compassion, and joy (Van Cappellen, 2017). Each of these takes us outside of ourselves, pushes against self-interest, and moves us toward a place of seeing others with understanding and compassion. Psychologist Patty Van Cappellen (2017) writes compellingly for the place of religion and spirituality in this process. Positive emotions are not necessarily religious in nature, but they can be, and various spiritual practices can promote positive emotions, compassion, and tranquility. We discuss this more in the next chapters.

SIMPLICITY

We mentioned the connection between tranquility and simplicity in Chapter 7. Not surprisingly, simplicity also shows up as one of the three treasures. While the treadmill of narcissistic prosperity tells us to move faster, accumulate and accomplish more, the gift of simplicity points us in the other direction.

An old Shaker hymn, written in 1848, still shows up in Quaker worship in the 21st century. It goes like this:

'Tis a gift to be simple, 'tis a gift to be free
'Tis a gift to come down where we ought to be,
And when we find ourselves in the place just right,
'Twill be in the valley of love and delight.
When true simplicity is gained,
To bow and to bend we shan't be ashamed,
To turn, turn will be our delight,
Till by turning, turning we come 'round right.

Whether it is found in Marie Kondo's (2014) five steps of tidying up or the current fascination with the minimalists (minimalists, n.d.), we see others joining this old Shaker chorus, stepping off the treadmill and seeking a sort of flourishing that is more about the "valley of love and delight" than the mountaintop of accomplishment.

The advertisements that fuel our favorite internet sites peddle a subtle but pernicious story that buying more stuff will make you fulfilled and happy. Most of these advertisements are honest, clever, and maybe even funny. They do not emerge from malicious intent. People are just doing their jobs, trying to sell their wares and do their part to help their business and the overall economy grow. But the story they sell is not true. More things do not, in fact, make us happier. Quite the opposite, materialism often contributes to poorer mental health and isolation (Kasser, 2002).

Why? The answer appears to be related to gratitude (Tsang et al., 2014). In our materialistic, narcissistic times, we focus on what we do not yet have, and on how to get it. If only I could have this car or that relationship or a bigger house, then my life would finally be just right. But when we get the car, we find something else we want. This is the way treadmills work. In contrast, consider moments when we settle into gratitude, where we need nothing more than to appreciate the gifts of the present moment. Tranquility prospers in places of quiet contentment.

A couple chapters ago we introduced William James's idea that tranquility involves shifting our equilibrium, and you may have noticed we have been returning to this idea over and over again. Tranquility means we shift from emotional volatility to stability, from doing more to being more attentive, from a selfie-gaze to an outward focus, from narrowed, stressed attention to self-transcended positive emotions. Another shift—closely related to the idea of simplicity—is in how we understand the good life.

Twenty-five centuries ago, Greek philosophers had some disagreements about the good life, as we do today. Epicurus promoted an ethical theory known as hedonism, suggesting that pleasure is good and pain is bad. Hedonism has been hugely influential throughout history, including in many philosophical systems in recent centuries.

Aristotle, a contemporary of Epicurus, was more interested in *eudaemonia* than *hedonia*. *Eudaemonia* also relates to the idea of happiness, but not just by seeking pleasure and avoiding pain. Rather, *eudaemonia* focuses on human flourishing and prosperity. What makes for a deeply good and satisfying life? Virtue ethics emerged out of Aristotle's work in this area. Many view tranquility as an outgrowth of a virtuous life. It follows from the natural order of things. It is not just doing good but experiencing peace and rest in the good.

Today, with positive psychology, we see renewed interest in virtue ethics, and this comes with an invitation to redefine the good life. While there is nothing inherently wrong with seeking pleasure and avoiding pain, it can lead to a shallow sort of understanding of happiness where we are always chasing the elusive end of the rainbow. We just need to buy the next gadget, take the newest pill, achieve the promotion, get the right dating app, and then we can be happy. But virtue points us toward a different, deeper sort of happiness that is about character formation, living well in a complex world, learning in difficult times, and getting our eyes onto others as well as ourselves. It is a simpler way of being, less acquisitive, deeply rooted in shared humanity, and intrinsically humble.

HUMILITY

Humility is the dragon slayer. In the *Tao Te Ching*, humility means not being an empire builder, not having to be the first or the best or the most visible. We do not have to be in the front of the line. We discussed in the last chapter how none of us wants to be average these days, so we perceive ourselves to be above average in most positive qualities, which is statistically impossible. Humility reverses this, making average a fine place to live.

At first glance, we may think of humility as self-deprecation, thinking and saying belittling things about oneself. "Look at me, I'm just average in an above-average world." But this misses the point. If I am constantly criticizing myself or comparing myself with others, I have still got the camera pointed inward. The point of humility is being content enough with ourselves and our place in life that we can turn outward, toward the other.

Stories of humility circulate on the internet, and they are poignant. Sam Rayburn, for example, speaker of the House of Representatives in the late 1950s, canceled a meeting with the president to have coffee with a friend in need. Or there is the time when George Washington, commander-in-chief, got off his horse to help some soldiers move a heavy log off the path while a mere corporal remained on his high horse, proclaiming, "I am the corporal. I give orders." Once President Obama served food to the homeless on Thanksgiving. These are all beautiful and inspiring examples, but notice how they involve the person at the head of the line voluntarily caring for someone further back in line. If we truly want to be inspired by humility, it will be by learning from those who never stood at the front of line. These are the stories of people who do not show up much on the internet. They volunteer at the homeless shelter, they take the bus to work each day because they do not need or want a car, they care for an aging parent with dementia.

A robust social science of humility has emerged in recent decades, much of it funded by the John Templeton Foundation. As with any scientific endeavor, the topic has to be defined in order to be studied well. Various definitions have been considered, but mostly they boil down to three main parts:

1. An accurate view of self, which is neither too high nor too low
2. Considering others
3. Being teachable, open to learning from those with different perspectives

The first two involve turning our focus outward, which is why we say humility is the dragon slayer. The third part of humility—about being teachable—is equally important.

We began this book by pondering the political divisiveness and polarization of our time, and how in times like this it is so easy, so natural, to cloister ourselves with like-minded people who tell us we are right. How much more difficult it is to be truly present to the other, to learn from those with whom we disagree. Paul Simon, the songwriter, once penned, "Still a man hears what he wants to hear and disregards the rest." Humility is hard. Being teachable does not come naturally some days.

It is not just that humility is hard; life is too. But it is precisely here, in the hard spaces of life, where we stand to learn and grow the most in wisdom. To be clear, it does not always work this way. Sometimes the difficulties of life drive us back into self-interest, but for some people, under the right circumstances, humility and wisdom grow in the face of difficulty. Glück and her colleagues (2005) collected written narratives from people about their lives, including times when they were wise and foolish. As people reflected back on their lives, one of the most prominent times for wisdom development occurred when life felt difficult and painful. Going through a divorce, or facing the sudden loss of a loved one, is a liminal time when some people are able to grow in self-transcendence and insight. We are not trying to put a Pollyanna spin on hard times. Stress has all sorts of detrimental effects, including enduring health problems, but it also holds the potential for growth if we are open to being teachable (Aldwin et al., 2009).

Wendell Berry wrote to his Buddhist friend Gary Snyder: "Dear Gary, I think it would be both surprising and disappointing if we agreed more than we do. If we agreed about everything, what would we have to say to each other? I'm for conversation" (Berry et al., 2014, p. vi). Here is a personal challenge for each of us to bring to our day: whenever we hear from someone who has a different perspective from us, and whenever we encounter something difficult, we ask ourselves what can be learned from this person or this situation. Perhaps we can come to second-guess our knee-jerk responses, as our first reaction is often one of defense. This is a posture of deep humility, and it might just help shift our equilibrium toward tranquility.

When we started Chapter 7 on the topic of tranquility, you were probably expecting us to take you to an inner sanctuary of meditation or to a warm, sandy beach where you feel a deep sense of calm, rest, and repose. Instead, we took you to a coffee shop where you are having conversation with a friend over matters of disagreement. Tranquility is fairly easy on the beach, but the tranquility that promotes wisdom shows up in the hard places of life, too. Notice the importance of humility in this example— that you would care enough to remain friends despite your disagreements, that you are teachable enough to discuss your differences and consider your friend's perspectives, that you are nondefensive and do not insist on being right. In all these ways, humility ushers you into a place of tranquility that does not require an inner meditative state or a beach. It shows up right in the middle of real life, and isn't that exactly where we would want tranquility to be?

PART 4

TRANSCENDENCE

CHAPTER 10

TRANSCENDENCE
AND WISDOM

D oes it sometimes seem we are supposed to leave religion and spirituality out of almost everything? It does not mix with politics, we
are told, or science, or polite conversation, or—perhaps—books on wisdom. If we consider transcendence at all, it is supposed to be like garlic
or profanity, used just enough to make things interesting but not so much
that it overwhelms what we are doing.

Perhaps no one mentioned this to Mahatma Gandhi, who may be
considered the 20th century's most successful proponent of utilizing
spiritual beliefs and principles to create positive social change. Gandhi—
who led a national movement against British colonial rule in India—
integrated religion into politics, believing that religion connects the human
and the divine.

Quite selfishly, as I wish to live in peace in the midst of a bellowing storm
howling around me, I have been experimenting with myself and my friends
by introducing religion into politics. Let me explain what I mean by religion. It is not the Hindu religion, which I certainly prize above all religions,
but the religion which transcends Hinduism, which changes one's very
nature, which binds one indissolubly to the truth within and which ever
purifies. It is the permanent element in human nature which counts no cost
too great in order to find itself, known its Maker and appreciated the true

correspondence between the Maker and itself. (Ghandi, as cited in Embree et al., 1988, p. 250)

As Gandhi points toward a transcendent element in us all, he admits to his own cultural and religious commitment—the Hinduism of India— while also acknowledging that the essence of religion goes beyond any particular expression of it. This reinforces one of the premises of this book, which is that wisdom unites people of different beliefs and worldviews by focusing on essential and eternal truths. This is a tall order in a time where demonization of the other gains a much quicker reaction with more "likes" and "followers" than seeking the deep truths uniting us all.

The transcendent dimension of wisdom in the KDTT model does not presume Christianity, or any particular religion. Just as Gandhi looked to the "religion which transcends Hinduism," in this final section (Chapters 10–12), we look beyond our beloved home of Christianity to attempt a more universal treatment of religion.

And not just religion, but spirituality, too. The Gallup organization recently reported that less than half of Americans (47%) are now members of a church, synagogue, or mosque (Jones, 2021). Over 70% were members of religious communities when Gallup started polling for this in the 1930s, and this stayed fairly constant through the economic rebirth following World War II, civil rights unrest of the 1960s, the hippie generation of the 1970s, technology transformation of the 1980s, and the fall of the Cold War in the 1990s. But when the century turned, so did the graph. A steady downward trend over the past two decades shows Americans decreasingly seeking spiritual connection through traditional systems of religious belief and practice.

Whether or not Americans belong to a church, synagogue, or mosque, most still believe in God (Hyrnowski, 2019), and our waning religiosity has not caused a decline in spiritual practices. The growing interest and research into mysticism, psychedelics, yoga, meditation, and ecological spirituality through connection with nature show people still desire something deeper. I (Paul) recently strolled through a Barnes & Noble store and noticed the expanded section labeled Self-Transformation where one can find many books pertaining to various spiritualities. What was previously relegated to a small New Age corner is now exploding in an easy-to-find central location. Finding the Psychology section of the store, which appeared about half the size by comparison, required a little bit more searching. This may not show much more than my own idiosyncrasies and obsessive nerdiness at noticing such things, but there seems to be a renaissance of alternative spiritualities now moving into the mainstream.

So what does this have to do with wisdom? Following the pattern used through the book, the goal of this chapter is to explore how transcendence relates to wisdom, and then in Chapter 11 we will discuss why wisdom is difficult in relation to transcendence. We will cap this off in Chapter 12 with some strategies for growing in transcendence and wisdom.

AN INTEGRATIVE CHALLENGE

Because we are both psychologists, our approach to writing this book is primarily motivated by psychological science and practice. At the same time, one of us (Paul) is theologically/philosophically trained, and the other (Mark) has spent several decades integrating psychology and faith. Put the two of us together, and you are bound to get a mix of science, clinical experience, philosophy, religion, and spirituality. We have approached wisdom this way, unapologetically, because it has deep roots in each of these areas.

But when we get to transcendence—a construct requiring both spirituality and psychology to understand—the integrative challenge is heightened. There is plenty of psychological research on spirituality, and lots on wisdom, too, but very little on the relationship between spirituality and wisdom (Takahashi, 2019). The seminal scientific book on wisdom (Sternberg, 1990), published in 1990, had no mention of spirituality at all, and when it was revised in 2005 (Sternberg & Jordan, 2005), only one index entry for spirituality showed up (Takahashi, 2019). Thankfully, a major wisdom handbook published in 2019 (Sternberg & Glück, 2019) has more references to religion and spirituality than earlier handbooks, but still quite little with regard to scientific exploration of how they are related. So we plant one foot in what little information is available in psychological science, the other foot in the heftier world of religion and spirituality, and we do our best to capture the essence of why transcendence is so important in wisdom.

Let's pause once again to ponder where we have been in the book so far, using a metaphor of expanding and constricting. We began the introduction by considering the constriction of ideological fortresses where we group together with like-minded people and keep our world intentionally small. Wisdom calls us outward, expanding our circles and perspectives. Then we looked at the first step—enriched knowledge—which expands how we understand the world around us. But the great obstacle to knowledge is being suffocated with data, which tends to isolate us in our silos and distract us from the big view. Detachment came next, which allows us to step back and gather an expanded view, but pain is the great obstacle, constricting our perspectives as we get swallowed up in stress and discomfort. Then we discussed tranquility, shifting our equilibrium toward a place of repose while opening ourselves up to a world of emotions and forging a path toward transcendence. But the obstacle of narcissism and self-focus easily shuts this down and restricts our focus back toward self-interest. The pattern shows up at every step, with wisdom broadening our focus and the obstacles being constricting influences that herd us back into narrow spaces. Transcendence, as with the other steps in the KDTT model, is like a big, life-giving inhale, expanding our perspectives and awareness, making us more alive and attuned to the world around us.

SELF-BUBBLES

The executive summary for this chapter goes like this: (1) transcendence helps move us out of our self-bubbles, (2) science supports the fact that this is good for us, and (3) it leads to elevated insight, and thus greater wisdom.

You may notice a hyphenated word you have not seen before: self-bubbles. Yes, we made it up. Here is a drawing we offer with the hope it may be worth 1,000 words.

At first glance, self-bubble may sound quite vile, as though we were talking about Narcissistic Personality Disorder, but that is not the case. It is actually quite natural. Most of us spend hours every day contemplating ourselves and the situations we are in, whether they be positive, negative, or neither. In traffic we ponder being late for a meeting, in the meeting we notice how well or poorly we are communicating, on the way home we notice a faint headache and wonder how we might spend the evening. None of these are wrong or bad, but just the way we are primed to think as humans who have made our way up the evolutionary ladder. We will refer to self-bubbles throughout this chapter because the point of transcendence is to give us a break from them. Transcendence moves us to some greater awareness and experience outside of ourselves.

TRANSCENDENCE MOVES US OUT OF OUR SELF-BUBBLES

To set the stage, consider this scenario from the wisdom curriculum we developed for Paul's dissertation. As you may recall from earlier chapters, young adults in a wisdom mentoring program met with mentors to ponder and discuss challenging situations such as this:

> *A friend shows up on your front porch asking for a place to stay for a few weeks until she finds a job and can afford a place to live. You know your friend has had problems with substance abuse and with keeping jobs in the past. In the past you have offered your place as a safe place for her to regroup when she has needed it. However you have recently gotten married, and you and your spouse are struggling with the transition to marriage and with communicating well. Your spouse feels strongly that the two of you need the space and privacy of your home to be able to work through this difficult time in your marriage.*

We are not going to be answering this problem for you, because there is no clear right or wrong answer, but we will use this scenario to consider how transcendence is part of wisdom. A reflexive and nonwise response to this would be to simply conclude yes or no based on self-interest. You simply announce to your spouse, "I haven't seen my friend for a long time, and I want to see her. I'm going to invite her to stay." Or you announce to your friend, "No, my life has changed and I can't help you anymore. You're on your own now." Quick, self-bubbled decisions will not do justice to the complexity of this situation. Transcendence invites us to consider how every person in this narrative is sharing a common humanity and, perhaps, a link with something bigger than humanity.

Transcendence is first a religious concept. Buddhism posits that one holds false selves, but by practicing meditation these can be shed, and the practitioner can reach toward enlightenment, where one is freed from self and experiences glimpses of the deeper truths of the world. In Christianity—especially the mystical traditions—one can learn to release a false, grasping self and discover a true self in union with God. This true self frees one to love God and neighbor. Sufism is the mystical branch of Islam, in which the goal is to be rid of the lower self in order to become more fully attuned to God. In each of these cases, the person of faith is attempting to move away from a self that desires and demands its own way and toward union with something greater (Aldwin et al., 2019; Trammel, 2017).

Some religious leaders once tried to trick Jesus by asking which of the commandments is greatest. Jesus offered an answer that has been reverberating for 20 centuries: to love God with our whole being, and to love our neighbor as ourself (Matthew 22:36–40). In this, he moved above the fray, transcended the self-interested question, and offered words that have served as a guide for faith and civility ever since. It is intriguing to wonder how an American might respond today if asked which political party or constitutional principle or amendment is greatest. Would we have the wisdom to move above self-interest, or would we be so trapped in our particular passions and persuasions that we end up settling for a strongly-worded rant?

In the mid-20th century, psychologists also became interested in transcendence. Some trace this back to Viktor Frankl, a Jewish psychiatrist who survived the horrors of a Nazi concentration camp before writing *Man's Search for Meaning* (Aldwin et al., 2019; Frankl, 1959). Frankl observed in the concentration camp that those who were able to get beyond their own suffering and be available to others did much better in the face of such atrocities. Early wisdom researchers became interested in transcendence late in the 20th century, as did psychologists of religion. Ralph Piedmont, a psychologist of religion who developed the Spiritual Transcendence Scale, defines spiritual transcendence as, "the capacity of individuals to stand outside their immediate sense of time and place to view life from a larger, more objective perspective" (Piedmont, 1999, p. 988). With spiritual transcendence, a person sees an overarching unity to all things and a persistent bond with one another. Examples of items on Piedmont's Spiritual Transcendence Scale include, "I feel that on a higher level all of us share a common bond," and "I find inner strength and/or peace from my prayers or meditations." Other psychologists have also developed transcendence scales.

In both domains—religion and psychology—transcendence is seen as the capacity to get beyond oneself, out of the bubble, to see a fundamental unity in all things, and to connect to this unity in some meaningful way that ends up shaping our thoughts, values, motivations, feelings, and behaviors. Most contemporary nonreligious spiritualities also emphasize connection with some unitive force or consciousness that transcends the human person.

Moving back to the friend on the front porch, we can now see a clear contrast between a self-interested response that is inclined to value self and disparage the other and a transcendent perspective that sees a common reality shared by each person involved. The easiest way to deal with the friend on the front porch would be to simply denounce one person or another. "She's just a loser, drug addict." Or, "my spouse is a clueless control freak." This leads to an easy decision, but not necessarily a wise one. It is much more challenging—and wise—to recognize three souls of enormous worth in this scenario—all trying their best to find peace and meaning in life, and finding it difficult.

TRANSCENDENCE IS GOOD FOR US

As we mentioned, there is not a lot of science on transcendence yet. What we do know is that men and women do not differ on transcendence, there appears to be a slight increase in transcendence with age (at least until one gets very old, at which point there may be some declines), and various physical and mental health benefits are associated with transcendence, as well as greater social support, spirituality, and positive emotions (Aldwin et al., 2019).

There has been more research done on self-transcendent positive emotions (STPEs), which were introduced in the previous chapter. Gratitude, for example, is an STPE because it gets us out of our self-bubbles as we place our thankful attention on another. The most widely researched of the STPEs, gratitude is related to a sense of well-being, positive mood, pleasantness, and life satisfaction. Those who are grateful are less likely than others to be depressed or anxious. They have fewer phobias and eating disorders and less alcohol and drug use. They are less motivated to accumulate material possessions than others and experience more daily motivation (Wood et al., 2010). Some early research showed those who practice gratitude are less likely than others to go to the doctor, and they sleep better and exercise more (Emmons & McCullough, 2003).

Another STPE is awe, which involves a sense of vastness—being amidst something bigger than words can contain (Keltner & Haidt, 2003). Psychologist Dacher Keltner (2016) reminds us not to underestimate the power of goose bumps. Awe requires us to challenge and change our existing mental structures in order to hold the new experience, and in the process, to move out of our self-bubbles. Science writer Summer Allen (2018) offers this beautiful description:

> If you've hiked among giant sequoias, stood in front of the Taj Mahal, or observed a particularly virtuosic musical performance, you may have experienced the mysterious and complex emotion known as "awe." Awe experiences are self-transcendent. They shift our attention away from ourselves, make us feel like we are part of something greater than ourselves, and make us more generous toward others. (p. 2)

In the midst of awe, we often feel humbled, attuned toward the greater good, and connected with the transcendent (Piff et al., 2015). Sometimes awe occurs in once-in-a-lifetime moments, such as standing atop a mountain and seeing for miles around, and sometimes it shows up in ordinary day-to-day experiences, such as seeing the smile of a newborn or observing the slow falling of an oak leaf on a crisp autumn day. Awe brings ecstasy, which is *ex stasis*, a standing outside of our selves. In this way, awe can serve to energize and elevate us toward the deeper call of wisdom. Religious conversion almost always comes with an accompanying sense of awe.

Like gratitude, awe is good for us. When researchers looked at how much various positive emotions predict lower levels of inflammatory cytokines in the body, they found awe to be a better predictor than amusement, compassion, contentment, joy, love, or pride (Stellar et al., 2015). In pondering their results, the researchers speculated that inflammation, injury, and sickness tend to cause us to retreat into social withdrawal, whereas awe pushes us in the other direction, toward exploration and curiosity. Put another way, pain puts us squarely in our self-bubbles, and awe invites us outward to explore the world of relationships, nature, and spirituality.

We should also mention some scientific evidence that links spirituality, religion, transcendence, and wisdom. Dilip Jeste and his colleagues conducted a survey of international experts on wisdom and learned that both wisdom and spirituality share a commitment to other-centeredness (Jeste et al., 2010). Some early studies show traditional religious beliefs and practices are not related to wisdom, but more recent studies suggest otherwise. Those who attend church frequently and those who report awe toward God score higher on a measure of practical wisdom, feel a deep sense of connection with others, and have greater life satisfaction than others (Krause & Hayward, 2015).

There is much more to be studied on these connections, but preliminary evidence suggests getting out of our self-bubbles, and moving toward transcendent perspectives and emotions, promotes health and well-being in various ways while also helping us grow in wisdom.

TRANSCENDENCE LEADS TO ELEVATED INSIGHT AND WISDOM

When today's fascination with spirituality meets the technological boom of the 21st century, one outcome is an explosion of websites on the existential meaning of dreams. If people dream about being a bird—able to fly above their normal terrain and get a birds-eye view of the world below—this is taken to be a symbol of transcendence, being free from the normal constraints of daily living For the purposes of explaining what we mean by elevated insight, we will use this example, while acknowledging that dream interpretation is complicated and more of an art than a science. The transcendent dimension of wisdom allows us to move above the normal details of life—above the pundits and blog posts and sponsored advertisements and op-ed articles—to capture a larger perspective, just as a bird sees more from the sky than from the ground.

We have been hinting at this need for a larger view throughout the book. Moving upward to glimpse a panoramic perspective keeps us from being suffocated in narrowly focused *knowledge*; then *detachment* further promotes the ability to look for the big picture. As we learn to do this, we come to experience the shifting equilibrium of *tranquility*. Transcendence brings this all together, helping us to view ourselves and our circumstances in a larger context, to hold the end in mind, to give perspective, to experience peace and equanimity, and to free us from the entrapment of self-bubbles.

Human development expert Carolyn Aldwin and her colleagues (2019) have speculated about four dimensions of transcendence related to wisdom, three of which we use to guide our discussion for the remainder of this chapter: interconnectedness, meaning and purpose, and emotional transcendence. We are saving the fourth dimension for Chapter 12.

Interconnectedness

Brené Brown (2018), a social science researcher and popular author, sees spirituality as "celebrating that we are all inextricably connected to each other by a power greater than all of us, and that our connection to that power and to one another is grounded in love and compassion." There is a bit more to her definition, which we will share soon, but for now it is worth pondering how our spiritual quest ties us together with one another in ways that bring out the best in us. Even the popular skeptic and agnostic Sam Harris acknowledges a transcendent connection with something beyond self:

I can say that the true goal of meditation is more profound than most people realize—and it does, in fact, encompass many of the experiences that traditional mystics claim for themselves. It is quite possible to lose one's sense of being a separative self and to experience a kind of boundless, open awareness—to feel, in other words, at one with the cosmos. (Harris, 2014, p. 43)

What does it mean to forge connections with a larger universe, to be at one with the cosmos? How do we become more like Gandhi and Jesus and the birds in our dreams? Most humans throughout history have carried a sense of being incomplete on their own, thus seeking a way to connect with something or someone beyond themselves (Takahashi, 2019). This helps promote the sort of humility we have discussed many times in this book—something essential for wisdom development.

Jocelyn came to my (Mark's) office to figure out a life pattern that had not worked well for her. She found herself drawn to impulsive men, time after time putting herself in harm's way. One past lover was in jail for dealing drugs, another had been physically abusive, a third had been married throughout his relationship with Jocelyn, without her knowledge. Sometimes the work of a psychologist seems much like the work of an endodontist, tracing tooth pain back to an infected root. In psychotherapy, Jocelyn did the hard work of noticing how lost she felt as a child. Both of her parents worked full-time jobs, plus overtime, her only sister was much older and almost out of the house, and her father had an explosive temper that often ended in physical abuse, making it important to be as invisible as possible around him. When a teenage boy started paying attention to her, it seemed remarkably healing for another human being to notice and apparently care about her. But the caring was superficial, and Jocelyn did not have enough experience with healthy relationships to understand that. By the time she reached her mid-thirties and my psychotherapy office she had been mistreated many times by many men, and a stifling depression had settled in. With time and hard work, Jocelyn got better. She looked courageously at her past, learned to set better boundaries with potential partners, and experienced the deep relief of seeing her longstanding depression recede. In terms of the KDTT model, Jocelyn gained knowledge about herself and her past, learned to detach and observe when men showed her attention, and experienced greater tranquility than she had known before. And then, as our treatment was winding down, the most remarkable thing happened.

Jocelyn's married neighbors had been asking her for years to come to a church service, but that seemed too weird and frightening for Jocelyn to consider. Faith had been part of her abusive family of origin, and she wanted nothing to do with it now. But as she became healthier, she also found herself curious about why her neighbors seemed so stable and kind, and on a whim she agreed one day to go with them to church where she ended up having a spiritual conversion experience. As she experienced loving interconnectedness with a higher being and with a new community of relatively healthy people, she blossomed and flourished in life. In each of our subsequent sessions her face seemed almost radiant, her voice strong and confident, and her sense of direction and values in life clear and precise. Psychotherapy helped her, but her connection with the transcendent helped her far more.

Psychologists of religion have studied conversion experiences since the seminal work of William James in the early 20th century. Jocelyn's story helps us understand why. Though not every conversion story has a happy ending, many do. Gaining a transcendent view on life—a sense of interconnectedness with something or someone bigger than oneself—can lead to remarkable psychological and spiritual change.

Contact with an absolute, however one may define it, is associated with being part of something infinitely greater than oneself. This sense of dependence helps us see our lives against a larger background. It is common to exaggerate the importance of our lives, especially for those growing up in the age of American exceptionalism and vertical individualism (more on this in the next chapter). Yet the actual freedom and control we have in determining the way life unfolds is to a certain extent illusory.

We are only authors of our own lives to a limited degree. When chaos and randomness descend, awareness of an absolute brings a presence that puts our experiences in context.

Elevated insight and interconnectedness reduce differences between people by reinforcing a shared common nature, a universal understanding of what it means to be alive. Astronauts seeing Earth from space often observe a profound sense of oneness. Sultan bin Salman Al-Saud, an astronaut on the international space station, put it this way: "The first day or so we all pointed to our countries. The third or fourth day we were pointing to our continents. By the fifth day, we were aware of only one Earth" (Wallace, 1999, p. 163). With interconnectedness, we are no longer a red team and a blue team kicking each other in the shins, but a collective humanity, united through our connection to the transcendent, trying to figure out how to live well in a complex world. The shared ground of ultimate being is not mine or yours, but ours.

In the year 622 CE, Muhammed lead a group of Muslims out of his native Mecca, after facing years of brutal persecution, to the city of *Yathrib*, which would later be known as Medina (the enlightened city). This *Hegira* (migration) denotes the beginning of the Islamic calendar. In doing this, Muslims see the creation of the *ummah*, a community of believers not composed of tribal kin but of all Muslims. This example of Muhammed's uniting of the Bedouin tribes of Arabia under the banner of Islam shows the universal and unifying aspects of religion; stemming from a transcendent understanding of human relations. Nothing happens that does not ripple out and impact farther than we can initially see. Seeing universally is the necessary precursor to building unity. Indeed, unity can be viewed as the core of spirituality, including a bridge connecting humanity with the divine (Hadot, 1963/1998).

Fifteen centuries later, in 2015, a group of a thousand Norwegian Muslims and other supporters surrounded a Jewish synagogue in Oslo after an anti-Semitic attack in Copenhagen. Together they chanted, "No to anti-Semitism! No to Islamophobia!" One of the organizers of the event, Zeeshan Abdullah, described the group's intent this way: "Humanity is one, and we are here to demonstrate that" (Good News Network & Weis-Corbley, 2018, p. 27).

With the friend on the front porch, it is easy to note the different perspectives of each person in this story. Your friend wants a place to stay, your spouse wants more time to work on your marriage, and you feel torn between your spouse and your friend. But imagine for a moment that all three of you are much more alike than you are different—all of you interconnected, yearning to be seen and known, all of you struggling to find the security and love you long for, and all of you wanting to be civil and virtuous as you work this out. It casts a different light on the problem, and while it does not make a solution easy, it does dignify each person in the story and shape the ways you might communicate with one another.

Meaning and Purpose

As we mentioned earlier, there is more to Brené Brown's (2018) definition of spirituality than we gave you. She goes on to suggest, "Practicing spirituality brings a sense of perspective, meaning, and purpose to our lives." The elevated insight that comes with spiritual transcendence gives life direction, as it did for Viktor Frankl in that Nazi concentration camp. Frankl drew repeatedly on a phrase he recalled from Friedrich Nietzsche: "Those who have a *why* to live, can bear with almost any *how*" (Frankl, 1959, pp. 69, 90). These words, paradoxically penned by an outspoken atheist, helped a religious Jewish man survive the most horrific circumstances one can imagine. We—like Frankl—search for meaning to organize and direct us in challenging times. We search for a *why* in a life filled with *whats* and *wheres* and *hows*. In this, transcendence helps us step forward toward wisdom.

You are likely immersed in a busy life, with more to do than time allows. Perhaps your morning routines involved getting yourself ready for work, engaging warmly with others in your family unit, preparing lunches for children, coordinating transportation needs, and anticipating evening plans. Then you arrive at work to an overflowing inbox, likely one you snuck a peak at on your phone even before walking into your office, or perhaps to an arduous day of labor. The office scurry keeps moving along even as the relational work of relating well with co-workers has its own drama. Eventually you walk back into your front door to figure out another meal and the comings and goings of another busy evening. Most lives in contemporary society involve lots of *whats, wheres, and hows*. They make more sense if there is also a *why*. Why is it that you scramble along day after day, working harder than you might have ever imagined a decade or two ago? Is it because you love the people you live with and want them to prosper and thrive in life? Maybe you truly care about the services or products your employer offers, and you are glad to be part of this work that helps people. Perhaps you care deeply about being a productive member of society, to help make the world a slightly better place than you found it.

Transcendence helps us glimpse a bigger purpose for life beyond just checking the items on the to-do list. These purposes often point us toward the transcendentals discussed in Chapter 3, which are common universal values based on philosophical assumptions about the nature of being and knowledge. The transcendentals put hands and feet on the transcendent, help give us a sense of *why* for living while allowing us to participate in something big and timeless as we grow toward understanding and make meaning of being alive and human. Transcendentals provide organizing principles for our values, thoughts, feelings, and actions, perhaps while connecting us to the essence of the universe.

Some may ask if we have fallen prey to spiritual mumbo jumbo. What does a particular value, such as appreciating beauty, have to do with a *why* for living or the essence of the universe? To probe deeper into this, imagine that beauty is not only in the eye of the beholder, but actually emanates from some greater source. If viewed this way, the transcendentals are specific manifestations of this larger transcendent source, which some name God. If truth, beauty, and goodness are primary colors, then the transcendent can be seen as color itself. Consider the way the ancient Greek philosopher Plotinus describes "the One," as the single unified and unifying source of everything whose being emanates down:

Only the Transcendent can be that; it is the great beginning, and the beginning must be a really existent One, wholly and truly One, while its sequent, poured down in some way from the One, is all, a total which has participation in unity and whose every member is similarly all and one. (Dillon, 1991, p. 110)

The transcendental experience of beauty is a unique experience as we focus on such things as symmetry, color, and aesthetic brilliance. Similarly, the experience of truth emphasizes intelligibility and order, growth through the light of knowledge, as it also reveals the basis of justice. And beauty, truth, and justice all point toward the possibility of a fountainhead, a source of everything.

Notice, though, that everyday life requires bridges between our daily experiences and the transcendent values that bring us meaning. We care about beauty, truth, and justice in the world, and then read about another law enforcement incident resulting in a person of color dying. This causes tension in ourselves and our communities as we recognize the gap between the values that bring meaning to life and the reality in which we live. How do we respond to such dissonance?

One option might be to simply resign ourselves to a life of passivity, or slip into apathy. It is quite natural to do this, but these are the folks Frankl observed who did not survive the horrors of a Nazi concentration camp. Those who made it through were those who kept wrestling with their values, trying to make sense of their lives amidst one of the worst atrocities of human history. Transcendence means that we keep struggling to cross the bridge between our ideals and the realities of everyday life, even when it seems almost impossible to do so.

Most of us have far lesser struggles than living in a concentration camp, but they still feel profound and powerful in the moment, allowing us to find meaning in the midst of our pain. Jonah Lehrer was a popular writer and blogger until some of his work was exposed for containing false quotes and facts. His devastating plunge from fame to shame was a pivotal point in his life. In telling his story on *The Moth*, he describes how he begged his wife to leave him because he was not worthy of her, but instead she stayed. He became an at-home father and learned more about parenting than he ever imagined, including searching through poop for the penny his daughter had swallowed. He reflects back now, with words of meaning and insight:

> But I also know that the worst parts, those scenes I most want to forget, they're also the most important parts: the look on the face of my wife when I tell her what I've done; the sound of my daughter crying in the hallway because I provide no comfort at all.
>
> There's a line from the Sufi mystic, Inayat Khan: "God breaks the heart again and again and again, until it stays open." That's what happened to me. (Lehrer, 2017)

Lehrer goes on to describe how this crisis event in his life taught him about love, and that love has been his consolation in the aftermath of shame. Love became Lehrer's *why* to allow him to endure this challenging season of his life.

Whether it relates to the latest police shootings, reflecting on the atrocities of a concentration camp, or learning love in the aftermath of shame, one of the most important values for daily wisdom relates to how we view people. Are others lesser human beings, nothing but tools to help us accomplish our own purposes, or do they possess ultimate dignity and worth just by virtue of being human? And if the latter, what gives human beings value?

Finding an objective foundation of self-worth is hard to come by these days. In prior times, the inherent value of the human person was based on a creator, an all-loving God. It is common these days for conditions of worth—those things we feel we must do in order to receive validation and love from others—to keep us striving for a love we can never reach, and we remain vulnerable to the opinion and judgment of others. But let's not rule out the divine altogether when considering human value because it may show up in human interactions, even among those who may not believe in God. Carl Jung saw contact with the numinous as the source of healing for his patients: "But the fact is that the approach to the numinous is the real therapy and inasmuch as you attain to the numinous experiences you are released from the curse of pathology" (Adler et al., 1973, p. 377). To Jung, the human psychotherapist is carrying some divinity that gets transfused to the client. As the client experiences this divine spark, a profound sense of being heard, seen, known, and valued emerges and healing ensues. In this way, psychotherapy is quite unusual and countercultural because most daily activities make self-worth both hard to identify and cultivate. Most of us carry on our daily business as consumers, mothers, fathers, children, employees, managers, laborers, but when we find our way to the psychotherapist's office we are perceived and treated as deeply valued human beings—a truth that longs to awaken in each of us, but often slumbers through the hustle and bustle of most days.

For the most fortunate, this way of being seen and valued occurs in some other relationship that does not require finding a licensed professional. It shows up in a patiently loving partner, a deep friendship, an exemplary parent, or a wise mentor. When this sort of human encounter happens, a divine spark awakens and transforms us, leading us toward grace, inviting us to experience deep self-worth, and propelling us forward toward meaningful values as we interact with others. The numinous shows up in a pulsing, breathing human, revealing an intentional presence that teaches us about ourselves, an intuitive knowledge revealing our core value and identity.

I (Mark) recently hit a speed bump in life that took me back into personal therapy, joining the throngs of people trying to find a mental health therapist amidst a global-pandemic-turned-mental-health-crisis. Patience and persistence paid off eventually. I submitted my Venmo payment, sat in a HIPAA-compliant electronic waiting room, then met the man on my MacBook screen who, over time, guided me deep into my psyche until I could glimpse my deeper self again. It was there in cyberspace, 50 minutes at a time, where I encountered a dignifying sort of grace, coupled with the spark of divinity that Jung wrote about 75 years ago. And as much as this may sound like a lesser form of grace than what I encounter in my Quaker church each week, that turned out not to be the case at all. The grace of a good psychologist dares to touch the silent places, and the hidden ones, and bears witness to the themes of sadness and threads of hope that hold a tattered life together. The only proper thing to do after this sort of unique grace is to weep in relief and sorrow and gratitude and the beauty of being seen and valued (even if through a webcam). So, I did. Over and over.

Emotional Transcendence

So far our discussion has been fairly cognitive—that elevated insight leads to a sense of interconnectedness and a sense of meaning and purpose in life. But as my tears in this recent psychotherapy experience show, emotions get fully engaged as we gain elevated insight. Perhaps you can recall similar experiences, whether in psychotherapy or not, where you felt incredibly connected to another person, as if there were a strong bond of compassion and empathy between the two of you. That bond illustrates how powerfully self-transcendence can happen between two people, and that it is bigger than either of you individually. And when you experience this, you likely have strong emotions.

This self-transcendent connection between two human beings is what Dr. Barbara Fredrickson (2013) calls *positivity resonance*. Our brains go wild in these moments, doing something called "neural coupling," oxytocin is released into our bloodstream, and the vagus nerve—one of 12 nerves that go directly into our brain rather than connecting through the spinal cord—stimulates facial muscles and the small muscles in the inner hear so that you can be more expressive and hear the other person's voice. This sort of self-transcendence fully engages the body, including our emotions.

If you attend religious services, perhaps you have experienced similar things during times of community worship. It is as if you move outside of yourself and begin experiencing the deep, abiding presence of God. In these moments, it is not at all uncommon to be moved by emotion.

Self-transcendent emotions free us to be curious, to explore the world around us with a sense of wonder and freedom. Once we are at peace with our own acceptance and value, we find freedom to expand the conceptual frames in which we learn, discern, and make decisions. We can boldly explore the world when we no longer feel a continual need to defend and protect ourselves. Transcendence introduces us to a land of rich new ideas and feelings that explode the usual categories and expectations we hold. Who we are, what we value, our sense of individuality, the purpose of our lives all expand by the seeing with a universal eye. There is beautiful freedom here: the more we grasp the ungraspable, the more we sense that, "in luminous presence, we encounter the purity of simple being" (Benner, 2014, p. 62).

We have already mentioned gratitude and awe, both of which are emotions that transcend our self-bubbles, pointing us outward toward others while elevating our insight toward the world around us. Other transcendent emotions include admiration, love, compassion, peacefulness, and joy.

These transcendent emotions share three things in common (Van Cappellen, 2017). First, they are other-focused. It is hard to experience gratitude or awe while confined in our self-bubble. Admiration requires us to notice another. So does compassion. Love is being fully present to another. Peacefulness may not involve another person, but it still takes us out of self-preoccupation to experience a sense of repose and calm.

Second, all these emotions incline us to be prosocial, thinking of others and acting kindly in the world. For those trying to follow Jesus' words to love neighbor as self, these positive emotions help a great deal because looking lovingly and compassionately at others changes the way we treat them. Imagine how important this is when confronted with the friend on the front porch. Of course, there will be some stressful emotions—surprise, fear, panic, insecurity, a quiet anger. But if we are also open to self-transcendent positive emotions, and to the interconnection of all things, the situation and the choices to be made will be bathed in love and compassion.

Third, all of these emotions have implications for religious and spiritual beliefs, and for how we go about making meaning in life. Those who are religious will likely identify with the sense of elevation and joy that comes with corporate worship through music, liturgy, or prayer. And faith—best conceived—makes us more loving and compassionate in a hurting world. Nonreligious spiritual practices do the same. And God knows, we could use more love and compassion in our world today.

CHAPTER 11

METRIC WORLD

W e are going to count down from three to one, and then reveal the great barrier to transcendence.

THREE: OUR OBSESSION WITH RATINGS

If you like this book, you may give it 5 stars on a website or two. If you do not like it, well, our ratings and sales may suffer a bit. This is not just the reality of authors, though, because metrics bubble up everywhere, from the places we dine to the employees we hire (and fire) to business and health care to movies and television to social media posts. There was a day when professors used course evaluations privately, to improve their courses. Typically they involved a couple open-ended essay questions: What did you find most useful about this course? What improvements would you suggest? But now professors are evaluated numerically, compared with peers at their institutions and around the country, and, in many cases, paid based on the ratings they receive. Physicians are in a similar situation, rated after each visit and then evaluated based on how many stars they average. One physician recently mentioned she feels like a waiter, filling prescriptions for her patients who seem to already know what they want and who happily wield the power of a rating to express satisfaction (or not) with how compliant their doctor is willing to be (Moore, 2020). Psychologists are now encouraged to give patient rating scales at the end of each session. The ratings go into a national repository where psychologists are then evaluated in relation to peers who offer similar services. In the not-too-distant future, it is possible that these ratings will determine insurance reimbursement rates. Our benchmarking Metric World is filled with acronyms: KPIs (key performance indicators), P4P (pay for performance), SEO (search engine optimization), and so many more.

Our goal is not to evaluate whether living in the world of metrics is a good or bad thing. It is undoubtedly both, and compelling arguments can be made on both sides. We are more transparent and accountable because of metrics, but we are also overwhelmed with surveys and any numerical system can be gamed. In his provocative book, *The Tyranny of Metrics*, Jerry Muller (2018) describes Campbell's law, named after social psychologist Donald Campbell who observed that the more we use metrics for social decision making, the more we are vulnerable to corruption. The pros and cons of metrics will continue to be debated, but what does our current fascination with numerical evaluation reflect about our broader social milieu? How might this serve as an obstacle to transcendence, and thus wisdom?

Just as narcissism is the great barrier to tranquility, there is a barrier to transcendence also. It is not exactly metrics, but we are marching toward it. As we continue the countdown, it is important to keep in mind that a barrier to one aspect of the KDTT model impacts the others. For example, an overconsumption of data and information limits our obtaining of real knowledge, as it also impedes our connection to tranquility and transcendence. Likewise, intense pain hinders detachment while limiting our pursuit of transcendence, as we become stuck in suffering's tyrannical clutches. Thankfully, the same is true on the other side of things. As we grow in wisdom, the four elements of KDTT also develop. For those who are able to gain insight and knowledge about themselves and maintain emotional balance in the wake of challenges, the work of detachment and growth can take place. The movement toward transcendence builds upon the natural order of knowledge, detachment, and tranquility, and then ultimately takes flight. But flying in some kinds of weather is harder than in others.

TWO: A MORE DETAILED LOOK AT INDIVIDUALISM

We introduced you to Ara and Sonja—two hypothetical teenagers—in Chapter 8, one of whom is being raised in a collectivist context and the other in an individualistic one. And while our goal is not to discredit either of these systems, we need to explore individualism further because at least one form of it leads to murky weather for the upward movement of transcendence.

It turns out describing a culture as individualistic or collectivistic is painting with too broad a brush. For example, both the United States and Sweden are considered individualistic countries, but they look and function very differently from one another. Similarly, both an Israeli kibbutz and Korea are considered collectivist places, but the disparity is remarkable. Harry Triandis and his colleagues offer a more detailed taxonomy in which both systems can be viewed as vertical, emphasizing hierarchy, or horizontal, emphasizing equality. We have summarized this in the table below (adapted from Triandis & Gelfand, 1998). As you look at

	Individualism	Collectivism
Vertical	High autonomy	Low autonomy
	Low equality	Low equality
	Authority ranking	Authority ranking
	Self as different from others	Self as different from others
	Market economy	Communalism
	Example: France	Example: China
Horizontal	High autonomy	Low autonomy
	High equality	High equality
	Equality matching	Equality matching
	Self as same as others	Self as same as others
	Democratic socialism	Communal living
	Example: Norway	Example: Monasticism

the table, it may be helpful to know that one—and only one—of the four cells is associated with low levels of self-transcendence. See if you might guess which one.

Let's consider some examples. In Norway, largely a horizontal individualist (HI) country, people want to do their own thing, but they do not care very much about status. People are perceived as equal, and rising to the top is just not that motivating to a Norwegian. In the United States, largely a vertical individualist (VI) country, we also want to do our own thing, but we want to be upwardly mobile as we do it. We arrange ourselves in hierarchies while insisting that average is not good enough. At the time we write this book, Norway has been rated the happiest country in the world four years running by the World Happiness Report (Helliwell et al., 2021), but it occurs to us that this is a very VI thing to measure and report. In Norway people may not care very much whether they are at the top of the heap, but we certainly look enviously at this from vantage point of the United States where we are not even in the top 10.

In horizontal collectivism (HC), people see themselves as similar to one another, interconnected, and interdependent, but they do not like submitting to authorities. In vertical collectivism (VC) people defer personal goals for the sake of their group, and they are generally respectful of and compliant with their group leaders.

ONE: THE REVEAL

As our countdown concludes, we are ready to reveal what we believe to be a major barrier to transcendence. It comes together with a somewhat obscure journal article published shortly after the turn of the century. Thao Le and Michael Levenson (2005)—two wisdom scholars at the University of California, Davis—collected data from an ethnically diverse sample of people living in America, including those identifying as Russian, Laotian, Vietnamese, Thai, Mien, Cambodian, and Tibetan. They also collected data from undergraduate students at UC, Davis, consisting mostly of European-American, Asian-American, and Hispanic participants. In both studies the researchers assessed the cultural identity of participants (HI, VI, HC, or VC) along with immature love and self-transcendence. Only one of the four cultural variants was related to immature love and low self-transcendence: vertical individualism. In contrast, an egalitarian stance promoted self-transcendence. This is not too surprising if we stop to reflect. In those cultures where people are perceived as fundamentally equal, people are more able to move out of their self-bubbles to perceive and experience the interconnectedness of all.

So what is the big barrier to transcendence? Vertical individualism, with all its predilection for competition, me-first perspectives, the dragon of narcissism, rising to the top, and seeing the individual as more important than the communities we belong to. And for many of us in Western countries, this is the water we swim in every day. It becomes so comfortable and natural to our ways of thinking and being in the world that we hardly even stop to notice.

Though the United States is a collection of many cultures, the dominant one is vertical individualism. We scramble toward upward mobility and play king of the mountain with our achievements and strivings. The Standard and Poor's 500 (S&P 500) is an index tracking the largest publicly traded companies in the United States. All 500 companies must report compensation to their chief executive officers as well as their median worker pay. In 2020, the average S&P corporation gave their CEO a $700,000 raise, bringing their compensation to $15.5 million for the year, an amount that is—on average—299 times as much as their median workers make (AFL-CIO, n.d.). The verticalism of such numbers is staggering, as the U.S. ratio of CEO pay to median worker pay is the highest in the world, and more than four times as high as Sweden, a more horizontal society (Duarte, 2019).

This is bad news for those of us living in vertical individualist countries, at least if we desire to grow in transcendence and wisdom. Our inclination to rank order, then provide troves of treasure and fame to those at the top flies in the face of the sort of unifying, transcendent movement described in the last chapter.

We rarely stop to consider that if one person moves up in our rank-ordered society, it requires another to move down. Search engine optimization (SEO) is both a metaphor and example of this. Individuals and companies spend big money on SEO audits to learn how they can rise in the ranks on Google searches, but every time one blogger or business rises a step, another one must fall. So then the falling blogger pays for a better audit, rises again, and then someone else falls. We are playing king of the mountain with metrics, as would be expected in vertical individualist cultures, especially when the mountain is built with a pile of money. But at what cost to our souls?

PSYCHOTHERAPY AS PAUSE BUTTON

Why psychotherapy works is a bit of a mystery, even to two psychologists writing a book on wisdom. But if we had to guess, it seems to have something to do with the opposite of what we have just been considering. Vertical individualism leads to a sort of striving, trying to get on top, be the best, win our way to success. Psychotherapy provides a pause button where people can breathe, reconsider, imagine their identity apart from accomplishments, see themselves as embedded in relationships and communities, and in the process find deeper meaning and hope for their existence.

Max would often arrive to sessions with a bright and jubilant demeanor, smiling and speaking about the progress he felt he was making in our treatment. The son of successful yet controlling parents, he felt a profound sense of responsibility to succeed and often projected a naive optimism about metrics of achievement. His sunny disposition was largely performative, masking anger, resentment, and fear. He would wake in the middle of the night afraid he was forgetting to do something, wrapped in guilt, and fearing time was quickly slipping away. During the day he remained fixated on his career in the business world, working long hours and struggling to find any personal time. Part of our work in treatment required a slow and steady climbing out of the burdening expectations of self and others. This ended up leading Max through a dark valley, a bleak psychological space, because his identity and sense of self and worth were constructed within a family and cultural structure that valued climbing high in the world of commerce and social status. Psychotherapy provided a different sort of relational frame for Max—one where he was not particularly valued for his successes and was not criticized for his failings. With time and the corrective relational work of psychotherapy, he began to glimpse in himself a center of innate self-worth and unconditional value. Such is the transcendent work of psychotherapy, moving a person toward a wholeness that cannot be measured by dollars or likes or 5-star ratings.

Knowledge, detachment, tranquility, and transcendence can be viewed as sequential moves in psychotherapy, as they were for Max. Knowledge is obtained through insight and self-awareness—changing lenses to look at life differently. Detachment from false identity often comes next, as people free themselves from previous modes of being that perpetuate painful thoughts and feelings. Tranquility represents an ideal feeling state, free of disturbance from sadness, fear, anger, anxiety, and depression. This comes and goes in treatment, as people glimpse what is possible and then slip back into old ways of being. With time, tranquility comes more than it goes, as a deep sense of peace settles in. Transcendence calls a person beyond the superficial markers of ego and success and allows for a greater sense of connection with self and others. This happens in two ways: moving beyond habits and patterns that confine the self, and ascending toward actualization where one gains clarity about values and meaning in life and shared human experiences.

This same rhythm of knowledge, detachment, tranquility, and transcendence may be helpful when the friend shows up unannounced on your front porch looking for a place to stay. The first step will be to accumulate knowledge. For how long will your friend be needing lodging? What other options might be available to her, and when? What alternatives seem possible to your spouse? What impact might you perceive on your marriage? Second, it will be important to detach from the immediacy of the situation so the rough edges of your emotions—and your partner's—can be smoothed. Good decisions for important matters are rarely made quickly. Looking at the situation from multiple perspectives will be important. Third, as the emotions calm, you and your partner will hope for a place of tranquility as you move toward a wise decision. The final decision can be made with transcendent awareness of the shared, common humanity of each of the people involved, and a clear sense of the prevailing commitments and values shaping your life, your marriage, and your friendships. These four steps (KDTT), which are far from simple, will ultimately guide whatever decision is made, and how it is communicated to everyone involved.

AFTER THE SESSION

Psychotherapy may offer a pause button, but after the session people still need to walk out of the office and back into Metrics World where many face the clamor of vertical individualism. The daily realities of immediacy, perfection, and even hatred show up again and again, and these impede our movements toward transcendence.

Immediacy

In vertical individualist countries, it seems there is a chronic urgency to do the next thing, and many things. When Max woke in the middle of the night, wondering what he might be forgetting and how it might impede his success, this is emblematic of contemporary life. As transcendence calls us to long, quiet contemplation, immediacy competes with this, telling us to hurry up, to remember everything, to scramble our way to the top of the heap. This makes wisdom difficult, because wise thinking and acting emerges from quiet spaces more than frantic ones.

When that friend shows up on the front porch asking for a place to stay, so many immediate concerns blast their way into awareness: do we have the space for another person? What might this mean for my tenuous marriage? My friend says it is for a few weeks, but what if she wants to stay longer? What financial implications will this have? In moments such as these it is incredibly difficult to gain elevated insight.

Most days, this challenge of immediacy shows up in smaller ways. Today's housing market in many areas requires a sort of frantic decision if one is to buy a new home. The house is listed on Tuesday and by Wednesday there may be seven offers, some of them well above market value. If one is to enter into such a market, there is no choice other than immediacy, but it also calls for a long, reflective consideration that just is not possible.

In noticing the immediacy of our world, we glimpse the inner struggle for transcendence. It is the same tension we face with our friend on the front porch, and that Max faced in psychotherapy. This is the dissonance facing us most days, and one of the reasons why wisdom is difficult.

Perfection

In scrambling toward the top of the heap, we face internal and external pressures to be perfect. The world of vertical individualism can be quite unforgiving and relentless, always calling us to be better, more productive, optimized in every way. Perfection is a double-edged sword. On the one hand, it presses us toward possibility and fullness, allowing us to meet our goals and improve the world. On the other hand, the notion wields power, making us vulnerable to great evils in the name of perfection, such as Nazis trying to take over Europe because they perceived the Aryan race to be the most perfect. In a metrics-dominated world, it is tempting to pursue perfection without seeing its complexity. Perfection is 5-stars, countless likes, abundant sales. Perfection means a pay raise, and anything short of perfection means demotion. Transcendence is also a call to perfection, but of a different sort.

Transcendence represents the highest ideals. It challenges us to pursue and follow paths to fullness, toward the *telos* discussed earlier. While this can lead to shame as we lament our inability to live up to lofty ideals, transcendence brings contact with that which is beyond. The more we taste of that something beyond the more we hunger for it. None of us plays the electric guitar like Jimi Hendrix, but in listening to his music countless musicians have been inspired to emulate his style, which has lead to degrees of perfection in his musical spirit as people press toward the fulness of what is possible.

We easily lose touch with both our value and our values; consequently, we play by the rules of others, acquiescing to their hierarchical rating systems and metrics. Achievements become slavish pursuits of cultural tokens. Touching transcendence breaks us out of this mold, allowing us to move toward completeness in relation to our unique gifts, passions, and abilities. At the same time, transcendence helps us see unity and interconnectedness among all humanity, meaning that perfection can never be accomplished by elevating one person at the cost of another.

Hatred

Hatred is such a strong word. We hesitate using it, except that it must be used if we are to understand the underbelly of vertical individualism in our day. Sixty-five years ago, Thomas Merton—a Trappist monk, mystic, poet, and author—warned of a hatred that eats away at society: "No amount of technological progress will cure the hatred that eats away the vitals of materialistic society like a spiritual cancer" (Merton, 1956, p. xii). We still have that cancer, maybe more than ever. According to the Federal Bureau of Investigation's most recent hate crime report (n.d.), we now have more hate crimes than any year since 2008—the year an African-American man was elected president of the United States. Hate crimes against Asian-Americans has surged 164% in the year we are writing this book (Center for Study of Hate & Extremism, 2021).

In vertical individualism we tend to compare ourselves with one another rather than viewing one another as equals, which is more characteristic of horizontal cultures. Vertical perspectives fuel our competitiveness, foster hatred, and hinder our interconnectedness with one another.

From time to time, we encounter a prophetic voice that calls us toward egalitarian views, toward the transcendent, but these voices are hard to hear amidst the clamor of hatred. Consider the work of Dr. Martin Luther King Jr. and his perilous pursuit of racial justice and equality. He had the transcendent wisdom to see the promised land even when the mountaintop was obscured by the ignorance of others and continual oppression. But while standing outside his Memphis motel room in early April of 1968, a shot of hatred rang out that stole a life and the hope of millions of people. It sometimes seems we will never recover from that day, yet we cling to Dr. King's words, steeped in a transcendent understanding of interconnectedness:

> Darkness cannot drive out darkness; only light can do that. Hate cannot drive out hate; only love can do that. Hate multiplies hate, violence multiplies violence, and toughness multiples toughness in a descending spiral of destruction. (King, 1963, p. 47)

Referring to the cancer of hatred, Merton (1956) goes on to say that the only possible cure is spiritual. Transcendence—seeing above the clamor and the hatred—is a spiritual task, and an exceedingly difficult one.

SOME PARTING REFLECTIONS ON IMMEASURABILITY

Perhaps we have been too hard on metrics in this chapter. They are here to stay, and there is some good that comes from measuring things precisely. Still, for the purposes of wisdom, there is also good in that which is immeasurable and transcendent.

The *Oxford English Dictionary* defines transcendence as "existence or experience beyond the normal or physical level." With it we step outside the measurability of the empirical world and sense a level of existence that requires a new lens of perception. Existential psychologist Emmy Van Deurzen notes how transcendence allows us "to shoot deeper roots into what we have understood and reach out further than we ever thought possible" (2015, p. 218). This allows us to expand our worldview, to soar "into the full flight of human existence" with a new sort of freedom (p. 218).

To comprehend transcendence solely with measurability or logic is impossible. Words themselves are inadequate. Try describing why you love your husband, wife, or closest friend or what it felt like when you lost a parent or the moment your first child was born. You may be able to capture some of the sentiment, but ultimately your description will fall short of its full meaning and significance. Lived experiences such as these cannot be fully described, let alone quantified. If it is difficult to capture these moments, how much more difficult are experiences of heightened transcendence, those hinge events where the natural world becomes enlivened by contact with the Transcendent Other.

Thomas Aquinas wrote volumes of some of the most important scholarly works of his time. He reportedly had a powerful encounter with the transcendent, a rapturous mystical experience near the end of his life which led him to put his pen down and never write again, even leaving his greatest work unfinished. When questioned by his friend Brother Reginald, "Master, will you not return to your work?" Aquinas stated, "I can write no more. All that I have written seems like straw" (Graves, n.d.). What did Aquinas see that rendered him so dismissive of his life's work and incapable of writing? Perhaps the patron saint of academics and universities touched something beyond scholastic analysis and words.

When intellectual pursuits have ended and the light of knowledge has been extinguished, next comes a move into darkness. This tradition is distinctly emphasized in Eastern forms of Christianity, as in the Orthodox Church. For example, Gregory of Nyssa, the fourth-century mystic, writes about the "luminous darkness," the penetration of the ineffable and infinite. As one moves closer to the mind of the divine, "this is the seeing that consists in not seeing, because that which is sought transcends all knowledge, being separated on all sides by incomprehensibility as by a kind of darkness" (Gregory, 2006, p., 80). This unknowing, sometimes called apophatic theology, shows our intellectual limitations when approaching the transcendent. Without a tranquil mind, which can bring forth elevated insight, the jewels of apophatic knowledge—that is, knowledge gained through negation—go unnoticed.

CHAPTER 12

THE FOURTH DIMENSION

If the title of this chapter makes it seem we will be ending the book with a compelling science fiction story, well, we may disappoint you. We are referring back a couple chapters when wisdom scholars suggested four dimensions to how transcendence may relate to elevated insight (Aldwin et al., 2019). We have told you three of them already—interconnectedness, meaning and purpose, and emotional transcendence—then promised to reveal the fourth dimension in this final chapter. Here it is: *development* of transcendence. Some people seem able to grow in transcendence and wisdom, while others struggle. What makes the difference?

Shanice spent months in anguish after a divorce she did not want. As her appetite and sleep waned, she spiraled downward into depression, intense anger, and hopelessness for her bleak-looking future. She worried incessantly about her three small children, her financial security, and her prospects for future happiness. The Christian faith of her childhood lost its luster and could not answer the big questions she faced, and she slipped ever further into helplessness as a result. Psychotherapy helped, but not as much as she hoped.

After a long season of grief, Shanice determined that the time of downward spiraling needed to stop. She invested herself fully into a new career and found renewed joy and confidence in her professional abilities. This gave her some social confidence also, and she started spending more time with friends as the spiral started to change direction from downward to upward. Loving her children and receiving support from her extended family became a place of deep meaning and refuge. Though she could not return to her religious home of Christianity, she began exploring spiritual practices that would help her find peace and wholeness, and move toward forgiving her former spouse. Each morning as part of her loving-kindness meditation she would hold Keon lovingly in her heart, wishing him goodness and peace. Several years removed from the divorce, after a long journey of forgiveness, she felt like a new person, whole and growing, in touch again with the mystery and goodness of life.

For every story like Shanice's, there are other stories of those who do not fully recover from such a trauma. After his unwanted divorce, Michael spiraled downward into cynicism, despair, and addiction. Seeking to find comfort for his immense pain, he made choices that ultimately made his pain worse, sinking further and further until he hit bottom and landed in a recovery program. So what makes the difference? Why does one person develop transcendence in the aftermath of pain and trauma while another sinks into a downward spiral?

TRAIT OR STATE?

Earlier, in the introduction, we explored the question of whether wisdom is a trait built into our personality (the *essentialist* view) or a state that can be learned and applied in specific situations (the *constructivist* view). As you may recall, the evidence suggests both are true. A similar question can be asked about transcendence. Is the ability to step outside ourselves and see a larger perspective something baked into some people's personality, and not so much for others, or is it something we learn with practice? Once again, the answer seems to be both.

The trait argument comes from research on personality styles. One of the most widely researched models of personality in the past few decades is The Five-Factor Model, sometimes called The Big Five (Costa & McRae, 1992). According to this model, the basic five components of personality are openness, conscientiousness, extraversion, agreeableness, and neuroticism. The Big Five is ubiquitous—a quick internet search will reveal many free online assessment tools. But what if there are six components of personality instead of five?

Psychologist Ralph Piedmont (1999) provided fascinating evidence for spiritual transcendence as a sixth domain of personality. This raises the possibility that some people are naturally inclined toward stepping outside of self-interest and taking a bird's-eye view as part of their heritable personality composition, just as some people are shyer and some are more naturally bold. If you are sitting with a group of friends and discussing a controversial topic, it is likely that one or two people in the group will naturally take this view-from-above posture, trying to help others consider multiple perspectives and different nuances. These friends are the ones with the personality trait of spiritual transcendence, and it is good to have them in the conversation because they help everyone else learn to move above self-interest also.

The trait part of transcendence is more or less a given. Some have it more than others. Period. The state part gives the rest of us hope, because if transcendence can be developed then we can change over time, just as an introvert can develop excellent social skills. In fact, it is quite natural to learn transcendence as we develop and grow through life, assuming a relatively healthy level of love and nurturing during one's formative years. At the beginning of life, an infant is self-interested, captured by bodily needs and the nurturance of caregivers, but as we grow, we naturally learn to move beyond caring for ourselves to considering others and the social contexts and quandaries that define human existence. As Shanice was determined to heal and bring more positivity into her world, so almost all of us can walk this path if we build particular patterns into our lives. The pathways toward transcendence have varied throughout time and cultures, although they typically involve effort, emotional expression and restraint, openness to experiential ways of being in the world (e.g., music, dance, meditation), stretching beyond one's natural limits, and religion or spirituality.

AN INDIRECT PURSUIT?

Recall the *hedonia/eudaemonia* distinction we made in Chapter 9—if we pursue happiness directly, it may be elusive, but if we pursue a life filled with virtue and meaning, then happiness often shows up. Similarly, with transcendence, it may show up when we do not seek it directly. Aldwin and her colleagues (2019) describe how a group of Benedictine nuns were somewhat amused when asked how they developed humility and love, because these were not direct pursuits but rather consequences of their lifelong focus of developing a meaningful relationship with God. They did this in three ways: by quieting themselves and opening their hearts to see how God is active in their lives, by being open and respectful toward others as they lived in community with others, and by confronting personal struggles and working toward the goals they perceived God had for them. These religious sisters did not take their vows in order to become more virtuous or transcendent, but those things naturally resulted from a life of discernment, listening, and intentional effort.

What about those who are not religious? A similar principle may be in effect. Abraham Maslow, the father of humanistic psychology, whose hierarchy of needs is still the standard model for psychological growth leading towards self-actualization, writes that "when we are well and healthy and adequately fulfilling the concept of 'human being,' then experiences of transcendence should in principle be commonplace" (1970, p. 32). Just as pests attack the weakest plants in the garden, so those furthest from the aspiration of self-actualization are most vulnerable to conflict, sectarian warfare, and the urge to dehumanize political and ideological opponents. With psychological growth comes deeper connections amongst people and all forms of life as we begin seeing that we are not all that different beneath our social identities.

Organic farmers know the main thing they grow is good soil; the crops are secondary. Similarly, the flourishing life fosters transcendence by creating an openness and broadened awareness of life in all its beauty, abundance, and goodness. How we create healthy soil for transcendence varies from one person to another. Some find centering prayer to be profound. Others walk in the woods. Some go surfing or star-gazing or bird-watching. Mindfulness meditation is important to millions, sometimes in conjunction with yoga. Many find connection with a faith community to be essential. Liturgy and worship foster transcendence for many. Others find God in the garden. The list is nearly endless, and our job is not to rank-order or critique these choices, but simply to observe that the common denominator is some sort of regular practice that helps us move beyond self-focus and gain a sense of connection with something larger. This larger connection, in turn, allows us to embody wisdom as we gain enlivened awareness, gratitude, and connection with humanity and nature.

The indirect path to transcendence begins with being fully alive, growing and flourishing, attentive to the numinous outside of ourselves. Transcendence shows up as a by-product of these pursuits. Shanice did not set out to become transcendent, she simply wanted to recover from her pain and grow toward being a whole person. In the process she found loving connections with her children, extended family, and friends; she found new confidence and competence in her work; she engaged in some new spiritual practices to help ground her and give her hope; and she worked toward forgiving her former partner. Transcendence and wisdom came naturally as Shanice learned to live more fully.

THE REFLECTIVE GAZE

Historically, transcendent awakenings have been associated with religious and spiritual practices, often coming from the reflective, contemplative traditions of major world religions. In his classic book, *Celebration of Discipline*, Quaker contemplative Richard Foster (1978) describes practices such as meditation, fasting, simplicity, service, confession, and worship. Elsewhere, in discussing prayer, Foster (1992) uses a winsome typology of outward, inward, and upward forms of prayer. Though we will not limit our discussion to spiritual practices, we are drawn to Foster's three directions and will borrow them to think about how we open ourselves to transcendence through deliberate reflection.

Outward Gaze

Scientists at Oregon State University recently published interesting findings on how people develop wisdom in the aftermath of difficult life events (Igarashi et al., 2018). Like Shanice, most people interviewed for the study had had life-turning painful moments that shook them to the core. These difficult experiences made people question their competence and value in a complex world, and the disruption was so big that prior ways of making sense of the world no longer worked. Strikingly, every person in the study who reported a life-altering event also described the importance of social interactions in reconstructing a sense of meaning. Friends rallied around them, or they found people who had gone through similar difficult life events; they sought expert advice, or they found some other way to gain social support. These social transactions helped participants get to know themselves better while also experiencing a sense of compassion and connection from others. Later, having experienced compassion from others, participants were able to show kindness and compassion toward others as well. Some of those interviewed described other ways they grew in wisdom as a result of these social interactions, including becoming more comfortable with uncertainty and accepting the complexity of life. It seems that wisdom often develops in this order:

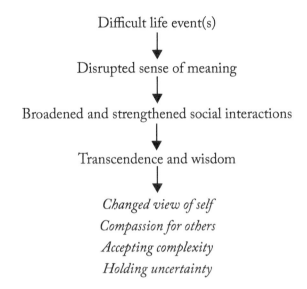

Difficult life event(s)

Disrupted sense of meaning

Broadened and strengthened social interactions

Transcendence and wisdom

Changed view of self
Compassion for others
Accepting complexity
Holding uncertainty

If we pause and consider this process, it makes sense. Living inside our self-bubbles does not promote either transcendence or wisdom, but as we are able to step outside of ourselves, to interact with, and learn from, others, to experience their care and compassion, we start gaining a larger view of interconnectedness with one another. Our horizons expand, the world around us takes on more complexity and nuance, and we grow in wisdom. It is worth remembering that all major religions occur in communities of faith. In the best cases, these social enclaves provide an ideal space for growing in wisdom and transcendence when life gets difficult (Aldwin & Levenson, 2019).

Loving-kindness meditation, described in Chapter 9, is another example of an outward gaze that promotes transcendence. It begins inwardly, as does most meditation, but then it moves outward as the meditator brings to mind another person and then holds that person in compassion and love.

Inward Gaze

If transcendence involves getting outside the self to see broader perspectives, it seems paradoxical to suggest this can be done with a more intent inward gaze, but some say the language of poetry and paradox is best for describing transcendent states. Carl Jung, for example, wrote that "paradox is a characteristic of all transcendent situations because it alone gives adequate expression to their indescribable nature" (1978, p. 70). Contemplative reflection, psychotherapy, and mindfulness meditation are all examples of seeking transcendence by looking inward. An inward gaze can transform and change a person, often spilling over onto others and moving toward essential outward action.

The contemplative and mystical traditions in religion involve a fair amount of looking inward, but not for the sake of becoming preoccupied with the self. To the contrary, this is a humble gaze inward with the goal of learning how we trip ourselves up. A classic example of this is the Daily Examen, a Christian practice described in Chapter 6. This sort of honest inward gaze assumes the most troubling facets of our personalities are the ones we do not look at or do not even know about because we have covered them with layers of defense and denial. By confronting our motives and desires we become available for an enhanced encounter with reality. Through repeated practice, contemplatives boldly confront their hidden shadows so they can bring what has been hidden into the light. This steady gaze inward is for the sake of ultimately seeing beyond the self and connecting more fully with the transcendent.

The first time I (Paul) attended a Buddhist temple, I happened to find myself in attendance of a rather well-known traveling monk. He was leading the evening service, an introduction into basic Buddhist concepts and practices. He spoke softly and with a well-measured cadence as he described the concept of "muddy-mind." This term struck a chord with me. This may have been the first time I thought about the mind as more than the place where thoughts live rather than as the center of consciousness that influences feelings and behaviors. Muddy-mind seems a rather fitting term for the distorted and distracted mental space many of us occupy. And there is something impactful about naming our struggles. How can we find enough tranquility to cultivate transcendence with minds clouded by our own judgments and preconceived notions? After the lesson and a brief guided meditation, I left the temple that night in a relaxed and curious mood. During the following weeks, the presence of this monk remained with me. I slept soundly, thought more clearly, and felt profoundly calm. The afterglow of this encounter revealed to me the power of transcendence. Still to this day, when I feel overburdened and stressed, I hear the refrain of this soft-spoken monk and "muddy-mind" echoes in my head, drawing me back to myself and the inward gaze of transcendence.

Psychotherapy, religious or not, bears some similarities to what contemplatives do. In psychotherapy, it is often a matter of sifting through the stressors and trauma and defenses of life to find a deeper, more transcendent self. Jung even suggested that an image of God—transcendent and eternal—resided deep in the self (Corbett, 1996). The process of psychotherapy, as with certain contemplative practices, makes it possible to become increasingly aware of this deeper person, while also developing a language based on our own experiences to describe it.

Initially a Buddhist practice, mindfulness meditation has become so widespread and well-researched that it is difficult to locate it in any particular religion or tradition these days. The meditation involves intentionally attending to experiences in the present moment, noticing both internal and external cues, and holding the moment nonjudgmentally. Mindfulness promotes both hedonic and eudaemonic well-being, and it is closely linked to a number of practices in positive psychology (Ivtzan & Lomas, 2016). Many books and other resources are available on mindfulness and mindfulness meditation. While it does appear to be a helpful tool, mindfulness can be misused as a method of suppression. We can imagine a major corporation initiating a workshop on mindfulness to help the overworked and underpaid employees be more productive and less in touch with their underlying feelings of anger and resentment at their being poorly compensated and exploited. Or consider Wall Street brokers who might apply techniques, originally designed to promote detachment from materialistic desires, to now help reduce feelings such as guilt or anxiety related to possible ethical qualms about their priorities. If used as a form of self-numbing and pacification, mindfulness serves as a barrier to depth and limits the inward gaze.

Still, mindfulness meditation can be useful when used to attune one to inward realities and present experiences. It first involves becoming still, setting aside some time just to stop and notice, then working to be fully present to this moment. Try not to focus much on the past or the future, but just say present to the now. Notice the weight of your body on the chair or the grass, or the breeze in the air, or the hum of the air conditioner. Pay attention to what is happening right now. As your thoughts roll in— and they always will—just notice them, and then let them slip on through to the other side of your consciousness. There is no need to judge yourself for having thoughts, or to judge the thoughts themselves. Just let them move along, much as a boat floating down a river would enter and leave your visual field. Come back to the present moment, over and over, never judging yourself for being distracted. When you are ready, open your eyes and lift your gaze back to the next thing in your day.

In its Eastern origins, mindfulness was used in psychological and spiritual development to help people toward enlightenment or transcendence. The more it has been imported into the Western allopathic medical model, it has been used as a tool to remediate illness (Ivtzan, 2016) where it has been quite effective (Goldberg et al., 2021; Khoury et al., 2013; Zhang et al., 2020). To illustrate just how prominent mindfulness meditation is in the research literature, consider that the gold standard of health care research is called a randomized control trial (RCT). In particularly robust research areas, once enough RCTs are published, researchers sometimes publish what is called a meta-analysis, which aggregates and summarizes all the findings from the RCTs. In the case of mindfulness meditation, there have now been at least 83 meta-analyses, and some researchers recently published a compilation of 44 of the best ones, involving a total of 336 RCTs and over 30,000 participants (Goldberg et al., 2021). Mindfulness meditation has been applied to topics as diverse as weight loss, depression, psychosis, cancer, anxiety, pain management, substance abuse, and more. The findings are promising, with mindfulness-based interventions performing as well as or better than other evidence-based interventions for a variety of psychological problems. But keep in mind this is a somewhat tepid application of mindfulness when it comes to transcendence because in its original religious context, it is intended not just to reduce stress or remediate symptoms but to elevate people into a state of transcendence, wisdom, and flourishing.

Upward Gaze

We mentioned earlier Richard Foster's (1992) book on prayer, which he begins with this invitation:

> God . . . is inviting you—and me—to come home, to come home to where we belong, to come home to that for which we were created. His arms are stretched out wide to receive us. His heart is enlarged to take us in. (p. 1)

Foster explores various types of prayer in his book, including several that help us gaze upward toward the divine: prayers of adoration and rest, meditative prayer, contemplative prayer.

Prayer spans history and religions, calling people to move beyond their own vantage point and consider something bigger. Gandhi famously referred to prayer as the "longing of the heart," helping us recognize our weakness and release ourselves into the numinous. Muslims begin their prayers with *Allahu Akbar*—God is great. The weekday Jewish prayer *Da'at* is a prayer for knowledge and wisdom. Buddhist prayers, often written centuries ago, remind people to release self-strivings and turn toward the spiritual.

> Give me energy for my heart to turn to the spiritual.
> Give me energy for the spiritual to become a way.
> Give me energy for this way to dispel confusion.
> Give me energy for confusion to arise as wisdom.
>
> *(McLeod, 2020)*

Across religions and time we see prayer pointing us toward the transcendent, moving us outside of self-reliance and into the arms of someone or something bigger.

The Pew Research Center's 2014 Religious Landscape Study (n.d.) suggests that over half of Americans pray daily, including Catholics, Evangelicals, Mainline Protestants, Historically Black Protestants, Eastern Orthodox, Hindus, and Muslims. The health benefits of prayer are clearly documented (Tolson & Koenig, 2003), but as with mindfulness, the health benefits are only part of the story. Prayer also helps us move outside of our self-bubbled existence to see and connect with a mystical force outside of our own skin, and, in this, it promotes transcendence.

Cynthia Bourgeault is an Episcopal priest, mystic, teacher, and author who has become known for her work in centering prayer (e.g., Bourgeault, 2004), an ancient Christian practice that emphasizes deepening consciousness through attentive silence. This is a prayer of surrender, letting go of thoughts as they enter the mind and the need to control the circumstances of life. Her welcoming practice is a derivative of centering prayer, and we will describe it in a moment. But first, it seems important to consider another dimension of gazing upward—one that demands attention, even when we do not welcome it.

Pain. We have our metaphors about whether it shows up in the butt or in the neck, but if we live long enough, it always shows up somewhere. Pain is part of life, and as we explored in Chapter 5, it gets right up in our face, demanding our attention and focus. Sometimes it can be alleviated—with counseling or ibuprofen or chemotherapy or any number of other solutions—but sometimes it cannot. There is no escape, no way to avoid or prevent the pain. This is what Carmelite theologian Constance Fitzgerald (1984) calls an impasse experience, noting that these experiences "cry out for meaning" (p. 93). For some, impasse is where the story ends. Life becomes a chronic struggle with disappointment and dysphoria. But somehow others are able to detach a bit (remember Chapter 6), and even to allow pain to transform and move them toward new possibilities, to gain some upward transcendent gaze outside of themselves.

For Shanice, the pain of losing her marriage felt intense and disorienting for several years, and then somehow she moved up out of it to gain a larger view. It is not that her pain went away entirely, but she learned to view it from above and to temper it with hope and social connectedness and spirituality. She learned to hold her pain with wisdom rather than allowing pain to grasp and evict her soul. When people learn to step outside pain, to transcend it and view life from above, we ought to celebrate such a thing because it may be one of the most difficult journeys of all.

Bourgeault's welcoming practice is a way to surrender ourselves to the transcendent in the midst of whatever life is bringing us. This is not passive acquiescence, but active surrender. It occurs in four steps (Contemplative Society, n. d.).

The first step is to sink in and feel the feeling. Let it wash over you. Where does it show up in your body? What emotions do you feel? Don't hold judgment about your feelings. Just feel.

Second, rather than pushing away what we are feeling, we actively welcome it. "Welcome, sadness." "Welcome, frustration." "Welcome, disappointment." "Welcome."

The third step is reminiscent of the 1970s Beatles hit, "Let it Be." Surrender any demands that things be fixed. Give up what we want or need. Those familiar with 12-step programs might say, "Let go, and let God." Experiencing God is the important thing here, not fixing any problem.

Fourth, we recognize the presence of the divine within us and embrace the fulness of the moment, including all of what we experience and bring to it. As we experience inner wholeness and transformation, we are then better prepared to deal with the situations we face moving forward. Sometimes we accept those situations, and sometimes we resist them, but in either case we approach the situation with a keen awareness that we are buoyed and connected to—and strengthened by—the divine.

We have offered examples of awakenings, ordering them as gazing outward, inward, and upward, but, again, this is a highly individualized matter. What brings some people to a place of transcendence seems weird and ineffective to others. Keep in mind the bigger point: for wisdom to flourish we need to find ways to get outside of our own self-bubble, to see things from a larger perspective, to recognize how interconnected we all are in our shared humanity, to claim and reclaim the values and meaning that propel us forward in a complicated world, and to immerse ourselves in transcendent emotions of joy, compassion, love, and awe. While there is a wisdom eclipse in our day, like the sun as the moon blocks its light to earth, we still see a glimmer of its radiance that we know and trust is ever-present. With upward gaze we long and hope for increased brightness that illuminates all around us.

JOURNEYING TOWARD WISDOM

We began this book with a metaphor of ideological fortresses where we hide away with like-minded people who reinforce how correct we are and how misinformed others are. It may feel like a safe place, but it is not. Dividing into competing fortresses is fueling deep division in our world, mass ignorance, vitriol, bitter anger, and violence. This is no way to live, at least not if we hold any hope of a harmonious world for the generations to come.

This is a time for wisdom—a time to wave our surrender flags, because even if we are not wrong we are not entirely right, either. Now is the time to emerge from our fortresses and discover our neighbors, to sit at a common table, share good food, and truly listen to one another. As we do this, we will gain important knowledge—things we could not have known because our data-driven world has shielded us by selective news feeds and custom advertisements. We will learn to stand at some greater distance, detach a bit from our passions and our pain to hold multiple perspectives and consider how others may know more than we think. With time, we will find tranquility, a shift of equilibrium as we move from that narcissistic dragon of self-inflated overconfidence toward a place of humility and compassion. Then maybe, if we have good fortune, we will begin seeing something bigger than ourselves, some benevolent presence of love in the cosmos that holds us together and calls us forward in wisdom.

Acknowledgments

This is a book about wisdom, yet we claim no special personal privilege of this virtue. As sojourners we have found the pursuit, and not necessarily the possession, of wisdom worthy and rewarding. Both of us have so many who have taught us along the path that we could never name them all. I (Paul) would like to thank Carl Fabrizio Jr., Kurt Free, Melvin E. Miller, and Nancy Thurston for their positive influence and encouragement during my clinically formative years. To Mark, I am ever grateful for your guidance, humility, and support, and in our shared quest over the past decade. I (Mark) am grateful to Lisa McMinn, Jeff Crosby, and Clark Campbell for your enduring and formative influence in my life over many years. And Paul, what a joy it has been to witness your transition from being a student to being a friend. Thank you for inviting me along on this book project, which has been a delight.

We offer our appreciation to the team at Templeton Press for believing in this project and making it strong. Susan Arellano, publisher, encouraged us to refine the project along the way, with a keen eye for keeping things relevant and current. Angelina Horst provided excellent conceptual guidance as well as a helpful critique of the first draft. Trish Vergilio (production) and Dan Reilly (marketing) helped bring our words into vibrant living color.

Finally, we acknowledge the pursuit of wisdom throughout the centuries. We are grateful to the scholars, sages, scientists, and researchers of various disciplines who have guided cultures and societies through difficult times before, and whose work and legacy help guide us still.

Appendix

The definition of wisdom we offer in the introduction is our attempt at distilling the essence of the various definitions we have discovered in our years of academic endeavors, including religion, philosophy, and psychology. Writing as two clinical psychologists, we focus on the psychological, emotional, and relational dimensions of wisdom. Yet we think it both unfair and unwise to exclude the time-honored and sage traditions of the world. The following table shows some of the definitions emerging from science and approaches to wisdom housed in the humanities and how our definition is connected to each.

PREVIOUS UNDERSTANDINGS OF WISDOM

Science of Wisdom		
Scientist(s)	Definition	How This Relates to Our Definition
Ardelt et al. (2019)	Wisdom is a personality type.	Wisdom is embodied in a person. It is a disposition that can be learned and formed.
Baltes & Staudinger (2000)	Expert knowledge in the fundamental pragmatics of life.	Wisdom includes purifying knowledge, which has practical implications for how we live. Knowledge of what is most essential.
Bangen et al. (2013)	Knowledge of life, prosocial values, self-understanding, acknowledgement of uncertainty, emotional homeostasis, tolerance, openness, spirituality, and a sense of humor.	Knowledge and spirituality are part of our definition too. Prosocial values, tolerance, and openness are part of elevated insight. Purgation and purification of knowledge include self-knowledge and acknowledging uncertainty. Emotional homeostasis as tranquility.

(continued)

Science of Wisdom

Scientist(s)	Definition	How This Relates to Our Definition
Glück et al. (2019)	MORE: Mastery, openness, reflectivity, and emotional regulation (including empathy).	Mastery involves recognizing life's unpredictability while also having confidence in one's ability to cope. Openness and reflectivity are part of elevated insight. Emotional regulation is included in tranquility.
Grossmann et al. (2020)	Morally grounded excellence in social-cognitive processing.	Morally grounded excellence is part of elevated insight. Social-cognitive processing is the purgation and purification of knowledge.
Peterson & Seligman (2004)	Knowledge hard fought for, and then used for good.	Purgation and purification of knowledge with practical implications. Elevated insight points toward the good.

History of Wisdom

Philosopher/ Sage	Focus	How This Relates to Our Definition
Socrates	Being aware of our ignorance on matters of virtue (epistemic humility).	Embodied disposition/act. Related to purgation and purification of knowledge.
Aristotle	Practical wisdom (how things can change) and theoretical wisdom (timeless truths).	Embodied disposition/act. Purgation and purification has practical implications. Self-transcendence opens the possibility of seeing time-honored principles.
Descartes	Wisdom comes from thorough rational knowledge and sound reason (scientific discourse).	Critical contemplation, purgation, and purification of knowledge in the ongoing pursuit of truth.
Buddha	Detachment from selfish desire and ego.	Purgation and purification of knowledge and tranquility are foundational to self-transcendence.
Laozi	Living in accord with nature and contemplative balance.	Tranquility is key as balanced emotions lead to insight into human nature and the hierarchy of values.
Jesus	Sacrificial love in the radical pursuit of truth, justice, and transcendence.	Self-transcendence and elevated insight lead beyond scientific forms of knowledge.

We are not trying to compete with other definitions, but rather to distill the insights offered by each. Of course our words fall short, because all definitions do, but this is our best effort to describe the ultimate goals for the KDTT model of wisdom that we outline in this book.

References

Adler, G., Jaffé, A., & Hull, R. F. C. (1973). *C. G. Jung Letters 1: 1906–1950*. London, UK: Taylor & Francis.

AFL-CIO (n.d.). Executive paywatch. Retrieved at https://aflcio.org/executive-paywatch

Aldwin, C. M., Igarashi, H., & Levenson, M. R. (2019). Wisdom as self-transcendence. In R. J. Sternberg & J. Glück (Eds.), *The Cambridge handbook of wisdom* (pp. 122–143). Cambridge, UK: Cambridge University Press.

Aldwin, C.M., & Levenson, M.R. (2019). The practical application of self-transcendent wisdom. In R. J. Sternberg, H. Nusbaum, & J. Glück (Eds.), *Applying wisdom to contemporary world problems* (pp. 293–307). Basel, Switzerland, AG: Springer International Publishing.

Aldwin, C. M., Levenson, M. R., & Kelly, L. (2009). Life span developmental perspectives on stress-related growth. In C. L. Park, S. C. Lechner, M. H. Antoni, & A. L. Stanton (Eds.), *Medical illness and positive life change: Can crisis lead to personal transformation?* (pp. 87–104). Washington, DC: American Psychological Association.

Allen, S. (2018). *The science of awe*. Berkeley, CA: Greater Good Science Center at UC Berkeley.

AllSides (n.d.). *Media bias ratings*. Retrieved at https://www.allsides.com/media-bias/media-bias-ratings

Andrew, S. (December 4, 2020). A Jewish doctor who treated a patient with Nazi tattoos says the pandemic has tested his compassion. Retrieved at https://www.cnn.com/2020/12/04/us/doctor-patient-swastika-tattoos-trnd/index.html#:~:text=(CNN)%20Dr.%20Taylor%20Nichols,compassion%20to%20do%20his%20job.&text=The%20patient's%20skin%20was%20covered,large%20swastika%20on%20his%20chest

Ardelt, M. (2000). Intellectual versus wisdom-related knowledge: The case for a different kind of learning in the later years of life. *Educational Gerontology, 26*(8), 771–789. https://doi.org/10.1080/036012700300001421

Ardelt, M. (2019). Wisdom and well-being. In R. J. Sternberg & J. Glück (Eds.), *The Cambridge handbook of wisdom* (pp. 602–625). Cambridge, UK: Cambridge University Press.

Ardelt, M., Pridgen, S., & Nutter-Pridgen, K. L. (2018). The relation between age and three-dimensional wisdom: variations by wisdom dimensions and education. *Journals of Gerontology: Psychological Sciences, 73*(8), 1339–1349.

Ardelt, M., Pridgen, S., & Nutter-Pridgen, K. L. (2019). Wisdom as personality type. In R. J. Sternberg & J. Glück (Eds.), *The Cambridge handbook of wisdom* (pp. 144–161). Cambridge, UK: Cambridge University Press.

Arterburn, S., & Felton, J. (2001). *Toxic faith: Experiencing healing from painful spiritual abuse* (1st Shaw ed.). Colorado Springs, CO. Shaw.

Baltes, P. B., & Staudinger, U. M. (2000). Wisdom: a metaheuristic (pragmatic) to orchestrate mind and virtue toward excellence. *American Psychologist, 55*(1), 122–136.

Baltes, P. B., Staudinger, U. M., Maercker, A., & Smith, J. (1995). People nominated as wise: A comparative study of wisdom-related knowledge. *Psychology and Aging, 10*(2), 155–166.

Bangen K. J., Meeks T. W., & Jeste D. V. (2013). Defining and assessing wisdom: A review of the literature. *American Journal of Geriatric Psychiatry, 21*(12), 1254–1266.

Barnard, J. (Ed.). (2015). *John Keats: Selected letters.* New York, NY: Penguin Classics.

Benner, D. G. (2014). *Presence and encounter.* Grand Rapids, MI: Brazos Press.

Berardino, M. (November 9, 2012). Mike Tyson explains one of his most famous quotes. Retrieved at https://www.sun-sentinel.com/sports/fl-xpm-2012-11-09-sfl-mike-tyson-explains-one-of-his-most-famous-quotes-20121109-story.html

Berenbaum, H., Huang, A. B., & Flores, L. E. (2019). Contentment and tranquility: Exploring their similarities and differences. *The Journal of Positive Psychology, 14*(2), 252–259. https://doi.org/10.1080/17439760.2018.1484938

Berry, W. (2002). *The art of the commonplace: The agrarian essays of Wendell Berry.* Berkeley, CA: Counterpoint.

Berry, W., Snyder, G., & Wriglesworth, C. (2014). *Distant neighbors: The selected letters of Wendell Berry and Gary Snyder.* Berkeley, CA. Counterpoint.

Bion, W. R. (1977). *Seven servants: Four works.* New York, NY: Jason Aronson, Inc.

Birren, J. E., & Fisher L. M. (1990). The elements of wisdom overview and integration. In R. J. Sternberg (Ed.), *Wisdom: Its nature, origins, and development.* Cambridge, UK: Cambridge University Press (pp. 317–332).

Blake, W., & Ostriker, A. (1791/1977). *The complete poems [of] William Blake.* New York, NY: Penguin.

Bourgeault, C. (2004). *Centering prayer and inner awakening.* New York, NY: Cowley Publications.

Brady, M. S. (2019). Why suffering is essential to wisdom. *The Journal of Value Inquiry, 53*, 467–549. Retrieved at https://doi.org/10.1007/s10790-019-09707-3

Brooks, D. (2015). *The road to character.* New York, NY: Random House.

Brown, B. (2015). *Rising strong: The reckoning. The rumble. The revolution.* New York, NY: Random House.

Brown, B. (March 27, 2018). Defining spirituality. Retrieved at https://brenebrown.com /blog/2018/03/27/defining-spirituality/#close-popup

Brueggemann, W. (2014). *Sabbath as resistance: Saying NO to the CULTURE OF NOW.* Louisville, KY: Westminster John Knox Press.

Center for Study of Hate & Extremism at California State University, San Bernardino. (2021). Report to the nation: Anti-Asian prejudice & hate crime. Retrieved at https:// www.csusb.edu/sites/default/files/Report%20to%20the%20Nation%20-%20Anti -Asian%20Hate%202020%20Final%20Draft%20-%20As%20of%20Apr%20 30%202021%206%20PM%20corrected.pdf

Chesterton, G. K. (1910/2007). *What's wrong with the world.* New York, NY: Dover Publications.

Chopik, W. J., & Grimm, K. J. (2019). Longitudinal and historic differences in narcissism from adolescence to older adulthood. *Psychology and Aging, 34*(8), 1109–1123.

Contemplative Society (n.d.). Welcoming practice. Retrieved at https://www .contemplative.org/contemplative-practice/welcoming-practice/

Corbett, L. (1996). *The religious function of the psyche.* New York, NY: Routledge.

Costa, P. T., Jr., & McCrae, R. R. (1992). *Revised NEO Personality Inventory: Professional manual.* Odessa, FL: Psychological Assessment Resources.

Cuddeback, J. A. (2013). Ordered inclinations. In R. Cessario, C. S. Titus, & P. C. Vitz (Eds.), *Philosophical virtues and psychological strengths* (pp. 61–80). Manchester, NH: Sophia Institute Press.

Day, D. (1963). *Loaves and fishes: The inspiring story of the Catholic Worker movement.* San Francisco, CA. Orbis Books.

de Botton, A. (July 27, 2009). A kinder, gentler philosophy of success. Ted talk. https:// www.ted.com/talks/alain_de_botton_a_kinder_gentler_philosophy_of_success ?language=en

Denny, F. M. (2006). *An introduction to Islam* (3rd ed.). Hoboken, NJ: Prentice Hall.

Dillon, J. (Ed.). (1991). *Plotinus: The Enneads.* New York, NY: Penguin Classics.

Domo (n.d.) Data never sleeps 5.0. Retrieved at https://www.domo.com/learn/data-never -sleeps-5?aid=ogsm072517_1&sf100871281=1

Duarte, F. (January 9, 2019). It takes a CEO just days to earn your annual wage. BBC Worklife. Retrieved at https://www.bbc.com/worklife/article/20190108-how-long -it-takes-a-ceo-to-earn-more-than-you-do-in-a-year

DuckDuckGo (December 4, 2018). Measuring the "filter bubble": How Google is influencing what you click. Retrieved at https://spreadprivacy.com/google-filter-bubble -study/

Eckhart, M. (2005). *Meister Eckhart: Selections from his essential writings.* New York, NY: Harper Collins.

Eliot, T. S. (1934). *The Rock.* New York, NY: Harcourt, Brace and Company.

Embree, A. T., Hay, S. N., & De Bary, W. T. (Eds.). (1988). *Sources of Indian tradition* (2nd ed.). New York, NY: Columbia University Press.

Emerson, R. W. (2006). The transcendentalist. In L. Buell (Ed.), *The American transcendentalists: Essential writings* (pp. 107–122). New York, NY: Modern Library.

Emmons, R. A., & McCullough, M. E. (2003). Counting blessings versus burdens: Experimental studies of gratitude and subjective well-being. *Journal of Personality and Social Psychology, 84*(2), 377–89.

Engel, G. (1977). The need for a new medical model: A challenge for biomedicine. *Science, 196*(4286), 129–136. http://dx.doi.org/10.1126/science.847460

Epley, N., & Dunning, D. (2000). Feeling "holier than thou": Are self-serving assessments produced by errors in self- or social prediction? *Journal of Personality and Social Psychology, 79*(6), 861–875.

Fatherly.com (December 22, 2017). The 2017 Imagination Report: What kids want to be when they group up. Retrieved at https://www.fatherly.com/health-science/what-kids-want-to-be-when-they-grow-up/

Federal Bureau of Investigation Uniform Crime Reporting (n.d.). 2019 hate crime statistics. Retrieved at https://ucr.fbi.gov/hate-crime/2019

Fitzgerald. C. (1984). Impasse and dark night. In T. H. Edwards (Ed.), *Living with apocalypse: Spiritual resources for social compassion* (pp. 93–116). New York, NY: HarperCollins Publishers.

Foster, R. J. (1978). *Celebration of discipline: The path to spiritual growth.* New York, NY: HarperCollins Publishers.

Foster, R. J. (1992). *Prayer: Finding the heart's true home.* New York, NY: HarperCollins Publishers.

Frankl, V. E. (1959). *Man's search for meaning.* Boston, MA: Beacon Press.

Frankovic, K. (February 15, 2021). Republicans used to call Ronald Reagan the best president in US history: Now it's Donald Trump. *YouGovAmerica.* Retrieved at https://today.yougov.com/topics/politics/articles-reports/2021/02/15/republicans-best-president-reagan-trump

Fredrickson, B. L. (2001). The role of positive emotions in positive psychology: The broaden-and-build theory of positive emotions. *The American Psychologist, 56*(3), 218–226.

Fredrickson, B. L. (2013). *Love 2.0: How our supreme emotion affects everything we feel, think, do, and become.* New York, NY: Penguin Group.

Fredrickson, B. L., Cohn, M. A., Coffey, K. A., Pek, J., & Finkel, S. M. (2008). Open hearts build lives: Positive emotions, induced through loving-kindness meditation, build consequential personal resources. *Journal of Personality and Social Psychology, 95*(5), 1045–1062.

Fredrickson, B. L., Tugade, M. M., Waugh, C. E., & Larken, G. R. (2003). What good are positive emotions in crisis? A prospective study of resilience and emotions following the terrorist attacks on the United States on September 11th, 2001. *Journal of Personality and Social Psychology, 84*(2), 365–376.

George, R. P., & West, C. (2017). *Sign the statement: Truth seeking, democracy, and freedom of thought and expression*—A statement by Robert P. George and Cornel West. https://jmp.princeton.edu/statement

Gilligan, C. (1982). *In a different voice: Psychological theory and women's development*. Cambridge, MA: Harvard University Press.

Glück, J. (2020). The important difference between psychologists' labs and real life: Evaluating the validity of models of wisdom. *Psychological Inquiry, 31*(2), 144–150.

Glück, J., & Bluck, S. (2011). Laypeople's conception of wisdom and its development: Cognitive and integrative views. *The Journals of Gerontology, Series B: Psychological Sciences and Social Science, 66*(3), 321–324.

Glück, J., & Bluck, S. (2013). The MORE Life Experience Model: A theory of the development of personal wisdom. In M. Ferrari, & N. M. Westrate (Eds.), *The scientific study of personal wisdom: From contemplative traditions to neuroscience* (pp. 75–97). Dordrecht, Netherlands: Springer.

Glück, J., Bluck, S., Baron, J., & McAdams, D. P. (2005). The wisdom of experience: Autobiographical narratives across adulthood. *International Journal of Behavioral Development, 29*(3), 197–208.

Glück, J., Bluck, S., & Westrate, N. M. (2019). More on the MORE Life Experience Model: What we have learned (so far). *The Journal of Value Inquiry, 53*, 349–370. https://doi.org/10.1007/s10790-018-9661-x

Goldberg, S. B., Riordan, K. M., Sun, S., & Davidson, R. J. (2021). The empirical status of mindfulness-based interventions: A systematic review of 44 meta-analyses of randomized controlled trials. *Perspectives on Psychological Science.* https://doi.org/10.1177/1745691620968771

Goldfield, A. (2014). The innate awareness of Buddhist wisdom. In R. N. Walsh (Ed.), *The world's great wisdom: Timeless teachings from religions and philosophies*. Albany, NY: SUNY Press.

Goleman, D. (1995). *Emotional intelligence*. New York, NY: Bantam Books.

Good News Network. (2021). https://www.goodnewsnetwork.org/

Good News Network, & Weis-Corbley, G. (2018). *And now, the good news: 20 years of inspiring news stories*. Santa Barbara, CA: Good News Network Publishing.

Good Project (n.d.). Value sort activity. https://www.thegoodproject.org/value-sort

Goodwin, D. K. (2005). *Team of rivals: The political genius of Abraham Lincoln* (1st Simon & Schuster pbk. ed.). New York, NY: Simon & Schuster.

Graves, D. (n.d.). I can write no more. All that I have written seems like straw. *Christian History Institute*. Retrieved at https://christianhistoryinstitute.org/incontext/article/aquinas

Green, B. P. (2012). Teleology and theology: The cognitive science of teleology and the Aristotelian virtues of Techne and Wisdom. *Theology and Science, 10*(3), 291–311.

Greene, J. (2013). *Moral tribes: Emotion, reason, and the gap between us and them*. New York, NY: Penguin.

Gregory of Nyssa. (2006). *The life of Moses* (1st ed.). New York, NY: HarperSanFrancisco.

Grossmann, I. (2017). Wisdom and how to cultivate it: Review of emerging evidence for a constructivist model of wise thinking. *European Psychologist, 22*(4), 233–246.

Grossmann, I., Karasawa, M., Izumi, S., Na, J., Varnum, M. E. W., Kitayama, S., & Nisbett, R. E. (2012). Aging and wisdom: Culture matters. *Psychological Science, 23*(10), 1059–1066.

Grossmann, I., Kung, F. Y. H., & Santos, H. C. (2019). In R. J. Sternberg & J. Glück (Eds.), *The Cambridge handbook of wisdom* (pp. 249–273). Cambridge, UK: Cambridge University Press.

Grossmann, I., Weststrate, N. M., Ardelt, M., Brienza, J. P., Dong, M., Ferrari, M., Fournier, M. A., Hu, C. S., Nusbaum, H. C., & Vervaeke, J. (2020). The science of wisdom in a polarized world: Knowns and unknowns. *Psychological Inquiry, 31*(2), 103–133.

Grubbs J. B., Exline J. J., McCain J., Campbell W. K., & Twenge J. M. (2019). Emerging adult reactions to labeling regarding age-group differences in narcissism and entitlement. *PLoS ONE 14*(5): e0215637.

Hadot, P. (1998). *Plotinus or the simplicity of vision*. Chicago, IL: University of Chicago Press. Originally published in 1963.

Haidt, J. (2013). *The righteous mind: Why good people are divided by politics and religion*. New York, NY: Vintage.

Hall, S. S. (2010). *Wisdom: From philosophy to neuroscience* (1st ed.). New York, NY: Alfred A. Knopf.

Hanh, T. N. (2015). *The heart of the Buddha's teaching: Transforming suffering into peace, joy, and liberation*. New York, NY: Harmony Books.

Hanh, T. N. (2020). Thich Nhat Hanh's health and updates. Plum Village. https://plumvillage.org/about/thich-nhat-hanh/thich-nhat-hanhs-health/

Hanson, R., & Mendius, R. (2009). *Buddha's brain: The practical neuroscience of happiness, love & wisdom*. Oakland, CA: New Harbinger Publications.

Harris, S. (2014). *Waking up: A guide to spirituality without religion* (First Simon & Schuster hardcover edition.). New York, NY: Simon & Schuster.

Harvey, P. (January 18, 2019). Howard Thurman: The Baptist minister who had a deep influence on MLK. The Conversation. https://theconversation.com/howard-thurman-the-baptist-minister-who-had-a-deep-influence-on-mlk-110132

Hayes, S. C., Strosahl, K. D., & Wilson, K. G. (2012). *Acceptance and commitment therapy: The process and practice of mindful change* (2nd ed.). New York, NY: Guilford.

Helliwell, J. F., Layard, R., Sachs, J. D., De Neve, J.-E., Aknin, L. B., & Wang, S. (2021). *World happiness report*. Retrieved at https://happiness-report.s3.amazonaws.com/2021/WHR+21.pdf

Huwe, M. (2018). Sustenance, for a healthy life. IMPROVECARENOW. Retrieved at https://www.improvecarenow.org/sustenance_for_a_healthy_life

Huwe, M. (2019). IGNITE—I choose to ask the hard questions. ImproveCareNow. Retrieved at https://www.improvecarenow.org/ignite_i_choose_to_ask_the_hard _questions

Huxley, A. (1945/2009). *The perennial philosophy* (1st Harper Perennial Modern classics ed.). New York, NY: Harper Perennial.

Huxley, A. (1954/2009). *The doors of perception: &, Heaven and hell* (1st Harper Perennial Modern Classics edition). New York, NY: Harper Perennial.

Hyrnowski, Z. (November 8, 2019). How many Americans believe in God? *Gallup News.* Retrieved at https://news.gallup.com/poll/268205/americans-believe-god .aspx

Igarashi, H., Levenson, M. R., & Aldwin, C. M. (2018). The development of wisdom: A social ecological approach. *The Journals of Gerontology. Series B, Psychological Sciences and Social Sciences, 73*(8), 1350–1358.

Ivtzan, I. (2016). Mindfulness in positive psychology: An introduction. In I. Ivtzan & T. Lomas (Eds.), *Mindfulness in positive psychology: The science of meditation and wellbeing* (pp. 1–12). New York, NY: Routledge.

Ivtzan, I., & Lomas, T. (Eds.). (2016). *Mindfulness in positive psychology: The science of meditation and wellbeing.* New York, NY: Routledge.

James, W. (1902). *The varieties of religious experience; A study in human nature; Being the Gifford lectures on natural religion delivered at Edinburgh in 1901–1902.* New York, NY: Modern Library.

Jaspers, K. (1951/2003). *Way to wisdom: An introduction to philosophy* (2nd ed.). New Haven, CT: Yale University Press.

Jeste, D. V., Ardelt, M., Blazer, D., Kraemer, H. C., Vaillant, G., & Meeks, T. W. (2010). Expert consensus on characteristics of wisdom: A Delphi method study. *The Gerontologist, 50*(5), 668–680.

Jeste, D. V., & Lee, E. E. (2019). The emerging empirical science of wisdom: Definition, measurement, neurobiology, longevity, and interventions. *Harvard Review of Psychiatry, 27*(3), 127–140. doi: 10.1097/HRP.0000000000000205

Jones, J. M. (March 29, 2021). U.S. church membership falls below majority for first time. *Gallup News.* Retrieved at https://news.gallup.com/poll/341963/church -membership-falls-below-majority-first-time.aspx

Jung, C. G. (1978). *Aion: Researches into the phenomenology of the self* (2nd ed.). Princeton, NJ: Princeton University Press.

Jurist, E. L. (2018). *Minding emotions: Cultivating mentalization in psychotherapy.* New York, NY: The Guilford Press.

Kahn, M. (2002). *Basic Freud: Psychoanalytic thought for the 21st century* (1st pbk. ed.). New York, NY: Basic Books.

Kasser, T. (2002). *The high price of materialism.* Cambridge, MA: MIT Press.

Kavanaugh, J. F. (2006). *Following Christ in a consumer society: The spirituality of cultural resistance* (25th anniversary ed.). Maryknoll, NY: Orbis Books.

Keltner, D. (May 11, 2016). Why do we feel awe? *Mindful*. Retrieved from http://www .mindful.org/why-do-we-feel-awe/

Keltner, D., & Haidt, J. (2003). Approaching awe, a moral, spiritual, and aesthetic emotion. *Cognition and Emotion, 17*(2), 297–314.

Khoury, B., Lecomte, T., Fortin, G., Masse, M., Therien, P., Bouchard, V., Chapleau, M., Paquin, K., & Hofmann, S. G. (2013). Mindfulness-based therapy: A comprehensive meta-analysis. *Clinical Psychology Review, 33*(6), 763–771.

King, M. L., Jr., (1963). *Strength to love*. Boston, MA: Beacon Press.

Kohlberg, L. (1984). *The psychology of moral development: Essays on moral development* (Vol. 2). New York, NY: Harper & Row.

Kondo, M. (2014). *The life-changing magic of tidying up*. Berkeley, CA: Ten Speed Press.

Korte, G. (January 18, 2021). Trump will end his historically unpopular presidency with lowest approval ever. *Fortune*. Retrieved at https://fortune.com/2021/01/18/trump -approval-rating-average-popularity/

Krause, N., & Hayward, R. D. (2015). Assessing whether practical wisdom and awe of God are associated with life satisfaction. *Psychology of Religion and Spirituality, 7*(1), 51–59.

Krumrei-Mancuso, E. J., Haggard, M. C., LaBouff, J. P., & Rowatt, W. C. (2020). Links between intellectual humility and acquiring knowledge. *The Journal of Positive Psychology, 15*(2), 155–170.

Kunzmann, U., & Glück, J. (2019). Wisdom and emotion. In R. J. Sternberg & J. Glück (Eds.), *The Cambridge handbook of wisdom* (pp. 182–201). Cambridge, UK: Cambridge University Press.

Le, T. N., & Levenson, M. R. (2005). Wisdom as self-transcendence: What's love (& individualism) got to do with it? *Journal of Research in Personality, 39*(4), 443–457.

Lee, E. E., & Jeste, D. V. (2019). Neurobiology of wisdom. In R. J. Sternberg & J. Glück (Eds.), *The Cambridge handbook of wisdom* (pp. 69–93). Cambridge, UK: Cambridge University Press.

Leeuw, M., Goossens, M. E. J. B., Linton, S. J., Crombez, G., Boersma, K., & Vlaeyen, J. W. S. (2006). The fear avoidance model of musculoskeletal pain: Current state of scientific evidence. *Journal of Behavioral Medicine, 30*(1), 77–94.

Lehrer, J. (January 31, 2017). Attachment. *The Moth*. Retrieved at https://themoth.org /storytellers/jonah-lehrer

Lim, K. T. K., & Yu, R. (2015). Aging and wisdom: Age-related changes in economic and social decision making. *Frontiers in Aging Neuroscience, 7*(120). doi: 10.3389 /fnagi.2015.00120

Lombardo, N. E. (2011). *The logic of desire: Aquinas on emotion*. Washington, DC: Catholic University of America Press.

Lubac, H. de. (1987). *Paradoxes of faith*. San Francisco, CA. Ignatius Press.

Manney, J. (2011). *A simple life-changing prayer: Discovering the power of St. Ignatius Loyola's Examen*. Chicago, IL: Loyola Press.

Maslow, A. H. (1970). *Religions, values, and peak-experiences.* New York, NY: Viking Press.

McLaughlin, P. T., McMinn, M. R., Morse, M., Neff, M. A., Johnson, B., Summerer, D., & Koskela, N. (2018). The effects of a wisdom intervention in a Christian congregation. *Journal of Positive Psychology, 13*(5), 502–511.

McLeod, K. (Summer, 2020). Say a little prayer. *Tricycle: The Buddhist Review.* Retrieved at https://tricycle.org/magazine/buddhist-prayer/

McMinn, M. (November 23, 2017). The generous soul: Why overcoming the Scrooge in all of us begins with gratitude. *Christianity Today.* https://www.christianitytoday.com /ct/2017/november-web-only/generous-soul-overcoming-scrooge-gratitude.html

Merton, T. (1956). *Thoughts in solitude.* New York, NY: Farrar, Straus and Giroux.

Merton, T. (1961). *Thoughts in solitude: Meditations on the spiritual life and man's solitude before God.* New York, NY: Dell Publishing Co., Inc.

Merton, T. (1969). *The way of Chuang Tzu.* New York, NY: New Directions.

minimalists. (n.d.). https://www.theminimalists.com/

Moon, H. G. (2019). Mindfulness of death as a tool for mortality salience induction with reference to terror management theory. *Religions* (Basel, Switzerland), *10*(6), 353. https://doi.org/10.3390/rel10060353

Moore, A. (March 10, 2020). On demand doctors: Are we becoming medical waiters? KevinMD.com. Retrieved at https://www.kevinmd.com/blog/2020/03/on-demand -doctors-are-we-becoming-medical-waiters.html

Moore, R. L., & Havlick, M. J. (2003). *Facing the dragon: Confronting personal and spiritual grandiosity.* Wilmette, IL: Chiron Publications.

Muller, J. Z. (2018). *The tyranny of metrics.* Princeton, NJ: Princeton University Press.

National Institute of Mental Health (n.d.). Mental illness. Retrieved at https://www .nimh.nih.gov/health/statistics/mental-illness.shtml#:~:text=Mental%20illnesses %20are%20common%20in,(51.5%20million%20in%202019)

Neff, M. A., & McMinn, M. R. (2020). *Embodying integration: A fresh look at Christianity in the therapy room.* Downers Grove, IL: IVP Academic.

Nerdbear. (2021). Get paid $1000 to watch James Bond movies. https://nerdbear.com /get-paid-1000-to-binge-watch-james-bond-movies/

Nguyen, J. H. (2018). *Apatheia in the Christian tradition: An ancient spirituality and its contemporary relevance.* Eugene, OR: Cascade Books.

Nouwen, H. (1981). *Making all things new: An introduction to the spiritual life.* New York, NY: Doubleday.

Oakes, H., Brienza, J. P., Enakouri, A., & Grossmann, I. (2019). Wise reasoning: Converging evidence for the psychology of sound judgment. In R. J. Sternberg & J. Glück (Eds.), *The Cambridge handbook of wisdom* (pp. 202–225). Cambridge, UK: Cambridge University Press.

Ogden, T. H. (2009). Bion's four principles of mental functioning. In T. H. Ogden (Ed.), *Rediscovering Psychoanalysis* (pp. 104–127). New York, NY: Routledge. https://doi .org/10.4324/9781315787428-12

Pasupathi, M., Staudinger, U. M., & Baltes, P. B. (2001). Seeds of wisdom: Adolescents' knowledge and judgment about difficult life problems. *Developmental Psychology, 37*(3), 351–361.

Pattison, J. (February 2, 2015). Sabbath as resistance: An interview with Walter Brueggemann. https://slowchurch.com/sabbath-resistance-interview-walter-brueggemann/

Peterson, C., & Seligman, M. E. P. (2004). *Character strengths and virtues: A handbook and classification.* Washington, DC: American Psychological Association; and New York, NY: Oxford University Press.

Peterson, J. B. (2018). *12 rules for life: An antidote to chaos.* Toronto: Random House Canada.

Pew Research Center Religious Landscape Study (n.d.). Frequency of prayer. Retrieved at https://www.pewforum.org/religious-landscape-study/frequency-of-prayer/

Piedmont, R. L. (1999). Does spirituality represent the sixth factor of personality? Spiritual transcendence and the Five-Factor Model. *Journal of Personality, 67*(6), 985–1013.

Piff, P. K., Dietze, P., Feinberg, M., Stancato, D. M., & Keltner, D. (2015). Awe, the small self, and prosocial behavior. *Journal of Personality and Social Psychology, 108*(6), 883–899.

Pinker, S. (2003). *The blank slate: The modern denial of human nature.* New York, NY: Penguin Books.

Pope Francis (2020). *Fratelli tutti: On fraternity and social friendship* [Encyclical letter]. Vatican City: Libreria Editrice Vaticana.

Ramos, A. (2012). *Dynamic transcendentals: Truth, goodness, and beauty from a Thomistic perspective.* Washington, DC: Catholic University of America Press.

Roberts, B. W., Edmonds, G., & Grijalva, E. (2010). It is developmental me, not generation me: Developmental changes are more important than generational changes in narcissism—Commentary on Trzesniewski & Donnellan (2010). *Perspectives on Psychological Science, 5,* 97–102.

Rohr, R. (January 6, 2020). Action and Contemplation: Part One. Retrieved on October 29, 2020 from https://cac.org/an-embarrassing-silence-2020-01-06/

Rolheiser, R. (2004). *The shattered lantern: Rediscovering a felt presence of God* (Rev. ed.). New York, NY: Crossroad Pub.

Ruane, K. A. (July 13, 2011). Fairness doctrine: History and constitutional issues. Congressional Research Service. Retrieved at https://fas.org/sgp/crs/misc/R40009.pdf

Ruisel, I. (2005). Wisdom's role in interactions of affects and cognition. *Studia Psychologica, 47,* 277–289.

Sacks, J. (2020). *Morality: Restoring the common good in divided times.* New York, NY: Basic Books.

Safi, O. (November 22, 2017). The wisdom of saying "I don't know." OnBeing. https://onbeing.org/blog/omid-safi-the-wisdom-of-saying-i-dont-know/

Salvanto, A., Khanna, K., Backus, F., & De Pinto, J. (January 17, 2021). Americans see democracy under threat—CBS news poll. Retrieved at https://www.cbsnews.com /news/joe-biden-coronavirus-opinion-poll/

Santos, H. C., Varnum, M. E. W., & Grossmann, I. (2017). Global increases in individualism. *Psychological Science, 28*(9), 1228–1230.

Schall, J. V. (2007). *The order of things.* San Francisco: Ignatius Press.

Senior, D. (1990). *The Catholic study Bible.* New York, NY: Oxford University Press.

Seppala, E. M., Hutcherson, C. A., Nguyen, D. T., Doty, J. R., & Gross, J. J. (2014). Loving-kindness meditation: A tool to improve healthcare provider compassion, resilience, and patient care. *Journal of Compassionate Health Care, 1*(5). DOI 10.1186 /s40639-014-0005-9

Shapiro, F. R. (April 28, 2014). Who wrote the Serenity Prayer? *The Chronicle of Higher Education.* https://www.chronicle.com/article/who-wrote-the-serenity-prayer/?bc _nonce=lm42b0k67ak9ha48g40fy&cid=reg_wall_signup

Siegel, D. J. (2012). *The developing mind: How relationships and the brain interact to shape who we are* (2nd ed.). New York, NY: Guilford Press.

Smith, C., & Davidson, H. (2014). *The paradox of generosity: Giving we receive, grasping we lose.* New York, NY: Oxford University Press.

Smith, J., Staudinger, U. M., & Baltes, P. B. (1994). Occupational settings facilitating wisdom-related knowledge: The sample case of clinical psychologists. *Journal of Consulting and Clinical Psychology, 62*(5), 989–999.

Snell, R. J. (2015). *Acedia and its discontents: Metaphysical boredom in an empire of desire.* Brooklyn, NY: Angelico Press.

Solzhenitsyn, A. (1978). *A world split apart.* Commencement address at Harvard University. Retrieved at https://www.solzhenitsyncenter.org/a-world-split-apart

Staudinger, U.M. (2019). The distinction between personal and general wisdom: How far have we come? In R. J. Sternberg & J. Glück (Eds.), *The Cambridge handbook of wisdom* (pp. 182–201). Cambridge, UK: Cambridge University Press.

Stefon, M. (December 30, 2018). Fairness doctrine. Encyclopedia Britannica. Retrieved at https://www.britannica.com/topic/Fairness-Doctrine

Stellar, J. E., John-Henderson, N., Anderson, C. L., Gordon, A. M., McNeil, G. D., & Keltner, D. (2015). Positive affect and markers of inflammation: Discrete positive emotions predict lower levels of inflammatory cytokines. *Emotion, 15*(2), 129–133.

Sternberg, R. J. (Ed.). (1990). *Wisdom: Its nature, origins, and development.* New York, NY: Cambridge University Press.

Sternberg, R. J. (2019). Race to Samara: The critical importance of wisdom in the world today. In R. J. Sternberg & J. Glück (Eds.), *The Cambridge handbook of wisdom* (pp. 3–9). Cambridge, UK: Cambridge University Press.

Sternberg, R. J., & Glück, J. (2019). Wisdom, morality, and ethics. In R. J. Sternberg & J. Glück (Eds.), *The Cambridge handbook of wisdom* (pp. 551–574). Cambridge, UK: Cambridge University Press.

Sternberg, R. J., & Glück, J. (Eds.). (2019). *The Cambridge handbook of wisdom*. Cambridge, UK: Cambridge University Press.

Sternberg, R. J., & Jordan, J. (Eds.). (2005). *A handbook of wisdom*. New York, NY: Cambridge University Press.

Sulmasy, D. (2002). A biopsychosocial-spiritual model for the care of patients at the end of life. *The Gerontologist*, *42*(suppl_3), 24–33. http://dx.doi.org/10.1093/geront/42.suppl_3.24

Svenson, O. (1981). Are we all less risky and more skillful than our fellow drivers? *Acta Psychologica*, *47*, 143–148.

Takahashi, M. (2019). Relationship between wisdom and spirituality. In R. J. Sternberg & J. Glück (Eds.), *The Cambridge handbook of wisdom* (pp. 626–646). Cambridge, UK: Cambridge University Press.

Taylor, C. (2007). *A secular age*. Cambridge, MA: Harvard University Press.

Tenzin Gyatso, Dalai Lama XIV, Tutu, D., & Abrams, D. (2016). *The book of joy: Lasting happiness in a changing world*. New York, NY: Penguin Random House.

Thomas à Kempis, (1998). *The imitation of Christ in four books* (J. Tylenda, Trans.). (Rev. ed.). New York, NY: Vintage Books. Originally published in 1580.

Thurman, H. (1953). *Meditations of the heart*. Boston, MA: Beacon Press.

Tippett, K. (July 25, 2013). David Gushee + Frances Kissling: Pro-Life, Pro-Choice, Pro-Dialog. *On Being with Krista Tippett*. Retrieved at https://onbeing.org/programs/david-gushee-frances-kissling-pro-life-pro-choice-pro-dialogue-2/

Tippett, K. (2017). *Becoming wise: An inquiry into the mystery and art of living*. New York, NY: Penguin Books.

Tolson, C. L., & Koenig, H. G. (2003). *The healing power of prayer: The surprising connection between prayer and your health*. Grand Rapids, MI: Baker Books.

Trammel, R. C. (2017). Tracing the roots of mindfulness: Transcendence in Buddhism and Christianity. *Journal of Religion & Spirituality in Social Work: Social Thought*, *36*(3), 367–383.

Triandis, H. C., & Gelfand M. J. (1998). Converging measurement of horizontal and vertical individualism and collectivism. *Journal of Personality and Social Psychology*, *74*(1), 118–128.

Tsang, J., Carpenter, T. P., Roberts, J. A., Frisch, M. B., & Carlisle, R. D. (2014). Why are materialists less happy? The role of gratitude and need satisfaction in the relationship between materialism and life satisfaction. *Personality and Individual Differences*, *64* (2014), 62–66.

Twenge, J. M., & Campbell, W. K. (2010). *The narcissism epidemic: Living in the age of entitlement*. New York, NY: Atria.

Underhill, E. (1990). *Mysticism: The preeminent study in the nature and development of spiritual consciousness* (1st ed.). New York, NY: Doubleday. Originally published in 1911.

United Nations (1948). Declaration of human rights. https://www.un.org/en/universal-declaration-human-rights/

Van Cappellen, P. (2017). Rethinking self-transcendent positive emotions and religion: Insights from psychological and biblical research. *Psychology of Religion and Spirituality, 9*(3), 254–263.

Van Deurzen, E. (2015). *Paradox and passion in psychotherapy: An existential approach* (2nd ed.). New York: John Wiley & Sons.

Vlaeyen, J. W., Crombez, G., & Linton, S. J. (2016). The fear-avoidance model of pain. *Pain, 157* (8), 1588–1589.

W., B., & Alcoholics Anonymous. (1976). *Alcoholics Anonymous: The story of how many thousands of men and women have recovered from alcoholism.* (3rd ed.). New York, NY: Alcoholics Anonymous World Services.

Wallace, L. E. (1999). *Dreams, hopes, realities: NASA's Goddard Space Flight Center—The first forty years.* Washington, DC: NASA History Office.

Wallin, D. J. (2007). *Attachment in psychotherapy.* New York, NY: Guilford Press.

Wayment, H. A., & Bauer, J. J. (Eds.). (2008). *Transcending self-interest: Psychological explorations of the quiet ego.* Washington, DC: American Psychological Association.

Webster, J. D. (2019). Self-report wisdom measures. In R. J. Sternberg & J. Glück (Eds.), *The Cambridge handbook of wisdom* (pp. 297–320). Cambridge, UK: Cambridge University Press.

Weeks, L. (May 28, 2015). The windshield-pitting mystery of 1954. NPR History Dept.: A fresh look at American history. Retrieved at https://www.npr.org/sections/npr -history-dept/2015/05/28/410085713/the-windshield-pitting-mystery-of-1954

Weil, S., & Leys, S. (1950/2013). *On the abolition of all political parties.* New York, NY: New York Review Books.

Westrate, N. M. (2019). The mirror of wisdom. In R. J. Sternberg & J. Glück (Eds.), *The Cambridge handbook of wisdom* (pp. 500–550). Cambridge, UK: Cambridge University Press.

Weststrate, N. M., Bluck, S., & Glück, J. (2019). Wisdom of the crowd: Exploring people's conceptions of wisdom. In R. J. Sternberg & J. Glück (Eds.), *The Cambridge handbook of wisdom* (pp. 97–121). Cambridge, UK: Cambridge University Press.

Wetzel, E., Grijalva, E., Robins, R. W., & Roberts, B. W. (2020). You're still so vain: Changes in narcissism from young adulthood to middle age. *Journal of Personality and Social Psychology, 119*(2), 479–496.

Whitehead, A. N. (1929). The rhythmic claims of freedom and discipline. In *The aims of education and other essays* (pp. 29–42). New York, NY: The Free Press.

Wilcox, B. L., Kunkel, D., Cantor, J., Dowrick, P., Linn, S., & Palmer, E. (2004). *Report of the APA Task Force on Advertising and Children.* Washington, DC: American Psychological Association.

Wood, A. M., Froh, J. J., & Geraghty, A. W. A. (2010). Gratitude and well-being: A review and theoretical integration. *Clinical Psychology Review 30*(7), 890–905.

Yang, S. (2013). Wisdom and good lives: A process perspective. *New Ideas in Psychology, 31*, 194–201.

Young, J. R. (May 24, 2018). Most professors think they're above-average teachers. And that's a problem. EdSurge. https://www.edsurge.com/news/2018-05-24-most -professors-think-they-re-above-average-teachers-and-that-s-a-problem#:~:text =A%20classic%20study%20found%20that,re%20in%20the%20top%20quarter .&text=Of%20course%20professors%20do%20get,of%20each%20term%2C%20 for%20instance

Zhang, Y., Xue, J., & Huang, Y. (2020). A meta-analysis: Internet mindfulness-based interventions for stress management in the general population, *Medicine*, *99*(28), e20493.

About the Authors

Paul T. McLaughlin, PsyD, graduated from the University of California, Santa Barbara, with a bachelor's degree in religious studies and a minor in philosophy. He received a master's degree in theology and Christian ministry from Franciscan University of Steubenville, Ohio, before obtaining a doctorate in clinical psychology from George Fox University in Newberg, Oregon.

Dr. McLaughlin has coauthored several published journal articles. His dissertation was published in the *Journal of Positive Psychology*. His research interest consists of integrating psychology, religion and spirituality, psychoanalytic thought, and positive psychology. He is currently a licensed clinical psychologist in Salem, Oregon.

Mark R. McMinn, PhD, is faculty emeritus and Scholar-in-Residence at George Fox University. Dr. McMinn is a licensed psychologist in Oregon, a fellow and former president of APA's Division 36, Society for the Psychology of Religion and Spirituality, and board-certified in clinical psychology through the American Board of Professional Psychology.

Dr. McMinn has authored or coauthored fourteen books, coedited four books, and published over 130 book chapters and peer-reviewed journal articles. His books *Finding Our Way Home* and *The Science of Virtue* received Awards of Merit in the annual *Christianity Today* book awards. He also is the author of *Psychology, Theology, and Spirituality in Christian Counseling*, which has sold approximately 100,000 copies over 25 years.